# CULTURE AND THE MEDIA IN THE USSR TODAY

# CULTURE AND THE MEDIA IN THE USSR TODAY

Edited by

## Julian Graffy

*Lecturer in Russian Language and Literature*
*School of Slavonic and East European Studies*
*University of London*

and

## Geoffrey A. Hosking

*Professor of Russian History*
*School of Slavonic and East European Studies*
*University of London*

St. Martin's Press   New York

© School of Slavonic and East European Studies, University of London, 1989

All rights reserved. For information, write:
Scholarly and Reference Division,
St. Martin's Press, Inc., 175 Fifth Avenue,
New York, N.Y. 10010

First published in the United States of America in 1989

Printed in Great Britain

ISBN 0-312-03457-1

Library of Congress Cataloging-in-Publication Data
Culture and the Media in the USSR today/ edited by Julian Graffy and
Geoffrey A. Hosking.
p. cm.
Includes index.
ISBN 0-312-03457-1 : $45.00 (est.)
1. Mass media—Soviet Union. 2. Soviet Union—Popular culture—
History—20th century. I. Graffy, Julian. II. Hosking, Geoffrey
A.
P92. S65C85 1989
302.23'0947—dc20                                             89-33421
                                                                  CIP

# Contents

List of Illustrations vi
Preface vii
Notes on the Contributors viii

1 Introduction
  Geoffrey A. Hosking 1

2 Soviet Television and *Glasnost'*
  James Dingley 6

3 *Glasnost'* and the Soviet Press
  Mary Dejevsky 26

4 The Cinema
  Ian Christie 43

5 Soviet Theatre: *Glasnost'* in Action –
  with Difficulty
  Michael Glenny 78

6 Soviet Music in the Era of *Perestroika*
  Christopher Rice 88

7 The Literary Press
  Julian Graffy 107

Index of Names 159

# List of Illustrations

1 Poster for Tengiz Abuladze's Film *Repentance*
2 Zeinab Botsvadze as Ketevan Barateli in *Repentance*
3 Poster for Kira Muratova's Film *Change of Fortune*, based on Somerset Maugham's story *The Letter*
4 Andrei Boltnev as Lapshin and Andrei Mironov as Khanin in Aleksei German's film *My Friend Ivan Lapshino*
5 Andrei Gradov as Nikita in Aleksandr Sokurov's film *The Solitary Voice of Man*
6 A scene from Larisa Shepit'ko's *The Homeland of Electricity*, the first episode in the collective film *The Beginning of an Unknown Century*
7 Rolan Bykov as Larsen in Konstantin Lopushanskii's film *Letters from a Dead Man*
8 Poster for Gleb Panfilov's film *The Theme*

(Film stills courtesy of Cannon Films, Sovexportfilm and the British Film Institute.)

# Preface

These papers originate from a Background Briefing held at the School of Slavonic and East European Studies, University of London, in March 1988 on 'Culture and the Media in the Soviet Union Today'. The authors were subsequently invited to develop and update their papers in whatever way seemed appropriate to their subject. They are thus very diverse in genre, but we present them for what they contribute to our understanding of a crucial aspect – some would argue *the* crucial aspect – of the radical changes taking place today in Soviet society.

*School of Slavonic and East European Studies*     JULIAN GRAFFY
*University of London*     GEOFFREY A. HOSKING

# Notes on the Contributors

**Ian Christie** is Head of Distribution at the British Film Institute. He has written, lectured and broadcast extensively on Soviet cinema and co-edited (with Richard Taylor) *The Film Factory: Russian and Soviet Cinema in Documents 1896–1939* (1988).

**Mary Dejevsky** read Russian and German at Oxford and worked for the BBC External Services before moving to *The Times* in 1986 as a Soviet and East European specialist.

**James Dingley** is Senior Lecturer in Russian Language at the University of London, and was educated at Cambridge. He was at one time editor of the *Journal of Byelorussian Studies*. His research interests lie chiefly in the history of Byelorussian language and culture, and he has published extensively in those areas.

**Michael Glenny**, an Honorary Fellow of the School of Slavonic and East European Studies, University of London, and Senior Associate Member of St Antony's College, Oxford, is a former Lecturer in Russian Studies at the Universities of Birmingham, Southern Illinois and Bristol. His translations of Russian plays have been performed in Great Britain, Ireland, Australia and the USA.

**Julian Graffy** is Lecturer in Russian Language and Literature at the School of Slavonic and East European Studies in the University of London. He has a particular interest in twentieth-century Russian literature.

**Geoffrey A. Hosking** is Professor of Russian History in the University of London and has published books on twentieth-century Russian and Soviet history and on contemporary Russian fiction.

**Christopher Rice** is a freelance writer, researcher and editor. He was educated at the Centre for Russian and East European Studies in Birmingham and has published on Russian politics and labour history as well as on cultural matters.

# 1 Introduction

## GEOFFREY A. HOSKING

Never before the Bolsheviks had any regime in history attributed such importance to the Word and the Image. Their mastery of mass propaganda contributed, perhaps decisively, to their victory over rival parties and movements in 1917–21,[1] and they have never abandoned the priority they accorded then to communication with the public. To this end they have made use of every means modern technology affords – newspapers, radio, cinema, television – to project information, outlook and ideology.

One compelling reason for the concern with culture was the abject and primitive state of Soviet Russia after the revolution and civil war. Lenin was well aware that in the light of schematic Marxism, the Russian revolution had taken place prematurely, before 'bourgeois' culture had had time to permeate the masses, as had happened in, say, Britain or Germany. This meant that the new government had a lot of catching up and teaching to do, especially in the broad field Lenin called 'culture', which included punctuality, cleanliness, honesty, and modern work practices – the characteristics, in fact, of the Swiss Post Office, which he so much admired and whose example he commended to his colleagues. Surveying the situation after the civil war, he admitted 'We have quite enough political power ... What then is lacking? Obviously what is lacking is culture among the stratum of the Communists who perform the administrative functions.'[2] How much more was it lacking among the ordinary people?

So the Communist Party has always interpreted the term 'culture' very broadly and assigned high priority to its inculcation by all possible means – education, propaganda, the mass media, and culture in the narrow sense in which we use the term in the West. To secure its own control, the party in 1932 abolished the squabbling sectarian movements which had tried to corner the market in cultural authority, and set up monolithic official 'creative unions' (like the Union of Soviet Writers) in their place. This step reflected the Communists' mercantilist approach to culture: they viewed it as part of the resources of a great power, to be marshalled and manipulated by the government like tank divisions or gold bullion. All cultural activity was to become an expression of the power of the Soviet state and its indwelling spirit, the Communist Party. To this end a mandatory doctrine, socialist realism, was promulgated *ex cathedra* by Stalin's cultural cardinal, Zhdanov, as an authoritative guide to practice in all the arts. In literature, inferior writers, enjoying their posts only by virtue of party patronage, were installed to police their (sometimes) more gifted colleagues. A similar means of control was applied in all the arts, while the party dominated the media directly through the Propaganda Department of the Central Comittee.

The result was a monotonous cultural output reflecting the tastes of the *vydvizhentsy*, the 'yuppies' of Stalinist Russia, who made meteoric careers, sometimes over the corpses of their predecessors, and combined dedication to the party's cause with humble background and rudimentary education. In the visual arts they preferred muscular, resolute, striding figures; in music, tunes which could be whistled at the workbench; in literature, positive heroes from the people tempered by the party's 'consciousness'. These were the stock-in-trade of Stalin's tame master craftsmen.[3]

In the end, however, the attempt to make culture a branch of state officialdom proved to be a contradiction in terms. The standardisation of the authoritative monological text (in whatever branch of the arts or media) became self-defeating. It could no longer fulfil even its pedagogical function, because it undermined normal communication between the artist or journalist and his public. Readers looked for information no longer in what the text *stated*, but rather in what it implied or even omitted. Whether reading literary works or newspaper articles, they became insensitive to the deadeningly omnipresent norm, and reacted only to the fleeting aberration. Cultural and media communication became either stupefyingly dull, or else a treacherous quicksand of veiled hints and implications in which all but the highly informed and engaged reader lost his footing. This dissolution of meaning frustrated the purposes of the media and threatened the death of culture. Society's communication channels, clogged with lifeless words and images, could no longer sustain any feeling of community.

Yet the institutions which existed to promote this pseudo-culture had become generous sources of patronage and material privilege. They provided jobs, homes, holidays, health care, retail services and secretarial help. People whose job was to promote the official ideology were given the resources to do it properly. To work for a newspaper, or to be a party propagandist, or to be a member of a creative union like the Union of Writers, was to enjoy a secure and on the whole respected existence – not perhaps a prosperous one, but at least cushioned from some of the primitive struggle for material goods which still disfigures Soviet life. These institutions became bastions of the establishment, protected by the party's solicitous concern, centres of rivalry and intrigue with an overwhelming interest in the preservation of the status quo – as one can see from Michael Glenny's description of theatre repertory companies, or Christopher Rice's account of the Union of Composers.

It does not follow that everyone working in culture and the media is ideologically orthodox. On the contrary they occupy an unusually good vantage point for identifying the defects of Soviet society, and also for lifting the veil on them. Khrushchev's 'thaw' of the late 1950s and early 1960s was a preliminary outburst of such plain-speaking, and, even after it ceased, a degree of *frondisme* never quite disappeared from at least the literary journals – which is why, as Mary Dejevsky points out, *Literaturnaia gazeta* alone among Soviet periodicals has always sold out. The prestige of literature in Russia, allied to the cunning and determination of certain editors, made discreet establishment non-conformity a regular feature of the literary scene in the 1970s and early 1980s.[4] It was not the Writers' Union as a whole which promoted such non-conformity, but rather its sub-units, individual journals and publishing-houses, like *Novyi mir* under Aleksandr Tvardovskii. In the theatre, the Taganka under its principal director, Iurii Liubimov, played a similar role. This has remained true in the Gorbachev period, as Julian Graffy shows, with individual courageous editors seizing the opportunities presented by a reduced censorship and a more relaxed political atmosphere.

Revitalisation of culture and the media has been the cutting edge of Gorbachev's 'Perestroika Mark 2', his bolder approach to reform which set in during the summer and autumn of 1986. He viewed them as essential contributors to the 'revolution in people's consciousness' at which he was aiming. They were to do the job of 'galvanising the intellectual and spiritual potential of society'.[5]

Because of the build-up of establishment non-conformity, however, when Gorbachev decreed *glasnost'* he was not so much impelling it as uncorking it – and once let out of the bottle, it will prove very difficult to stuff back in, unless the party is prepared to resort to terror of Stalinist dimensions, which seems unlikely. But the effects of *glasnost'* have not all been favourable to the institutions of culture and the media. Their business may be publicity, but they are also institutions of the Soviet establishments, with much to defend and a certain amount to conceal. The utterance of long-suppressed complaints and grievances has increased not only the honesty of the media and creative unions but also their cliquishness, the 'group passions and personal ambitions' of which Gorbachev himself complained at the Party Conference.[6]

Besides, the centralised and hierarchical traditions of the creative unions are threatened by the accompanying process of *perestroika*, which requires them to become more autonomous, internally democratic and financially self-reliant. In theatre and cinema, the requirement that each troupe, each studio earn its own way without central subsidy imposes disciplines of a new, unfamiliar kind. It may be that the theatre workers set up their own creative union in 1986 precisely because without one they were less well placed to defend themselves against the pressures of the market-place. This may also have been one consideration underlying the radical change in the Union of Film-Makers, a more obvious effect of which has been to open the way for the screening of hitherto banned films. Even here, as Ian Christie shows, benefit has mostly accrued to works from the *past*: there has been no rush to create new films, not least because of worry that their commercial prospects might be poor.

*Glasnost'* also demands higher standards, increased professionalisation. This usually requires the imitation of Western models – as James Dingley shows in his study of television – a process which can lay its practitioners open to the charge of importing bourgeois ideology. This was the burden of the criticisms of Nina Andreeva, a Leningrad lecturer, who in March 1988 had a brief hour of glory in the newspaper *Sovetskaia Rossiia* as the flag-bearer of those in the party hierarchy wanting to rein back *glasnost'*.[7]

The combination of commercial pressure with western example threatens men and women of conservative taste with the irruption of youth culture, which they have long resisted. This can be seen especially clearly in the case of music, as Christopher Rice demonstrates. In the condemnation of rock music, establishment non-conformists are as vehement as party stooges, indeed perhaps more so, for they see the values they have long fought for under a new kind of siege. Thus the well-known rural writers Vasilii Belov and Valentin Rasputin joined the war novelist Iurii Bondarev in warning of rock music's 'drug-like ability to warp the minds of defenceless adolescents'.[8]

Up to now the arts have enjoyed a semi-sacral status as purveyors both of the official ideological monopoly, and also (paradoxically but thanks to that status) of small helpings of taboo-breaking nonconformity. Now they are losing some of their official status at the very time when taboo-breaking is also gradually shedding its fascination. This means the arts have to descend into the market-place, with consequences that many find distasteful. As for the media, they are learning Western public relations techniques, partly because they find them attractive, partly because the party now wants them to. The stately dullness has given way to lively and more penetrating reporting, whose relationship with the official ideology is much less clear than it used to be. But then the ideology itself is in flux. The Soviet system is torn between two conflicting political priorities; on the one hand the *pravovoe gosudarstvo* – the 'state ruled by law' – and on the other the leading role of the party. The condition of culture and the media faithfully reflects that fundamental ambivalence.

## Notes and References

1. See R. Pethybridge, *The Spread of the Russian Revolution* (London: Macmillan, 1972).
2. Political report to the 11th Party Congress, 27 March 1922, *Collected Works*, vol. 33, pp 287–9. Robert Tucker has recently argued that Bolshevism was from the very outset primarily a 'revitalisation movement' aiming to transform the *culture* of the mass of the working people. See the second chapter of his book, *Political Culture and Leadership in Soviet Russia: from Lenin to Gorbachev* (Brighton: Wheatsheaf Books, 1987).
3. See Hans Günther (ed.), *Culture of the Stalin Period* (London: Macmillan, forthcoming).
4. See my paper, 'The institutionalisation of Soviet literature', pp 55–75 of Geoffrey A. Hosking, George F. Cushing (eds), *Perspectives on Literature and Society in Eastern and Western Europe* (London: Macmillan, 1989).
5. Gorbachev's speech to the 19th Party Conference, June 1988. *Summary of World Broadcasts*, SU/0191, 30 June 1988, C/9.
6. Ibid, C/10.
7. *Sovestkaia Rossiia*, 13 March 1988, quoted in *Summary of World Broadcasts*, SU/0126, 15 April 1988, B/1–6.
8. *Pravda*, 9 November 1987.

# 2 Soviet Television and *Glasnost'*

## JAMES DINGLEY

The controlling body of both television and radio in the Soviet Union is a committee called Gosteleradio SSSR. The Party Central Committee has its own committee with the special task of overseeing the work of the broadcasting media but the nature of the connections between Gosteleradio and the Party is not always clear. Suffice it to say that the Chairman of the Committee, A. Aksenov, is also a member of the Party Central Committee. The organisational structure of radio and television in the USSR has not yet received the detailed attention it deserves; this article will therefore cover the most immediate aspect of TV broadcasting – the actual output, the programmes.

The role ascribed to the broadcasting media in Soviet society today is quite clear. A. Aksenov states categorically that television and radio are 'key factors in the renewal of society, essential tools for influencing millions of people, for the formation of public opinion, convictions and actions, the development of healthy tastes ... they raise issues connected with education in matters of music, ideology and morals, and aesthetics' (Aksenov 1988). Television 'does not issue directives; its task is rather to arouse and shape public opinion, to raise problems, not to attempt to solve them'. This role was emphasised and developed by Mr Gorbachev in his speech at the media workers' conference on 10 May 1988 (reproduced in *Literaturnaia gazeta* 1988, 19); journalists in both the print and broadcasting media will obviously take their cue from a statement such as 'the key to everything is democratisation, involving the people in all activities'. The importance attached to television can be measured by the increase in broadcasting time that has taken place over the last year or so, and by the number of agreements recently made in several countries to enable them to receive Soviet TV broadcasts (Yasmann 1988).

It has been possible to receive Soviet television live by satellite in this country for five or six years. What we actually receive is in fact only one of two channels that cover the whole of the Soviet Union. This channel (channel 1) carries a wide range of programmes of all kinds, reaching more than 260 million people; channel 2 shows school and other teaching programmes during the daytime, and offers films, sport and news in the evening. Currently it can be received by 190 million people. (The figures are taken from Askokova 1988, p. 33.)

The weekly programme schedule *Govorit i pokazyvaet Moskva* (Moscow speaks and shows), available in this country only in its Moscow edition,[1] apart from listing the programmes on the two main all-Union channels, also gives information about an adult education channel which starts broadcasting at 8 p.m. every evening; the Moscow local station; and the Leningrad local programmes which can be received by those who have the necessary adapter for their set. Both local stations broadcast only in the evenings. (Despite the existence of an educational channel, there is as yet no Open University or Open College as such, probably because many institutes of higher and specialist education have sections to deal with distance learning.) There are many other local TV centres throughout the country, but little information is as yet available on the programmes they have to offer.[2] Adverse criticism in the newspapers implies that they have not yet felt the full impact of *glasnost'* and *perestroika*. Nevertheless, the importance now attached to local broadcasting may be judged by the fact that 67 new studios are planned.

It is evident that, in the Soviet Union, as in most other countries of the world, television is playing an increasingly important role in people's lives. The number of sets in the country grew from a mere 400 in 1940 to 10 000 in 1950 and 4.8 million in 1960. The Soviet Union was producing 7 million TV sets every year by 1976. Only 5% of the population could see TV programmes in 1960; 93% could do so in 1986. Eighty-six per cent of the territory of the USSR can be reached by TV signals. During the 1960s, television still ranked third after radio and newspapers as the major source of information on current affairs. There can be little doubt that TV is now the major source of such information. Given this new dominant role for television, Gosteleradio has recently established a section for conducting 'sociological research' – that is, public opinion polls. The polls conducted so far amount to little more than asking viewers what they thought about, for example, the programmes on New Year's Eve or youth programmes (Mel'nikova 1988), but the programme producers are clearly beginning to realise that they have a viewing public who expect satisfaction from the goods on offer. The presentation of television news underwent a major change on 1 January 1968. For the first time the main news of the day was broadcast in a new format and perhaps most important of all, at a fixed time. This was the beginning of *Vremia* (Time), now on the air at 9 p.m. Moscow time every night of the week on all channels, including those local ones which are listed in the Moscow weekly programme schedule. It lasts 40–45 minutes (longer, if a major policy speech has just been made by the current General Secretary), of which the final five minutes or so are taken up by sport and weather. In a recent comparative study of the approach adopted by *Vremia* and the main US TV news broadcasts (primarily ABC) to the events of one week (Mickiewicz & Haley 1987), the authors found that in the 35 minutes allocated to actual news each day, *Vremia* could cover an average of 22 items, devoting just over two minutes to each one. (By comparison, the American score was 22 minutes of news time, 13.5 items on average, 1 minute 39 seconds devoted to each item.)

The structure of the programme was in many ways reminiscent of the central Soviet daily newspapers: domestic news always had precedence over foreign, items that in other countries would either go unreported or be consigned to specialist programmes, such as harvesting campaigns or technological innovations, were relentlessly included. There are signs that things are beginning to change. In several of the recent broadcasts of *Vremia* domestic matters still lead, but in a sometimes more open way. It was, for example, a pleasure some months ago to watch the public discomfiture of the Minister of School Education of the Russian Republic when he was closely questioned about the poor availability of school textbooks. A more recent programme carried an item on moonshine distilling, an obviously burning issue at a time when alcohol is less easily available than it once was. Moreover the item was introduced without the high moral tone previously associated with revelations of similar criminal activity. A. Aksenov says in a moment of what under Gorbachev is routine candour (Aksenov 1988: 1) that people once used to wait until 9.15 before switching on *Vremia* because that was when the foreign news would begin, but now more of the population is watching the programme in its entirety. Unfortunately he does not elaborate on the methods used to reach this conclusion, but it is certainly true that attempts are being made to hold the viewers' interest to a much greater extent than previously. The Sunday edition of *Vremia* makes room for a considerable amount of material culled from foreign TV stations, by no means all of it serious: there are occasional 'silly' items about animals, or people who have done/are doing strange things. So far items of similar levity do not seem to have been made actually within the Soviet Union. Kuznetsov (1988) gives an account of the history and present development of the programme.

*Vremia* is also the subject of a short article by an American researcher, M. Dimmock, in the newspaper *Argumenty i fakty*, 1988, 30.[3] The author remarks on the predominant position of domestic news items, the importance attached to tractors and 'interviews with workers' and the generally formal, stilted manner of the newscasters. There are two replies. One is by G. Shevelev, chief editor of the Central Television news department who comments, not without justification, that Dimmock's views on the excessive number of items dealing with tractors are now somewhat outdated. Steps are being taken to enliven the presentation.[4] The second reply is by a psychologist, S. Roshchin, who criticises *Vremia* for continuing to reproduce major speeches by the Soviet Union's leading political figures either in their entirety or at least in large chunks. *Vremia*'s method of reporting the opening and closing of the 19th Party Conference confirmed this criticism, by being extended to upwards of 90 minutes on both occasions. Criticism has also been levelled at *Vremia* together with the print media, for being slow to respond to Nina Andreeva's now notorious letter of 13 March 1988 to the newspaper *Sovetskaia Rossiia* opposing perestroika;[5] TV news programmes were also uncertain about how to handle events in Nagorny Karabakh. One of *Vremia*'s earliest contributions to public information on the unrest in Armenia and Azerbaidzhan was an unhelpful interview with an Azeri scholar who 'had devoted her life to the discovery of documents revealing the age-old friendship of the Armenian and Azeri peoples'.

There are regular news slots in the breakfast programme *120 minut*[6] and throughout the day (usually about five minutes each). Other programmes are specifically devoted to foreign news. The most regular of these, the daily *Segodnia v mire* (The World today), has recently been extended from 15 to 20 minutes. Until now the commentator (there are about five or six regular ones) has devoted the time to the in-depth discussion of just a few items, sometimes only one, of direct relevance to Soviet foreign policy and/or ideological preoccupations; there has been nothing for the viewer to watch except the talking head and, very occasionally, a map. Efforts are now being made to enliven the proceedings by an increased use of video material.

The Sunday evening prime-time (6 p.m.) weekly *Mezhdunarodnaia panorama* (International panorama) shows material from Gosteleradio's foreign correspondents. Previously this almost always tended to be critical, certainly as far as items from western countries were concerned; there is a noticeable trend now to include more items showing where the USSR can learn from the experience of others. A similar approach is also discernible in the regular programme showing items specifically from countries within the Socialist Commonwealth. A recent edition of *Kamera smotrit v mir* (The camera looks at the world), another regular programme used as a vehicle for conveying specialist domestic and foreign news, contained items on a leading Soviet fashion designer of the 1920s, a follow-up to an item in a previous edition on the fate of Soviet Germans who have emigrated to the Federal Republic, and a piece on the use of electronic spying devices in the USA. In general it can be said that the Soviet viewer receives information about foreign countries not only, and indeed not so much, from formal news programmes such as *Vremia* as from the *telemosty* (spacebridges) such as have been held with Americans and Britons in various centres, and uncensored interviews with Western political leaders. Of particular interest in this respect were the five parts of the programme *Vstrechi s Amerikoi*, hosted by the unbelievably smooth (and obviously highly professional) bilingual Vladimir Pozner. The first four broadcasts consisted of studio discussions with audiences in the United States on a wide range of topics. The fifth was a discussion by a small panel of experts in Moscow, led by Pozner, on the basis of questions phoned in by Soviet viewers. Clearly the most impressive aspect of the programmes for many of those who phoned in their comments and questions was the freedom with which Americans expressed their opinions. Inevitably a series of uncensored programmes that gave Americans a chance to talk about themselves gave rise to serious thoughts about the situation in the Soviet Union. Given the obvious importance attached to news programmes of all kinds, it is not surprising that there are hints (emanating from the chief news editor G. Shevelev himself, in *Govorit i pokazyvaet Moskva* 20, p. 19) at the possibility of the establishment of a separate news channel.

The second most important programme (after *Vremia*) on Soviet TV at the moment, at least because of its timing and regularity – 9.40 p.m. most evenings except Sunday – is the 10-minute *Prozhektor perestroiki* (Spotlight on *perestroika*) (Olenin 1988). It first went on the air on 3 August 1987, since when it has continued to cast light on many areas of Soviet society that need the fresh air of *perestroika*, such as the scandalous waste of resources represented by large and frequently meaningless slogan hoardings found all over Soviet cities, the practice of sending anonymous letters to the authorities, a shoe factory in Belorussia which – quite literally – ran out of money to pay its workers, why the theatre in Volgograd is about to close, the scandal of flats belonging to the regional party committee in Archangel being left empty while the housing queue grows and grows, and so on. Perhaps because of its regularity the programme is now being criticised for its 'lack of bite': it is all very well to make the exposures, but what then happens? We are witnessing the beginnings of investigative journalism, with journalists acquiring the courage (probably because they have official permission from on high) to tackle bureaucrats who previously would have been beyond open criticism in the media.

The main programme for young people has for a long time been *Do 16 i starshe* (For 16-year-olds and over). A recent broadcast included a visually powerful item on vandalism in a Moscow technical school; not surprisingly the youngsters interviewed did not seem to know the meaning of the word *vandalizm*. More surprisingly, some of them appeared to show no concern about the damage caused to their school. Other programmes aimed at the young are also beginning to play a vital role in opening up all areas of Soviet life to public scrutiny. The occasional *12-i etazh* (12th storey) has produced outspoken comment from young people – seated, for some obscure reason, on a staircase – on virtually taboo subjects such as the 1941–45 war (why talk about it so much?), patriotism, authority.

This programme has not been included in the schedules for some time now. It may possibly have been replaced by *Do i posle polunochi* (Before and after midnight), described as a musical and news programme (broadcast monthly), and its companion late-night programme *Vzgliad* (Glance) (now broadcast once a week,[7] usually on Fridays at about 11.30 p.m.). The two programmes have done much to reduce the stiff formality that is elsewhere still frequently encountered on Soviet TV. Both are broadcast live, and are clearly intended to combine serious comment and discussion on current affairs with entertainment. *Vzgliad* also acts as a phone-in programme. Both programmes must make a disturbing impression on their more staid viewers, in this country as well as in the Soviet Union. The presentation tends on occasion to the chaotic, but in their comparatively brief lifetime the programmes have so far held interviews with Moscow rocker and punk gangs, and shown Western rock videos and an increasing number of inventive Soviet ones as well. There have been interviews with senior figures in the Russian Orthodox Church; recent broadcasts of *Vzgliad* have had as one of the studio guests (who was therefore asked to comment on other items in the programme) Father Mark of the Moscow Patriarchate administration, described as a 'church journalist' in charge of the Patriarchate's 'video department'. One of the broadcasts with Fr Mark also included discussion of, and extracts from the controversial play about modern Soviet teenagers *Dorogaia Elena Sergeevna* by Liudmila Razumovskaia and continued discussion of Iurii Poliakov's story about the violent treatment of conscripts in the Soviet armed forces, *100 dnei do prikaza* (100 days to demobilisation) which appeared in the young people's journal *Iunost'*, 1987, 11. A letter from a conscript was read out complaining that the political officer of his detachment had removed the offending issue of the journal from the library. In addition there was an item about a Soviet cruise ship that caught fire in Osaka harbour because of the stupidity of some of the tourists themselves, with the loss of twelve lives. The ensuing studio discussion centred on the insistence of the remaining tourists that they must stay another day in order to complete their purchases of 'defitsitnye tovary' (goods in short supply). Not overtly expressed, but almost certainly implied, was criticism of the news programme *Vremia* for not having covered the tragedy in such detail. This particular broadcast also continued to raise the question of the Soviet troops still held prisoner by Afghan rebel groups, in two very particular ways. First, Aleksandr Rozenbaum's song about them was repeated by popular request (it had first been broadcast in May, 1987); secondly, there was an extract from an Orthodox memorial service held at Zagorsk '*za voinov na pole brani vo Afganistane ubiennykh*' (Church Slavonic: for the warriors slain on the field of battle in Afghanistan).

In several broadcasts of *Vzgliad* before the 19th Party Conference specific items were devoted to the election of delegates – or rather, as it turned out on numerous occasions – to the method whereby delegates were imposed on local Party organisations. These items contained some fascinating 'vox pops'; most noteworthy were the interviews conducted outside the gates of the Lenin Komsomol Motor Works (complete with bleeped-out expletives), because the senior management and factory Party committee would not admit the TV crew.

Irina Zaitseva, whose reports for *Do i posle polunochi* have taken her inside a convent and a prison, showed viewers of the programme on 31 July 1988 the inside of a hospital for the criminally insane in

Leningrad. Quite apart from her direct question to the senior doctor about Western allegations of the use of psychiatric hospitals as prisons for political dissidents, she raised the very pertinent issue of the need for Soviet society as a whole to rethink its attitude to mental illness.

*Glasnost'* implies the possibility of open, frank discussion about the history of the Soviet Union. As far as television is concerned, this discussion has taken several different forms. There have been interviews in *Vzgliad* and *Do i posle polunochi* with individuals who suffered during Stalin's repressions of the 1930s, or who became political dissidents in the Brezhnev era; performances of songs by Aleksandr Galich; or Roi Medvedev arguing for political pluralism. A heightened interest in events of the 1920s and apparent greater freedom of access to contemporary newsreel archives has led to the incorporation of a large amount of material in the new documentaries that are now flooding on to the screen. Of the 1700 documentaries shown annually on Soviet TV most doubtless fall into the category of solemn variants on the late, unlamented 'Look at Life'. However, as producers expand the range of their newly-found creative freedom, it is evident that television documentaries will play an increasingly important role in educating and informing the viewing public about past events. The results are already impressive.

The first of these recent documentaries really to catch the attention of Western observers was *Bol'she sveta* (More light), in effect a newsreel-based history of the Soviet Union with a clear message: the social and economic experiments of the 1920s were beginning to bear fruit when they were so abruptly smashed by Stalin; collectivisation ruined the peasantry; Stalin was responsible for the widespread destruction of the Party and the armed forces and so must be blamed for the country's unpreparedness for war in 1941; Khrushchev made brave attempts to undo the damage caused by Stalin, but unsystematically and without involving the people to the necessary extent; under Brezhnev corruption and 'ochkovtiratel'stvo' ('eye-wash') flourished to such an extent that people led double lives, saying in public things they knew to be untrue.

Of equal significance in the range of topics covered are the two parts of *Risk*. Both parts are essentially concerned with the malignant role of Stalin in the development of Soviet science. His treatment of Sergei Korolev in the 1930s effectively delayed a rocket programme that could have made the country much stronger in the face of aggression. The development of atomic physics in the Soviet Union was similarly affected. The second part of *Risk* goes further than any other programme I have seen so far in drawing a direct parallel between Stalin and Hitler, a parallel that is of especial relevance in dealing with the two dictators' treatment of their scientists. Atomic physicists fled Nazi Germany in large numbers; those who remained were pressed into government service for the development of the ultimate weapon. The problem in the Soviet Union, says the commentator, was different: here it was a question of people simply disappearing. Later the commentator informs viewers that at the meeting of the Academy of Sciences called to discuss the possible expulsion of Andrei Sakharov in the 1960s, the eminent physicist Kapitsa reminded his fellow academicians that Einstein had been expelled from the Prussian Academy of Sciences on orders from Hitler. When war broke out in 1941, it was to the Church that the people turned: there are extracts from Metropolitan Nikolai's rallying speech. The commentator notes icily that when Stalin finally spoke to the nation, he addressed them as '*brat'ia i sestry*' (brothers and sisters), terms that were forgotten when, after 1945, the returning deportees and those who had been in the areas under German occupation began the long journey to prison and Siberian exile. Interestingly the film, directed by Dmitrii Barshchevskii, was made for the department of Central TV dealing with programmes for young people, not for the propaganda division. *Protsess* (The trial) includes footage of Andrei Vyshinskii as presiding judge at the 'Prompartiia' trial of 1930 and as prosecutor at the trial of Nikolai Bukharin in 1938. Some of the people interviewed in the film seek to justify Stalin's methods with the usual well-tried arguments: industrialisation was possible only because of collectivisation, there were no food shortages, society was disciplined, Stalin's leadership was the crucial factor in ensuring a Soviet victory in 1945. The director of the film, Igor' Beliaev, uses these arguments to demolish Stalin's reputation as a peacetime and wartime leader. We learn that in 1937 Stalin destroyed 40 000 army officers, among them 80 per cent of the top leadership. A moving interview with Ivan Tvardovskii (brother of the poet and editor Aleksandr) sheds light on the experiences of one 'kulak' family caught up in the collectivisation process, and serves to put human flesh on the brutal figures of the number of people 'dekulakised' presented by Academician Tikhonov. Towards the end of the film Tikhonov goes a long way towards blaming the emergence of Stalin on Lenin, without actually mentioning Lenin by name. This could be the most outspoken documentary film to have emerged so far.[8] Less universal in scope, but with enormous human interest, is a documentary made by the Sverdlovsk TV studios: *A proshloe kazhetsia snom* ... (And the past seems like a dream). It shows the reunion after fifty years of the authors of the book *My iz Igarki* (We come from Igarka) published in 1937. They were the children of *'spetspereselentsy'* (specially resettled persons) who were forcibly moved up the river Enisei to Igarka, a settlement that was to become the only Soviet town inside the Arctic Circle. With the help of a mixture of old footage and the participants' own retelling of their experiences, the film builds up an impressive picture of the survival of the human spirit against almost overwhelming odds. Particularly memorable are the shots of the now empty shell of the Stalin museum built on the site where he had spent his Siberian exile before the Revolution. The documentary includes shots of a young participant on the cruise singing the song *Tovarishch Stalin, Vy bol'shoi uchenyi* (Comrade Stalin, you're a great scholar), which is particularly appropriate in this context, since it includes a reference to Stalin's exile in the Turukhanskii krai.[9]

*Literatura. Istoriia. Obshchestvo* is a two-part televised account of a conference held jointly by the Writers' Union, the History Section of the Academy of Sciences and the Social Sciences Institute of the Party Central Committee. Conference speeches and interviews with delegates do not normally make riveting television. On this occasion what was important was not the presentation, but the content. It must have startled many viewers to hear the playwright Shatrov talk about the 'thin ice' of the present political situation with people still trying to work out how they should behave, or Iurii Afanas'ev, historian and rector of the Moscow Archive Institute, state categorically that 'there is probably no other country in the world with a history as falsified as ours'. How did they react when the whole of the official history of the Great Patriotic War was effectively consigned to the dustbin? Or to the description of Brezhnev's rule as *'mertviashchaia stalinshchina'* (the dead weight of the Stalin legacy)? Academician Kukushkin (the name means 'cuckoo'!), co-author of several history textbooks for schools, appeared to be experiencing considerable embarrassment in seeking to explain to his audience exactly why the latest post-1985 editions of his textbooks still failed to treat Stalin and the 1930s openly and honestly. It may well be that programmes such as this, broadcast to the whole country at peak viewing time, will ensure that current trends are indeed irreversible.

The major documentary on Chernobyl' is *Chernobyl': dva tsveta vremeni* (Chernobyl': two colours of time). The first two parts were shown in 1987; the third part was broadcast on 28 July 1988. This third part, on the basis of interviews with leading participants in the clean-up operation still in progress, develops into what can only be described as an indictment of nuclear power, or at the very least of nuclear power in the Brezhnev era. This is achieved by skilful intercutting of shots of the power station and the desolate surrounding area as they are now, with newsreel clips from 1977, full of pompous boasts about the earlier-than-planned completion of building work. A journalist from Canada is given full opportunity to stress – in Ukrainian – the need for openness in distributing information. There are accusations of cover-ups and lying on the part of members of the investigating commission. The First Deputy Minister of Health is reported as having informed *Izvestiia* in May 1986 that all the serious cases of radiation sickness were being treated in Moscow. Not so, says Aleksandr Kovalenko, the man now in charge of the information service on site. Many people were successfully treated in Kiev. He cites this as an instance of the medical rivalry between the two cities. There are harrowing shots of a man who returns with official permission to his flat in the town of Pripiat' to look for some birth certificates, only to find that his home has been burgled. This documentary is a fine example of *glasnost'* in action in dealing with the contemporary Soviet scene. Its chief criticism is that no preparations had been made for a disaster of this kind, in contrast to what happens in the West.

Clearly ecology and the preservation of the environment feature very strongly in this film. These issues are also important in the three parts of *Na putiakh perestroiki* (On the paths of *perestroika*). Part two contains clips of speeches at the conference of the Union of Writers that denounced the grandiose schemes to divert the course of major Siberian rivers, and footage shot in the Karakalpak ASSR, where similar 'improvement' schemes have had disastrous results for the population, leading to poisoned wells and disease. The third part contains material about farmers who are taking over disused land on a cooperative basis, one of whom expresses certain misgivings about the future – *A vdrug ... ?* (What if [Gorbachev falls/the reforms are reversed]?).

Other documentaries have dealt with very specific issues, but are none the less products of the new atmosphere, and evidence that the process of reconstruction is underway in the media: among these are *Byvshie* (Those who once were ...) dealing with large-scale corruption in the supply sector and including interviews with prisoners who face the death penalty for their crimes, and *Bez orkestra* (Without the orchestra), on what happens to orphan children once they leave the orphanage. The element common to all the documentaries discussed above is a reappraisal of the moral values of Soviet society, both in its view of the recent and more distant past, and in its attitudes today. Equally challenging to established views was the documentary *Madonny XX veka* (Madonnas of the twentieth century), which posed the hoary old question of the position of women in Soviet society in a new way by broadcasting extracts from a show by women body-builders in Vilnius, and interviews with women weightlifters. Not so far shown on TV are the documentaries *Aura* dealing with drug-trafficking by a militia chief in Turkmenia (with the profits knowingly being used for the purchase of guns by the Afghan mujahedin) and one about the activities of the Uzbek mafia leader Adylov. There is evidence, according to a recent broadcast of *Vzgliad*, that this later film has been barred from the screen at the moment by Party officials in Uzbekistan and Moscow.

The millennium of the adoption of Orthodox Christianity as the officials state religion of Kievan Rus' has not been overlooked by Soviet television. *Vremia* has carried several items devoted to specifically Church matters, and a number of short (occasionally unscheduled) programmes under the general title *Tysiacheletie kreshcheniia Rusi* (Millennium of the Baptism of Rus') have also been shown. Of special importance is the documentary *Khram* (Temple), directed by Valentin Tolmachev and shown on 11 June 1988. It contains old newsreel shots of the destruction of churches, scenes from the everyday family life of an Orthodox parish priest in the USSR (Fr Dmitrii from Vladimir), the everyday work of monks and nuns showing the sanctity of ordinary human labour, an extract from the service for Thursday in Holy Week and the funeral service for Anna Akhmatova. Almost the last thing the viewer hears in the programme is the hymn of Easter joy (*Khristos voskrese iz mertvykh/Smert'iu smert' poprav* ... Christ is risen from the dead/by his death trampling Death). The half-hour documentary *Ia zovu zhivykh* (I call the living) was devoted to the bell-ringing traditions of the Orthodox Church.

It is much too early to conclude that religious matters will now receive a fair hearing on television. So far there have to the best of my knowledge been no programmes devoted to other Christian churches in the USSR, and no non-Orthodox Christian leaders have appeared, although there was a brief item on the Baptists (together with short interviews with newly-baptised young people) on *Vzgliad* on 5 August

1988. All items on the Orthodox Church have stressed its patriotic role in Russian history, and thereby serve to confirm the current presentation of that history.

It has long been evident that social policy has laid great stress on the wellbeing of the young. (Whether the results have always been positive is another matter.) At the same time the old have been pushed to the very margins of society. Soviet television, in its role of moulder of public opinion, appears to be seeking to change attitudes to the elderly by the introduction of a new programme, *Esli vam za* ... (If you're over ...). This will be a worthwhile area for future study.

Important for its role in arousing patriotism and military enthusiasm is *Sluzhu Sovetskomu Soiuzu* (I serve the Soviet Union), a weekly that goes on the air at 10 every Sunday morning. It cannot and does not shun Afghanistan, but has inevitably concentrated on the positive presence there of Soviet soldiers, dwelling particularly on acts of individual heroism. The presenters of *Vzgliad* have mentioned several forthcoming documentaries on Afghanistan; on 12 August 1988 extracts were shown from a film made as a final-year project by a graduate of VGIK (the All-Union Cinematography Institute), Andrei Goncharov: *Proshchaite, muzhiki* (Farewell, lads). The title in fact comes from the last words spoken over the radio by a helicopter pilot before he crashes.

Cultural issues are raised in confrontational programmes, often between a studio audience and the editors and contributors of the major literary journals. Music programmes are largely classical (and still traditional in repertoire), folk, variety (of a type that recalls similar programmes on British TV in the 1960s). Rock has featured in the Leningrad programme *Muzykal'nyi ring* (Musical ring), as well as on the late-night programmes mentioned above, and there is a regular spot for jazz-lovers, about once a month.

The closest approach to a 'soap opera' in recent months was the multi-part *Gardemariny, vpered!* (Forward the Marines!), a carefully designed and apparently successful attempt to produce an adventure story with a wide appeal on the model of *The Three Musketeers*, but with the essential patriotic ingredient that the young heroes are eighteenth-century Russians fighting in defence of their homeland. Political drama in general is given considerable prominence, especially as a means of exploring past and current social issues. The series *V.I. Lenin: stranitsy biografii* presents a less mythological, more human Lenin, and is especially remarkable for its treatment of figures such as Bukharin (Loginov 1988, Sharapov and Aizenberg 1988).

TV is criticised for the number of old films it still shows:[10] none of the recent Soviet films such as *Repentance* have been shown on the all-Union channels. The regular review of new films, *Kinopanorama*, lost its regular presenter El'dar Riazanov (see Riazanov 1988) some time ago and is now, in the words of Simanovich (1988, p. 35), looking rather tired. It suffers from having more than one presenter, and therefore lacking an 'image'. An equally difficult area is that of films made specially for television. This had obviously been the subject of acrimonious debate at the fourth plenum of the board of the Union of Cinema Workers.[11] Nikich (1988) raises fundamental issues, connected not only with the showing of films on TV, but also with the whole process of the democratisation of television. Who, he asks, is to control the managers of the television network? The three chief words of these managers are, he claims, 'propaganda', 'ideology' and 'politics', with no mention of the cultural and educational role of television stressed at the February 1988 Plenum of the Central Committee of the Communist Party of the Soviet Union. He proposes that programme-makers should become independent by having their own budget limits; it would then be up to them to fight for their audience. In connection with this he advocates the restoration of the *abonementnaia plata* (TV licence payments, which before their abolition had been set at 3 roubles a month), on the grounds that the viewer will be willing to pay for information and entertainment.

Certain regular programmes occasionally act almost as consumer guides; this has been particularly true of some editions of *Dlia vsekh i kazhdogo* (For each and everyone) and *Nash dom* (Our home). There are no advertisements as such on Channel 1 – the curious experiment with an excruciating advertisement for a particular make of portable TV on *Do i posle polunochi* about a year ago seems not to have been repeated – although there is an occasional five-minute programme on Channel 2, called bluntly *Reklama* (Advertising). Among other regular programmes are *Chelovek i zakon* (Man and law) (a clear attempt to raise the legal awareness of the population) and *Dvizhenie bez opasnosti* (Keep danger off the roads) (containing much of interest to that harassed sector of Soviet society, private-car owners). There is abundant evidence in the vast range of topics now being broached that Soviet television is actively responding to the Party leadership's call for more openness. A long distance has been covered since the time when television 'existed to serve the tastes and views of one man' (that is, Brezhnev) (Riazanov 1988, p. 26). Nevertheless, problems still exist. Censorship and what he views as an unprofessional approach to showing films on television prompted El'dar Riazanov to resign as presenter of *Kinopanorama* and to vow never to work for television again (Riazanov 1988,[12] Leibovskii 1988, Tsvetov 1988). There have been complaints about censorship in a documentary about Chernobyl' (Panov 1988), and cuts in musical programmes (Gradskii 1988).

What of the future? Foreign contacts are being developed. The naturalist Gerald Durrell recently made a film in the USSR *Darrell v Rossii* (shown in January 1988). An Italian series on the life of Verdi has recently been occupying most evenings immediately prior to *Vremia*. The contacts that began in 1984 with a Soviet Television Week at the National Film Theatre in London were continued this year by the visit of a delegation of six Soviet television professionals (Doyle 1988). To counter complaints of the paucity of foreign feature films on Soviet TV, an organisation called Gosteleeksport is to be set up, with the aim of promoting and selling Soviet TV programmes abroad, thereby earning vital foreign currency (Kravchenko[13] 1988). Television criticism is still an underdeveloped area. The rubric *7 x 7* in *Literaturnaia gazeta* disappeared several months ago and has not been replaced; in any case it had not become identified with one specific writer. Such criticism as there is in the press tends to concentrate on the political role of TV – that is, the value of this or that programme in promulgating *glasnost'* and *perestroika*.

As far as domestic programmes are concerned, the kind of *glasnost'* advocated by Professor Iasen Zasurskii, Dean of the Faculty of Journalism of Moscow State University, in his interview in *Literaturnaia gazeta* (Zasurskii 1988) might well – if adopted – lead to open government of a kind that we scarcely have in this country. Among other things, he urges the direct broadcasting of the proceedings of Party and government bodies. Indeed a start may already have been made in this direction with the broadcast of the speeches on Nagorny Karabakh made at a special meeting of the Presidium of the Supreme Soviet. Information and entertainment programmes like *Vzgliad* and *Do i posle polunochi* will inevitably increase in importance, as will those programmes concerned with giving the 'man in the street' a chance to have his say. Whether the criticisms of the current 'pure entertainment' offerings will be heeded remains to be seen. All that can be said is that television in the Soviet Union, as with the other forms of mass media, will probably not become a force completely independent of Party policy.

## POSTSCRIPT

Important evidence of the discussions on reorganisation now taking place within Gosteleradio is provided in *Televidenie i radioveshchanie*, 1988, 10, pp. 8–11. The report gives some details of a round-table discussion that followed a *'mozgovoi shturm'* (brainstorming) business-games session in Central TV in May this year. The first useful information given in the article is a series of photographs enabling the researcher to identify individuals and their functions within the organisation. Two possible lines of development for television in the USSR were apparently identified: *'vnutrennii khozraschet'* (internal profit-and-loss accounting) and *'konkuriruiushchie kanaly'* (rival channels). The possibility was raised in discussion of the establishment of financially independent programme-making brigades. The success or failure of a particular programme could be reflected in the salaries of the brigade members. It is clear that for payment by results to work properly, a proper system of rating ('reiting') will have to be set up, including, for example, a *'tsentr izucheniia obshchestvennogo mneniia'* (Centre for the Study of Public Opinion); there was obviously a clear difference of opinion as to whether such a centre should be attached to or completely independent of Gosteleradio. At present the 'sociological service' of Gosteleradio is being computerised in order to provide the beginnings of a ratings analysis; 500–600 registering devices are to be attached to TV sets in selected homes in the Moscow area. Kravchenko identified the need for an *'otdel nauchnogo ili perspektivnogo planirovaniia'* (Department of Scientific or Forward Planning) to study social attitudes and trends in public opinion.

In the opinion of some participants in the discussion, rival channels will be feasible only when the whole country can receive at least two channels. Channel 1 is received by 97 per cent of the population, whereas only 71 per cent can watch Channel 2. It will take ten years to remove the gap. On the other hand there appears to have been general agreement that some form of rivalry is necessary for the stimulation of greater creative effort. Equally essential is the establishment of a *'tvorcheskii soiuz rabotnikov televideniia'* (Creative Union of TV Professionals), on the lines of analogous bodies now active in the cinema and theatre. The current situation fails to provide adequate opportunities for professional development. There is no single set of criteria by which the output of each TV employee can be evaluated, and opportunities for creative experimentation are almost completely lacking.

*Vremia* has shown a tendency to be both as consistently conservative as ever and yet more innovative in some areas over the last few months. The reporting of the recent meeting of the Supreme Soviet of the USSR still gave Gorbachev's speech in full, as if the programme controllers were unwilling to take responsibility for cutting anything out. On the other hand, there has been a great deal of live reporting from Armenia. The reports have not hesitated to show the real shortcomings in the rescue efforts, also mentioning the looting and continuing civil disturbances and giving full credit to the role of foreign aid.

The earlier criticisms of *Prozhektor perestroiki*, that it was a programme that highlighted problems but failed to show whether anything was ever done to solve them, have at least partially been answered by making the Monday issue of the programme one that deals with readers' letters and follow-up.

*Vzgliad* has contained little of interest over recent months, except an interview with Andrei Sakharov just before his departure for America and live coverage of a demonstration outside the Pakistani embassy in Moscow by relatives of prisoners-of-war held in Afghanistan. Perhaps the most remarkable part of this report was the speech by the journalist Iona Andronov urging the relatives not to rely on any initiative from the state but to set up their own committee. A Sunday morning version of *Vzgliad* was broadcast for the first time on 27 November 1988; unfortunately it showed the same lack of clear purpose in the items included that has dogged many of the Friday night broadcasts. The programme will be shown on the last Sunday of every month, or such is the intention.

A curious new departure was heralded by the first showing on 11 November 1988 of what will be a twice-monthly advertising programme, *Progress, informatsiia, reklama* (Progress, Information, Advertising). Made in conjunction with the Italian firm 'Fininvest', it consists of a series of short video films advertising foreign companies and their products. One such included an advert for Allied Lyons, informing the Soviet viewer that the English drink beer in pubs. Given that the goods and services advertised are unobtainable by ordinary mortals in the Soviet Union, the programme must be aimed at Soviet ministries and firms. Indeed this is made abundantly clear by the studio commentaries and discussions with economists that form an integral part of each broadcast.

Two documentaries are worth special mention. *Khronika ostanovlennogo vremeni* (Chronicle of time stopped), dealing with the private fiefdom set up in Uzbekistan by state farm chairman Akhmadzhan Adylov in the 1970s, finally reached the screen on 19 October after difficulties with the authorities. It is a lengthy indictment of the grand-scale corruption that flourished unhindered under Brezhnev. The other documentary is *Ochishchenie* (Purification), shown on 22 November. The immediate subject material for this film stems from an article published by the Belorussian writer Ales' Adamovich in the newspaper *Sovetskaia kul'tura* on 19 May 1988. The article, entitled '*Nakanune*' (On the Eve), deals with those who still seek to defend Stalin, and refers in particular to a '*torzhestvuiushchii zashchitnik palachei*' (triumphant defender of the torturers). This was understood (rightly) by one Ivan Timofeevich Shekhovtsov, a lawyer who has been active in writing to newspapers attacking those who 'seek to denigrate the achievements of the 1930s', to be a personal reference to him. Shekhovtsov brought a civil action for slander against Adamovich and the editors of *Sovetskaia kul'tura* on the grounds that Stalin had not been found guilty of crimes in a court of law, and therefore he (Shekhovtsov) was slandered by being described as a 'defender of torturers'. After passionate statements by Adamovich and witnesses for the defence (Shekhovtsov produced no witnesses), and partisan participation by the audience, the judge threw out the case. The plaintiff plans to appeal.

The complaints that too few recent films are shown on TV were in part countered by the screening on 20 November of the Lenfil'm 1988 version of Mikhail Bulgakov's long-suppressed *Sobach'e serdtse* (Heart of a Dog). The preceding *Kinopanorama* has an item about the making of the film.

**Notes**

Abbreviations:   *GiPM: Govorit i pokazyvaet Moskva*
                 *TR: Televidenie i radioveshchanie*

1. Regional editions of *GiPM* are called 7 *dnei* (7 days). According to information in *GiPM*, 1988, 33, p. 20, regional editions are published in: (for the RSFSR) Leningrad, Novosibirsk, Altaiskii Krai, Krasnoiarskii Krai (including Kemerovo and Tomsk regions); Ukraine, Latvia, Lithuania and Estonia. Norr (1985) gives some information on the use of languages other than Russian in Soviet television.
2. Askokova (1988) and Ivanov (1988) contain general information about

local stations, Malikov (1988) has information on the station in Chita, Tsvik (1988) on the situation in Riazan'.
3. Soviet and American television news are also compared in *Sovetskaia kul'tura* 11 June 1988 under the title *Dva mneniia o sovetskom TV* (Two opinions of Soviet TV), on the basis of an article by David Remnick in the *Washington Post*.
4. Elsewhere (*GiPM*, 1988, 20, p. 19) Shevelev concedes that *Vremia* is '*ofitsioznoe*', a word which actually means 'semi-official', but in the context is apparently being used to mean something like 'stiff', 'formal'.
5. See the round-table discussion in *Moskovskie novosti*, 24 April 1988.
6. Lengthened from its original version of 90 minutes. Before the development of this new format, there had been an early-morning version of *Vremia*.
7. According to an announcement in *GiPM*, 1988, 2, p. 19, *Vzgliad* was to be broadcast twice a week, on Tuesdays and Fridays. The Tuesday programme has not so far materialised. For a survey of both *Vzgliad* and *Do i posle polunochi* see Liashenko (1988). Riazanov (1988) shows that censorship still exists, even on a programme like *Do i posle polunochi*.
8. For a detailed analysis of *Protsess* see Wishnevsky (1988).
9. This song, long thought to have been written by Vysotskii, is in fact by Iuz Aleshkovskii, a writer living in emigration. It was published in *Novyi mir* in December 1988.
10 *GiPM*, 1988, 7 carried a questionnaire on films on television. The results are reported in 1988, 14.
11. The text of decisions and recommendations from the plenum concerning films on television is given in *TR*, 1988, 6, p. 15.
12. The difficulties of which Riazanov speaks in his *Ogonek* article concern arbitrary cuts made by Central TV in a number of his programmes: *V krugu druzei* (broadcast in March 1986 in full via the Orbit satellite to the Soviet Far East and Siberia, but subsequently cut for broadcast to the European part of the country), his interview with V. Molchanov on *Do i posle polunochi* about his film *Zabytaia melodiia dlia fleity*, his televised meeting with a studio audience in Ostankino, and finally the enormous problems with the making and showing of his four-part series about Vysotskii. Riazanov questions the competence of the recently appointed head of films at Central TV, a former figure-skater and sports commentator. S. N. Kononykhin.

Leibovskii's article recalls difficulties with the documentary *Trinadtsatyi*, about Garri Kasparov. Tsvetov's article argues for the establishment of a rival TV station.
13. L. P. Kravchenko is First Deputy Chairman of Gosteleradio.

## Bibliography

Aksenov A. (1988) 'Vremia velikikh peremen', *TR*, 1 pp. 1–3.
Askokova, L. (1988) 'Poisk svoego lista', *TR*, 3, pp. 32–34.

Doyle, T. (1988) 'Take six Soviets', *Sight and Sound*, 57, 3, pp. 159–62.
Gradskii, A. (1988) '... i pust' budut luchshie obraztsy', *TR*, 4, pp. 36–38.
Ivanov, A. (1988) 'Oblastnoe TV: v poiskakh svoego litsa', *TR*, 1, pp. 12–13.
Kravchenko, L. (1988) 'Snova o fil'makh na teleekrane', *GiPM*, 26, p. 19; 27, p. 19.
Kuznetsov, G. (1988) 'Mir v zerkale ekrana', *TR*, 1, pp. 4–8.
Leibovskii, V. (1988) 'Kak prorvalsia "trinadtsatyi" ', *Ogonek*, 25, p. 27.
Liashenko, B. (1988) 'Razmyshleniia do i posle polunochi', *TR*, 2, pp. 14–16.
Loginov, V. (1988) 'Istoriia dlia millionov', *TR*, 6, pp. 13–14.
Malikov, E. (1988) 'Zagolovki i rubriki ne v schet', *TR*, 4, pp. 18–19.
Mel'nikova, O. (1988) 'Net "srednego" zritelia', *TR*, 3, pp. 36–38.
Mickiewicz, E. and Haley, G. (1987) 'Soviet and American News: Week of Intensive Interaction', *Slavic Review*, 46, 2, pp. 214–28.
Nikich, O. (1988) 'Esli ne my, to kto zhe?', *Iskusstvo kino*, 7, pp. 3–7.
Norr, H. (1985) 'National Languages and Soviet Television:' a statistical report', *Nationalities papers*, 13, 1, pp. 84–105.
Olenin, B. (1988) 'V svete prozhektora', *TR*, 1, pp. 9–11.
Panov, A. (1988) 'Z vidomym ukhylom?', *Literaturna Ukraina*, 19, p. 5.
Riazanov, E. (1988) 'Pochemu v epokhu glasnosti ia ushel s televideniia?', *Ogonek*, 14, pp. 26–27.
Sharapov, Iu. and Aizenberg, A. (1988) 'Novaia interesneishaia glava', *TR*, 4, pp. 1–5.
Simanovich, G. (1988) ' "Kinopanorama": vremia molodet' ', *TR*, 4, pp. 35–36.
Tsvetov, V. (1988) 'Teleprogramma na zavtra', *Ogonek*, 25, pp. 28–29.
Tsvik, V. (1988) 'Sdelaet li vesnu pervaia lastochka?', *TR*, 4, pp. 15–17.
Wishnevsky, J. (1988) 'Soviet Television discusses Stalin's Legacy', *Radio Liberty Research Paper*, RL 205/88.
Yasmann, V. (1988) *'Glasnost'* and Soviet Television in 1987', *Radio Liberty Research Paper*, RL 31/88.
Zasurskii, Ia. (1988) 'Nuzhny li glasnosti granitsy?', *Literaturnaia gazeta*, 22, p. 2.

# 3 *Glasnost'* and the Soviet Press

## MARY DEJEVSKY

In the two years after Mikhail Gorbachev became General Secretary of the Soviet Communist Party, there was much debate both in the West and in the Soviet Union about whether *glasnost'* – variously translated as 'openness', 'publicity', 'voicing opinions' – was genuine and if it was, how far it would be allowed to go. In the third year, even some of the most sceptical analysts had begun to concede that the policy of *glasnost'* had wrought profound change in the character of the Soviet media.[1] The official press had been in the forefront of that change.

The most visible sign of change is that the reputation of Soviet citizens as voracious newspaper-readers, a reputation which had been in abeyance through most of the Brezhnev years, is being restored. People are buying and reading newspapers and magazines, and frequently, they are surprised.

Before Mr Gorbachev came to office in March 1985, people might read newspapers to find out the official 'Kremlin' view of the world. They might comb the columns and read between the lines to detect changes in that view. But they were unlikely to read newspapers to find out what had happened or to participate in discussion. Nor would they usually read more than one: if they read *Pravda*, the official Communist Party paper, or *Izvestiia*, the official organ of the Soviet government, they had gained a good idea of what was printed in the other papers, too.

By the middle of 1987, press articles had become a constant subject of Moscow conversation, both in the drawing-rooms of intellectuals and in the streets and on the metro. Five years before, the only newspaper that regularly sold out at news kiosks was *Literaturnaia gazeta*, the paper of the Writers' Union. In the summer of 1987, people would queue from early morning to buy the weekly *Moscow News* – in whatever language it happened to be available[2] – and the magazine, *Ogonek*. They also read the daily papers far more attentively then before.

Among the many changes of approach is a more adventurous attitude to layout and the use of pictures, which makes the papers more attractive and easier to read. The traditional idea of a newspaper as four broadsheet pages of solid print is very slowly being abandoned. The extreme conservatism of picture editors, who seemed to like nothing better than posed portraits or shots of happy workers among the machines, is also giving way to greater enterprise. The action photographs from the Afghan warfront published in *Ogonek*[3] offer one example; a picture purporting to show drug addicts trading in the Moscow metro, another.[4]

By far the greatest changes, however, are not in the way Soviet newspapers look, but in what they say. Four specific changes can be noted: previously taboo topics are gradually being discussed in the press, there are the beginnings of an internal debate between different publications; the prescriptive attitude which dominated the press treatment of social and political issues is less pervasive, and articles by foreign journalists and politicians are being published without the hitherto compulsory editorial disclaimer.

## BREAKING TABOOS

Soviet history, social and economic problems (including corruption and juvenile crime), and the military presence in Afghanistan have all been covered by the press. These subjects, and others like them, were barely touched in official Soviet sources before Mr Gorbachev came to office. To some extent, their emergence follows the General Secretary's own frankness about the extent of the problems facing Soviet society and those facing his reform programme in particular.[5] Once given the green light, however, the press has moved further and faster in opening up new subjects for public discussion.

Nowhere has the role of the press – or rather a section of it – been greater than in developing the discussion of Soviet history, especially in reappraising the role of Stalin and Stalinism. In the second half of 1987 and through 1988, the press raked over the past and uncovered facts and figures which were widely known, but had not been publicly acknowledged before in the Soviet Union. The period from the 1930s to the 1950s provided fertile ground. *Ogonek* offered estimates of the number of people sent to camps under Stalin and gave accounts of camp conditions and the attempts of relatives to locate victims.[6]

*Moscow News* acknowledged the falsity of the so-called doctors' plot against Stalin.[7]

Articles in those same two weekly publications[8] argued for the rehabilitation of Nikolai Bukharin for several months before he, Rykov and those tried with them in 1937 were formally rehabilited.[9] *Ogonek* published the plea which Bukharin had made his wife learn by heart before he was arrested and executed. She had, on his instructions, written it out every month to keep it in her mind until such time as it could be published in the Soviet Union. That happened on 4 February 1988, fifty years after his death.[10]

While the press has concentrated on the Stalin era, more recent Soviet history has occasionally come under the journalistic microscope. An analytical article by the historian Professor Iurii Poliakov accused the late Soviet leaders, Leonid Brezhnev and Konstantin Chernenko, of creating personality cults and exaggerating their war records. It was especially critical of Brezhnev's literary endeavours, including his autobiographical account of the war, *Malaia Zemlia*, which, the article suggested, bore little resemblance to the truth.[11] And *Literaturnaia gazeta* published a full page article by Fedor Burlatskii recounting his memories of Nikita Khrushchev, a nonperson since he was removed from the leadership in 1964, in a way which mixed the positive and negative traits of his character.[12]

Although economic problems have been discussed in the columns of the official press, with senior economists like Professor Abel Aganbegian and Nikolai Shmelev floating hitherto heretical ideas about market economics, price reform and unemployment,[13] the complexity of the arguments has meant that their most ambitious designs tend to be set out more often in monthly journals. Trenchant economic criticism has figured in the daily press: *Izvestiia* ran a series of articles questioning the value of Brezhnev's great enterprise, the second trans-Siberian railway, the BAM;[14] and several papers have sprung to the defence of would-be founders of cooperative ventures frustrated by Soviet red tape.[15] But in general social issues have provided more scope for the daily and weekly papers.

Among the social problems 'discovered' by Soviet journalists in the past three years have been alcoholism (in the wake of Mr Gorbachev's campaign against vodka), drug addiction and prostitution. *Literaturnaia gazeta* published a full-page article about prostitution in hard currency bars in Moscow,[16] while the punishment meted out to prostitutes by friends and relatives provided lurid stories with a moral.[17] The moral angle is also preferred in articles which recount serious crimes or expose corruption or miscarriages of justice. Such cases are now being reported, but usually well after the culprit has been caught and the sentence carried out.[18]

Categories of statistics which cast Soviet social achievements in a less than flattering light have begun to be published, including those for crime and infant mortality.[19] Severe journalists have given accounts of the defects of Soviet medical facilities and the practice of psychiatry, including the wrongful committal of individuals to mental hospitals.[20] Mostly, however, the articles conclude by saying that the criticisms have been acted on and the worst is now over.

Special attention has been paid to the problem of orphans and abandoned children, of whom there are reported to be more now than at the end of the Second World War.[21] In August, after a long campaign in the press – mostly in *Komsomol'skaia pravda*, the Communist Party's youth paper, and *Literaturnaia gazeta*, which gave distressing accounts of homes where children shared outdoor clothes and were given inadequate food – a special fund, the Lenin Children's Fund, was set up to help abandoned children and improve orphanages.[22]

The foreign and domestic repercussions of the Soviet involvement in Afghanistan were another area where the press became increasingly bold. Throughout 1987 and 1988, the press had started to bring to public attention both the fact that Soviet troops were engaged in armed combat – something the media had been reticent about before – and the plight of war veterans returning home. This was even before Mr Gorbachev had put his personal authority publicly behind the decision to withdraw Soviet troops.[23]

*Pravda* was one of the official papers which devoted attention to the Afghan veterans who returned wounded and the difficulties faced by bereaved families. Initially based on letters received by the paper, the articles later investigated individual cases.[24] *Ogonek* printed a series of articles about service in Afghanistan and the problems of fighting a guerrilla war.[25] The initial pretence that Soviet troops were engaged only in humanitarian projects was replaced by harrowing accounts by Soviet soldiers who have seen combat, and the exposure of the high-handed and bureaucratic treatment of disabled servicemen requiring help from the state.

## THE INTERNAL PRESS DEBATE

The breaking of many – though by no means all – taboos in official Soviet press coverage has been accompanied by two related developments: first, different newspapers have begun to reflect different viewpoints, according to the standpoint of their editor; and secondly, newspapers and their editors have engaged in sporadic debates with those representing an opposing line on a particular subject.

Newspapers can be classified on a scale from pro-*glasnost'* to non-*glasnost'*, according to their subject-matter and their treatment of it. *Sovetskaia Rossiia* (the official paper of the Russian Federation's government), and *Moskovskaia pravda* (the Moscow regional party paper), tend towards *glasnost'*;[26] *Komsomol'skaia pravda*, *Vecherniaia Moskva* (the local Moscow evening paper), *Krasnaia zvezda* (the official paper of the Soviet armed forces), and *Trud* (the paper of the Soviet trade union organisation) – against. *Izvestiia* (the Soviet government paper) comes somewhere in the middle.

Responsibility for the attitude taken by the publication appears to rest with the editor and with the particular interest group he feels he represents. The editors of the two journals which became pioneers of *glasnost'*, Vitalii Korotich of *Ogonek* and Egor Iakovlev of *Moscow News*, have come under attack both implicitly, from the man assumed to be Mr Gorbachev's deputy, Egor Ligachev,[27] and explicitly in the columns of other publications,[28] for exaggerating the negative aspects of Soviet life and history. *Pravda* made specific charges against *Ogonek* for its exposure of corruption among members of the Writers' Union.[29]

As the decision by the Soviet leadership to withdraw its troops from Afghanistan was clarified, so the post-mortem began on the correctness of their presence there in the first place. The argument was waged largely in the columns of the press, between those who argued that specialists in the area had advised strongly against military involvement,[30] and those like a senior correspondent of the military paper, *Krasnaia zvezda*, who argued not only that they had an obligation to go in, but also that they had acquitted themselves well.[31]

Nor was this the only political argument to be fought between rival organs of the official press in the spring of 1988. Perhaps the most consequential debate of all, by virtue of its political content, was initiated by *Sovetskaia Rossiia* in the weeks before the special all-union Communist Party conference in June 1988.[32] The article in question, which purported to represent the views of a chemistry lecturer at a Leningrad college, Nina Andreeva, was an eloquent exposition of the platform of those believed to be in the vanguard of opposition to Mr Gorbachev's reform programme. Many regarded it as representing the views of Mr Ligachev, and there were indeed echoes of earlier Ligachev speeches.[33] The article queried the ideological and theoretical basis for the reform programme, attacked the denigration of Stalin and the materialism of the present generation, and called for the revival of the nationalist and egalitarian spirit which, it said, had inspired the revolution.

Two weeks later, in its editorial commemorating the third anniversary of the April 1985 Central Committee plenum – Gorbachev's first as General Secretary, *Pravda* published its riposte, attacking the premises of the Andreeva article and defending the reform programme as the only way forward.[34] A day later, a point-by-point ideological reply to Andreeva was published by Fedor Burlatskii in *Literaturnaia gazeta*. This was the end of this particular argument and the beginning of Mr Gorbachev's victory as a reformer. A Central Committee plenum which followed endorsed both his economic programme, including greater freedom for cooperative ventures, and the programme of political reform he had advanced, which included proposals for limiting the tenure of party officials to two five-year terms.[35]

## LESS PRESCRIPTION

Even before he was called on to defend the Gorbachev reform programme against its conservative detractors, the political publicist, Fedor Burlatskii, had argued in *Pravda*[36] and elsewhere for the acceptance of a right to disagree and hold divergent opinions. The publication in some papers of letters attacking published articles – *Ogonek*, for instance ran a series of letters from people angrily defending Stalin's leadership[37] – is one way in which editors have chosen to represent contrary views. The notion that individuals should always be obedient to the collective has also been attacked. A journalist in *Komsomol'skaia pravda* criticised what he called the 'slavish philosophy' which stopped people from going into a polling booth to cross out the names of unworthy candidates and from speaking out against injustice.[38]

The press also started to attack cherished myths: in 1987, the project to divert the flow of the great Siberian rivers from north to south so as to provide irrigation to the desert lands of Central Asia was halted after a campaign waged by intellectuals on ecological grounds, partly in the columns of learned journals, but also in the press.[39]

## FOREIGN ACCESS

*Moscow News, Izvestiia* and some other papers have introduced as a regular feature articles reprinted from Western newspapers or contributed by foreign politicians. These appear to have been selected in order to give Soviet readers the 'enemy's' view and may be coupled with an article representing the official Soviet view. This technique was followed last year when *Moscow News* printed an open letter signed by 10 Soviet émigrés, which had been published in a number of Western papers – including *The Times* – and replied to it.[40] The traditional Soviet practice of preceding an otherwise unacceptable viewpoint with censorious editorial comment is followed less frequently.

## WHERE IT ALL BEGAN

There is still no agreement about when *glasnost'* first came to the Soviet media, or why. According to one view, it can be traced to the nuclear disaster at Chernobyl in April 1986. The theory runs that Mr Gorbachev was so concerned by the way Soviet secrecy had hampered relief measures at home and damaged the Soviet image abroad, that a policy of *glasnost'* was introduced forthwith in an attempt to ensure that there would be no repetition.[41] Although Chernobyl may have hastened the process, however, *glasnost'* seems rather to be part of Gorbachev's recognition, voiced early in his leadership, that there could be no progress – economic, political or cultural – in the Soviet Union unless people were given more information and more individual responsibility.[42]

When *glasnost'* became official policy, the press had an advantage over the other branches of the official Soviet media. Despite its reputation as dull and hidebound, a true servant of the state, the press – especially the provincial press – had a tradition of campaigning and investigating injustice. Often, its investigations were restricted to local economic crimes, such as bribery and corruption or black-marketeering in food and consumer goods, and were kept within strictly defined boundaries. Such cases were generally covered only when the rights and wrongs had already been established and the criminal brought to justice. They had a didactic and deterrent aspect.[43]

In the first three years of Mr Gorbachev's leadership, the range of subjects open to investigative journalists has been expanded. They can tackle, for instance, blatant corruption in large enterprises or even ministries. The incidence of crime, including juvenile crime, and camps for offenders are discussed, as is the incidence of corruption in hospitals and old people's homes. In one case, the local KGB came under scrutiny.[44]

Many constraints, however, are still in place. The problem for editors is in deciding where the constraints lie. Individual editors seem now to have more freedom to decide which subjects to tackle and how to do it, but this carries risks – that they may unwittingly go beyond the unmarked border of the permissible, that they may incur the wrath of influential people – and not everyone is prepared to take these risks. Individuals with a grievance now feel freer to take it to the press; a correspondent may be sympathetic, but the topic may still be vetoed by the editor as too sensitive or unsuitable for discussion in his paper.[45]

The overriding question about *glasnost'* is still: is it an end in itself, or is it merely a means to an end? Is its prime purpose to give the people of the Soviet Union access to more information because the leadership recognises that as a good and necessary aim in itself, or is its main purpose to help Mr Gorbachev consolidate his authority, discredit his predecessors and his opponents, and improve his image in the Soviet Union and abroad?

Before Gorbachev, most manifestations of *glasnost'* had a clear political purpose. Details of local corruption scandals were commonly designed to discredit particular individuals; there was a settling of scores. When, in the early 1980s, details of scandals implicating the Brezhnev family were printed, this was assumed to be an attempt by Brezhnev's opponents, with the connivance of the KGB – to ensure that the then head of the KGB, Iurii Andropov, became the next General Secretary.[46] Viktor Grishin was removed as First Secretary of the Moscow Communist Party organisation in December 1985 after a similar press campaign during which he was accused of inefficiency, incompetence and, indirectly, of corruption.[47]

Mr Gorbachev has been able to use criticism of the economic stagnation which set in in the late Brezhnev years to discredit his predecessor and spur on his own programme of economic reform, or *perestroika*. The press has followed his example.[48] Exposure of the evils said to derive from that time, such as corruption, nepotism, black-marketeering, alcoholism, is used by Mr Gorbachev to show how necessary change is and how the time has come for hard work and honesty to prevail.[49]

The policy of *glasnost'* can also be used to assuage some of the dissatisfaction felt by intellectuals. Their restricted access to information and the distortions they sensed in their own media encouraged many to listen to foreign radio stations in the Brezhnev years. It turned some, like the physicist Dr Andrei Sakharov and his wife and numerous writers and artists, into dissidents or émigrés. The greater freedom given to the press to cover current social and economic issues can be seen as just one part of a wider campaign to recover the loyalty of intellectuals. The publication of books which had earlier been banned, like Pasternak's *Dr Zhivago* and Grossman's *Life and Fate*, and the freer discussion of cultural and historical questions reflect the concern of the Gorbachev leadership that it has lost the very people it needs if *perestroika* is to have any chance of success.[50]

The extent of change in Soviet press coverage since Gorbachev became leader suggests, however, that even if *glasnost'* was intended to do no more than clear Mr Gorbachev's opponents from his path and reduce dissatisfaction within the intelligentsia, it could in time assume a momentum of its own.

Even at this early stage, *glasnost'* in the press has had one unexpected consequence. Perhaps because of their increased contact with Western correspondents and greater access to Western publications, younger Soviet journalists are starting to ask, at open press conferences, the sort of questions about the Soviet Union that their Western counterparts have been asking for many years. Many of these correspondents come from highly privileged party backgrounds and work for central Communist Party and government newspapers.

In late 1987, they asked questions such as these: (of the head of the visa section at the Ministry of Internal Affairs) Why is it so difficult to emigrate from our country? Why do you not simply let anyone go who wants to?; (of a senior government statistician) Why are there gaps in economic statistics?; and (of a first deputy prime minister) Is defence policy being properly run? 'Does the Soviet acceptance of the "double zero" and its decision to dismantle medium-range missiles in Asia as well as in Europe not jeopardise Soviet security? After all we were told only last week that these missiles were essential to safeguard our defence.' These points are not yet made in print, but it can only be a matter of time.[51]

In April 1988, as ethnic unrest erupted in the Soviet republics of Armenia and Azerbaidzhan, one journalist on the staff of no less orthodox a paper than *Pravda* broke with his colleagues to disclaim responsibility for an article he was supposed to have written. The

*Pravda* correspondent in Armenia, Iurii Arakelian, was one of three journalists whose name appeared beneath an authoritative article on the source of the unrest: the disputed region of Nagorno-Karabakh. The article foreshadowed the official decision not to transfer the region to Armenian administration and condemned the Armenian case.[52] Arakelian sent a telegram to the editor of *Pravda*, dissociating himself from the contents of the article and complaining about the use of his name. When it came to a choice, his loyalty to Armenia was greater than his loyalty to the Soviet Communist Party. He was immediately suspended from his job.[53]

## TEST CASES: THE LIMITS OF *GLASNOST'*

The divergence between the sort of questions Soviet journalists are asking and the articles which appear in print, and the treatment of a journalist who chose to forsake his paper's editorial policy, demonstrate that *glasnost'* has distinct limits. A few test cases will serve to illustrate how narrow those limits are and the extent of the constraints that still hamper the Soviet press.

**Accidents.** If *glasnost'* was already official policy before the disaster at Chernobyl nuclear power station, then Chernobyl was its first and greatest failure. It failed at local level, when officials failed or feared to inform the central authorities, then at national and international level when the truth was not told. While the compilation and publication of the accident report showed how far the Soviet authorities were prepared to meet international criticism under pressure, the subsequent trial of Chernobyl employees held responsible for the accident was for the most part closed, and little more than the verdicts appeared in the Soviet press.[54]

Even after Chernobyl, the Soviet press still finds it difficult to report what is negative and unpredicted. Throughout 1986 and 1987, plane crashes were reported in a few lines, and days or even weeks after the event. A rail accident in August 1987 near Rostov-on-Don, in which more than 70 people were killed, was reported more than 24 hours after it happened and without casualty figures, although speculation about how it had happened was printed.[55]

Similarly, details of hijackings, including the one attempted by the musical ensemble, *The Seven Simeons*, on a flight from Irkutsk to Leningrad in March 1988, have been reported, but only when the 'incident' is safely over.[56] The 'Simeons' hijack was unusual, however, in that the conduct of the police who stormed the plane at Leningrad and killed or injured innocent passengers was criticised by one newspaper.[57]

**Ethnic unrest.** Unrest which has not been predicted (the Alma Ata riots in December 1986, the Crimean Tatar demonstrations in July 1987, and the Armenia/Azerbaidzhan protests in March and April 1988) has received scant coverage in the official press. The first hints of difficulty are given in official condemnation or through a formal announcement that a committee has been set up to investigate the grievance.[58] For instance, it would not have been until a month after the disturbances began that Soviet newspaper readers would have known about the violence in Azerbaidzhan and the territorial dispute that had given rist to it.[59]

Ethnic unrest is particularly difficult to monitor because of Soviet travel restrictions. At any hint of disturbances, the Soviet authorities can seal the area off, as they did in Kazakhstan in December 1986 and in the trans-Caucasus in the spring of 1988. The result is a virtual news-blackout. Most information comes from unofficial sources and is impossible to verify.

Demonstrations in the Baltic States, which usually coincide with national anniversaries, have been treated more openly in the official press – perhaps because they are a more familiar and predictable phenomenon and so regarded as less menacing. They can also be prepared for: both by the use of police at the scene, but also in advance through counter-propaganda and warnings on the radio and in the local and national press. The fiftieth anniversary of the Ribbentrop–Molotov pact on 23 August 1987 was the subject of massive press and radio analysis in the Baltic States which gave only the Soviet view of the treaty – as the salvation of the Baltic states from the Nazis – in advance of the anniversary.[60]

**Communist Party, Nomenklatura and the KGB.** The Communist Party and the KGB have largely been exempt from *glasnost'* and shielded from the prying press. The one exception was the case of a KGB officer in the Ukraine who was exposed in the press for hounding a journalist to his death in early 1987, but this may have been the result of a local vendetta. Unless senior figures fall foul of still more senior figures, their personal lives are still out of bounds to reporters. The lavish Western press coverage of Mrs Raisa Gorbacheva is not replicated in the Soviet press, and questions about her answered by Soviet officials are not reported in the Soviet papers.[62]

In political matters, the press is still used to uphold only the party line, or what is believed to be the party line. Andreeva's article, which was published in March 1988, was reproduced elsewhere and used as the basis for discussion in the belief (welcome to many party officials) that it represented official thinking.[63] After the rebuttal had appeared in *Pravda*, retractions were printed.[64] The previous November, the press was used to vilify the Moscow first secretary, Boris El'tsin. *Pravda* and other papers published an account of his condemnation and dismissal in November,[65] but his earlier speech to the Central Committee which led to his dismissal has not been published.

**Foreign affairs and defence.** Aside from the limited access to the Soviet media given to foreign correspondents and politicians, these subjects have barely been opened up for public debate. Differing emphasis and interpretation (within bounds) is permitted in print among recognised Soviet specialists, like Fedor Burlatskii, Aleksandr Bovin and Georgii Arbatov, but informed discussion about foreign policy and defence spending and priorities is conspicuous by its absence from the press.

## THE UNOFFICIAL PRESS

The diversification of views and approaches represented in the official press since Mr Gorbachev came to power has been accompanied by a proliferation of unofficial publications. Some observers reckon there are now over 100 titles appearing more or less regularly.[66] An unofficial journal, *Zhurnal zhurnalov*, has even been founded to provide a guide to the world of the unofficial press.

Most of these 'independent' publications are *samizdat* in the strict sense that they are private initiatives undertaken without the approval or cooperation of the state. Unlike earlier *samizdat*, most have been tolerated and some circulate openly. Their legal position, however, is still ambiguous. In mid-1987 it appeared that the authorities might be prepared to give unofficial publications some recognition, perhaps allowing the establishment of publishing cooperatives, and enshrine their position in law. But towards the end of the year, there were reports that this intention had been shelved.[67]

Not all these unofficial journals are new creations; some are the successors of *samizdat* publications begun in the 1960s.

The unofficial journal best known abroad is *Glasnost'*, edited by Sergei Grigoriants, which publishes in part dissident and human rights material, but has also included accounts of and complaints about working conditions in Soviet industry. The high public profile taken by Mr Grigoriants has brought him regular censure from the authorities,[68] but it may also have ensured him a measure of protection. His journal continues to appear.

Among other unofficial publications is *Ekspress-khronika*, which specialises in human rights affairs. It is edited by Aleksandr Podrabinek, who has served terms in prison camp for political offences. There are also a number of environmentalist journals, the most well-known being Mikhail Talalai's *Vestnik soveta ekologii kul'tury*. Until recently, ecology and the conservation of the natural environment and traditional architecture were subjects the official press preferred to ignore.[69]

Up to now, most unofficial journals have been based in Moscow, the Baltic and Leningrad, where the first meeting of their editors took place in October 1987.[70] In 1988 journals have also begun to appear in the Ukraine, the Caucasus and the Russian provinces, though it is too early to get an overall impression of them.

## CONCLUSIONS

The impact of *glasnost'* on the Soviet press over the past two years has been considerable, but, as the test cases show, it has also been limited. There is little evidence that any part of the official press, even those publications in the forefront of *glasnost'*, is running out of control. When the Armenian correspondent of *Pravda* broke ranks, he was at once suspended.

The coverage of hitherto taboo subjects – historical controversies, social or economic problems, and Afghan casualties – is carefully planned and thought out in advance. Newspapers still hesitate before covering the new and unexpected: accidents, protest demonstrations, setbacks in Afghanistan, and so on. Reliable information about such incidents is hard to come by. The editor may be waiting for instructions about how to handle the material, or simply to see how others react. The official account, when it comes, is often as anodyne and uninformative as in pre-Gorbachev times.

Under *glasnost'*, editors appear to have more discretion as to what they publish, and correspondingly greater responsibility. There has been high-level criticism of editors, but no editor of a central publication has lost his job. The editor of *Moskovskaia pravda*, who left his job in the wake of the dismissal of El'tsin, appears to have been removed because of his sympathies, not because of what he published. Sergei Grigoriants, the editor of the most widely circulated unofficial journal to be published in the new climate, has been vehemently criticised in the official press, but each new issue of his journal *Glasnost'* has appeared. Whether he would have been able to continue publishing if he lived in the provinces and had not taken the precaution of making himself known to Western correspondents must be open to question.

The two measures which could transform the Soviet publishing scene have yet to be enacted. A plan to allow cooperative publishing ventures, in the same way in which cooperative restaurants and service outlets are now permitted in a limited way, was mooted in 1987, but subsequently shelved.[71] A new law on the press has also been mentioned but has not so far materialised and there have been no indications of what it might contain. In March 1988 a Soviet spokesman said that a law on *glasnost'* was being drafted, in which the limits would be set out in a short paragraph.[72] The speaker said that the authorities had considered introducing a law on secrecy that would declare everything open which was not specifically designated secret, but this would not be enacted yet. It had been decided, he said, that Soviet legal and democratic standards were not yet high enough to accommodate such a law. There had also been opposition.

The last word rests with Mr Gorbachev. In January 1988 he addressed media workers for the second time in twelve months. His address contained a gnomic statement on the subject of *glasnost'* and its limits:

> We are for *glasnost'* without reservation or limitations, but for *glasnost'* in the interests of socialism. To the question of whether *glasnost'*, criticism and democracy have limits we answer firmly: If *glasnost'*, criticism and democracy are in the interests of socialism and the interests of the people they have no limits! This is our criterion.[73]

This is the authoritative definition of journalistic freedom in the Soviet Union. It suggests that for the time being at least, *glasnost'* in the Soviet press will mean exactly what Mr Gorbachev and the Communist Party leadership want it to mean: no more and no less.

## Notes and References

1. Peter Reddaway, 'The battle for Moscow', *The New Republic*, 1 February 1988.
2. *Moskovskie novosti* (*Moscow News*), printed in Russian, English, French and – from April 1988 – in German, is intended primarily for foreign consumption. (*Tass*, 11 March 1988.) Under the editorship of Egor Iakovlev, it has been one of the pioneers of *glasnost'*.
3. *Ogonek*, 1987, 27.
4. *Izvestiia*, 12 August 1987.
5. For example, Gorbachev's address to CPSU plenum, *Pravda*, 26 June 1987.
6. For example, 'Tainaia sud'ba Mikhaila Kol'tsova', *Ogonek*, 1987, 31.
7. *Moscow News*, 1988, 6.
8. *Moscow News*, 1987, 49, and *Ogonek*, 1987, 48.
9. *Izvestiia*, 7 February 1988.
10. See *Ogonek*, 1987, 48.
11. *Literaturnaia gazeta*, 29 July 1987.
12. F. Burlatskii, *Literaturnaia gazeta*, 24 February 1988
13. A. Aganbegian, *Ogonek*, 1987, 28, 29; N. Shmelev, 'The rouble and perestroika', *Moscow News*, 1988, 6.
14. *Izvestiia*, 20 August 1987.
15. *Sovestskaia Rossiia*, 19 August 1987; *Sovetskaia kul'tura*, 3 August 1987.
16. *Literaturnaia gazeta*, 1 August 1987.
17. *Trud*, 31 July 1987.
18. *Sovetskaia Rossiia*, 23 July 1987, on an embezzlement case.
19. *Nedelia*, 20 February 1987.
20. *Pravda*, 25 July 1987; *Izvestiia*, 11 July 1987; *Komsomol'skaia pravda*, 15 July 1987.
21. *Komsomol'skaia pravda*, 9 August 1987.
22. *Izvestiia*, 17 September 1987
23. Gorbachev, on Soviet television, 8 February 1988, in *BBC Summary of World Broadcasts*, SU/0071/C/1, 10 February 1988.
24. *Pravda*, 5 August and 25 November 1987.
25. *Ogonek*, 1987, 27 and 28.
26. The character of *Moskovkaia pravda* changed after November 1987 when its editor left following the sacking of Boris El'tsin as first secretary of the Moscow Communist Party organisation.
27. E. Ligachev, speech to teachers, *Pravda*, 27 August 1987.
28. *Pravda*, 29 January 1988.
29. *Ogonek*, 1988, 2.
30. See 'Soviet aims achieved in Afghanistan', *BBC Summary of World Broadcasts*, SU/0100/i.
31. Ibid.
32. *Sovetskaia Rossiia*, 13 March 1988.
33. See above, Note 27.
34. 5 April 1988.

35. *Tass*, 27 May 1988.
36. F. Burlatskii, *Pravda*, 18 July 1987; also V. Korotich, editor of *Ogonek*, interviewed by Moscow radio in English, 2000 GMT, 19 November 1987, published in *BBC Summary of World Broadcasts*, SU/0009/B/1.
37. Letters in *Ogonek*, 1987, 33 and 44.
38. *Komsomol'skaia pravda*, 10 January 1988.
39. 'Sibaral – an end to the great debate?', *Soviet Analyst*, September 1987; S. Voronitsyn, 'The river diversion scheme ...', *Radio Liberty Research*, 28 July 1987.
40. *Moscow News*, 25 March 1987.
41. Xan Smiley, 'Did Chernobyl really teach the Russians candour?', *Daily Telegraph*, 26 April 1987.
42. M. Gorbachev, closing address to Central Committee plenum, 28 January 1987, 'We need democracy as we need air', in *BBC Summary of World Broadcasts*, SU/8480/C2/1, 31 January 1987. See also Vera Tolz, 'A chronological overview of Gorbachev's campaign for *glasnost*' ', *Radio Liberty Research*, 23 February 1987.
43. See above, Note 18.
44. *Pravda*, 8 January 1987.
45. See *Literaturnaia gazeta*, 16 December 1987.
46. Christian Schmidt-Häuer, *Gorbachev*, London, 1986, pp. 87–88.
47. *Pravda*, 25 December 1985.
48. For example, Iurii Poliakov in *Literaturnaia gazeta*, 29 July 1987.
49. Gorbachev's plenum speech, June 1987.
50. Reddaway, 'The battle for Moscow', op. cit.
51. Based on my experience of attending Moscow press conferences, July–August 1987.
52. *Pravda*, 21 March 1988.
53. *Tass*, 25 March 1988.
54. *Sovetskaia Rossiia*, 30 July 1987; Tolz, 'A chronological overview', op. cit.
55. *Sovetskaia Rossiia*, 9, 10 August 1987.
56. *Izvestia*, March 11 1988.
57. *Komsomol'skaia pravda*, 13 March 1988.
58. See the announcement of the establishment of a commission into the complaints of the Crimean Tatars, *Izvestiia*, 24, 29 July 1987.
59. *Pravda*, 21 March 1988.
60. *Pravda*, 21, 22 August 1987.
61. See above, Note 44.
62. Interview with Tom Brokaw of NBC, 2 December 1987.
63. *Izvestiia*, 10 April 1988.
64. *Sovetskaia Rossiia*, 5 April 1988.
65. *Pravda*, 13 November 1987; A. Rahr, 'The ouster of Boris Yeltsin', *Radio Liberty Research*, 18 December 1987.
66. Peter Reddaway and Mariia Rozanova in private conversations, spring 1988.
67. Vera Tolz, 'Independent journals proliferate in USSR', *Radio Liberty Research*, 27 January 1988.

68. *Vecherniaia Moskva*, 6 August 1987.
69. Tolz, 'Independent journals', op cit.
70. Communiqué, published in political information letter from the Association for a Free Russia, 18 December 1987. On unofficial journals see also Boris Kagarlitsky, 'Glasnost', the Soviet press and red greens', *The Times Literary Supplement*, 25 December 1987, pp. 1430, 1442; reprinted in his *The Thinking Reed. Intellectuals and the Soviet State, 1917 to the present* (London: 1988), pp. 341–47.
71. Viktor Yasmann, 'Drafting a press law', *Radio Liberty Research*, 8 January 1987.
72. Iurii Baturin, interviewed by Soviet television, 26 March 1988.
73. Gorbachev's speech to journalists, *Pravda*, 13 January 1988.

# 4 The Cinema

## IAN CHRISTIE

Like Viktor Shklovskii's evocation of Petrograd in 1921 – 'poised between the present and the future' – Soviet cinema stands today on the brink of a perilous experiment. For the first time since it was fully centralised and given heavy state subsidy under Boris Shumiatskii's leadership in the early 1930s, it faces the daunting prospect of justifying its existence by paying its way – or rather, since the cinema has always been a net contributor to state revenues, of submitting itself to the disciplines of self-financing and consumer demand. In line with the same principles introduced by Gorbachev in other areas of the Soviet economy, the cinema henceforth has to recover its expenditure from domestic box-office receipts and any foreign sources of revenue it can tap, while showing itself responsive to the needs and interests of a no longer passive domestic audience.

On the face of it, this should be quite possible with an average attendance rate still one of the highest in the world at an estimated 10–12 visits per head of the population each year (compared with the USA's 4.5 or Britain's 1.5). But such an apparently healthy position disguises a multitude of problems, all threatening more or less simultaneously to attack the Soviet tradition of near-universal cinemagoing. For the bitter irony is that Soviet cinema's unshackling comes just as Soviet television has also been freed to make its programming highly competitive (with unrestricted access to the whole legacy of Soviet cinema), while home video is spreading rapidly and, thanks to liberalised foreign trade relations, there is the prospect of many more important films soon becoming available.

Soviet cinema indeed has so long enjoyed a vast audience lacking any real alternative entertainment that it could hardly be worse equipped to counter these rival attractions and seize the initiative. The very tempo of daily life under Gorbachev has so accelerated that many people report having no time to see films – they are too busy grappling with the demands of *perestroika*, reading the newspapers and journals that are now eagerly passed from hand to hand as demand far outstrips supply, and watching television to catch the latest sensations of *glasnost'*. Indeed Soviet cinema itself has been so dominated by the fruits of *glasnost'* during the last three years that its present runs the risk of appearing a pale shadow of its newly-revealed past.

After the annual 'national' festival (at which the year's new releases from all Soviet studios are shown in competition) was won in 1988 for the second year running by an 'unshelved' film – in this case Andron Mikhalkov-Konchalovskii's 20-year old *The Story of Asia Kliachina Who Loved But Did Not Marry* – one critic remarked ironically that if Eisenstein's lost *Bezhin Meadow* (1935–37) were suddenly to appear it would undoubtedly be acclaimed as the best new film.[1] Both at home and in festivals and sales abroad, attention has focused almost exclusively on a handful of previously censored films, ranging from the three shelved in that *annus mirabilis* 1967 (*The Commissar* and *The Beginning of a New Century*, in addition to Konchalovskii's *Asia*) to such relatively recent, though still pre-Gorbachev, casualties as *Repentance* and *My Friend Ivan Lapshin*.[2] The result, as so often in the past, has been a new myth challenging the old – both of them extreme simplifications, not to say distortions, of any adequate critical history of Soviet cinema since the death of Stalin.[3] In place of a shackled, servile cinema redeemed only by a few brave dissidents, we now have the tantalising prospect of a wholly suppressed cinema 'on the shelf' starting to be revealed. Both myths ignore the sheer scale and diversity of cinema as a cultural institution in the Soviet Union, and undervalue the large body of responsible, non-complaisant work produced *and shown* during the 'era of stagnation'. The challenge in writing at this juncture, therefore, is how to convey the genuine novelty and excitement of the last three years' extraordinary events, while keeping in focus what had already been achieved before Gorbachev, and the range of problems which will still remain after the present euphoria (or exhumation) has run its course.

It was in May 1986 that the fifth congress of the Film-Makers' Union found itself in the unprecedented situation of having no pre-arranged list of candidates for automatic election to the 50-strong board.[4] On the evidence of some participants, there was a distinct feeling of expectation at the congress, prompted more by the unusual absence of Central Committee officials than by any explicit guidance to delegates. And it has been strongly rumoured that the man who would be elected to replace Lev Kulidzhanov as First Secretary was only consulted at the highest level shortly beforehand. But delegates were certainly aware of the revolt that had broken out in April among students at the central film school, VGIK, who were calling for the resignation of the elderly ultra-conservative Rector Vitalii Zhdan.[5] And there had been some sense of victory for creative film-makers in the air since 1985, when two major 'shelved' films, *Agonia* and *My Friend Ivan Lapshin*, were finally released, although the latter was still pointedly excluded from the Moscow Film Festival of that year.

Nothing, however, could have prepared those gathered in the Kremlin's Palace of Congresses for the removal of some two-thirds of the Brezhnev-era board, including the First Secretary and Secretary of the Board Aleksandr Karaganov. Perhaps the most revealing rumour from the proceedings concerned the prominent (and well-connected) actor and director Nikita Mikhalkov who, when he spoke in defence of the widely-disliked Brezhnev favourite Sergei Bondarchuk, was promptly also voted off the board. The mood among delegates was for radical reform, and no one suspected of ambivalence was given the benefit of the doubt. Among the members of the new board were such uncompromised directors as Vadim Abdrashitov, El'dar Shengelaia, Andrei Smirnov; the critic Andrei Plakhov, then writing for *Pravda*; and the new First Secretary, Elem Klimov.

Klimov's surprise election – clearly engineered from above, but nonetheless widely welcomed – was the most public evidence thus far in the cultural field of a radical new scale of priorities. For his record surpassed even that of Tarkovskii: no less than *five* of Klimov's six features had been 'arrested' (as the old euphemism had it) for varying periods. Even his scarifying *Come and See*, it later transpired, had been vetoed when first initiated in 1976, before being restarted in 1983 and going on to win first prize at the 1985 Moscow Festival.[6]

The succession of Klimov to Kulidzhanov's old post could not have been more symbolic. While the latter (b. 1924) had been one of the early hopes of the uncertain years immediately following Stalin's death, and had done much to make possible the explosion of a post-Thaw 'new wave', Klimov was a member of that new generation – and one who experienced its characteristic trajectory, from hitherto undreamed-of creative freedom in his first works to censorship and near-suppression. Kulidzhanov's first films (co-directed with Iurii Segal) *This is How it Began . . .* (1954) and especially *The House Where I Live* (1958) are usually credited with having brought a human scale and lyricism into the Soviet cinema of the period (although these qualities were in fact typical of many films of the late 1950s, such as Raizman's *Can This Be Love?* (1955) and the celebrated 'breakthrough' works, *The Cranes Are Flying* (1958) and *The Ballad of a*

*Soldier* (1959). But Kulidzhanov's films soon became fewer and more conventional, while he began to climb the ladder of political patronage as First Secretary of the Union, Supreme Soviet Deputy and eventually Central Committee member.[7]

Klimov (b. 1933), meanwhile, emerged from VGIK soon after the debuts of Abuladze (*Someone Else's Children*, 1958), Khutsiev (*Two Fedors*, 1959) Daneliia (*Serezha*, 1960) and Ioseliani (*April*, 1961); and at the same time as Tarkovskii, Shepit'ko (whom he subsequently married), Shukshin and Konchalovskii. His diploma film was an outrageous satire on Young Pioneer summer camps, *Welcome, or No Entry for Unauthorised Persons*, produced with great difficulty and released only in 1964 after first being banned because a fantasy funeral sequence (somewhat akin to *Billy Liar*) involving the hero's grandmother, who bears a passing resemblance to Khrushchev, was interpreted by a zealous editor as implying Khrushchev's death![8] Thereafter he continued to meet opposition and censorship with *The Adventures of a Dentist* (1965), *Sport, Sport, Sport* (1970), *Agonia* (shelved for nine years) and *Farewell* (shelved for four years). All of which, as he explained in a 1987 lecture in London, made the call of Gorbachev's *perestroika* irresistible:

> People of my age and circle were all very aware that this was a turning point for the Soviet Union, a moment we had to grasp because who knows when it might come again? Whatever our personal desires, we had to put them aside because there was a common cause to serve.[9]

Almost immediately, Klimov and his new board launched a two-pronged attack on the bureaucratic inertia that still gripped Soviet cinema. Realising that a responsive and candid press was essential to promote their aims, they insisted that the film journals 'had to change, which meant changing the people who ran them'.[10] Why should the popular *Sovetskii ekran* or the heavyweight *Iskusstvo kino* routinely praise the latest inflated productions of Bondarchuk, Rostotskii or Talankin, when these films were manifestly mediocre – and their overprivileged directors had just been voted off the Union board by their peers? Staff and attitudes changed, and soon the Soviet film press began to speak with a new independence. Controversial films were praised for their outspokenness, while the former mandarin 'untouchables' began to be criticised for their complacency and extravagance.

The onset of a new pluralistic film criticism was signalled by the appearance of a comparative 'critics' chart' in the weekly paper *Nedelia*.[11] And shortcomings in the distribution and exhibition system, which could wreck any new initiatives, are now at least regularly reported.[12]

It was this new climate which made possible a highly significant programme change at one of Moscow's largest cinemas, the Rossiia in Pushkin Square, in the Autumn of 1986. There Bondarchuk's ponderous *Boris Godunov* was moved from the main auditorium after attracting only small audiences, to the smaller screen, where huge crowds had been fighting to see Juris Podnieks's revealing Latvian documentary *Is It Easy to Be Young?*, which scanned the full range of youth 'problems' for the first time in any Soviet film. Apart from being one of the few recorded instances of audience demand producing a direct response, this minor incident could also symbolise the profound change underway in Soviet cinema. No longer will the self-indulgent extravagances of the 'masters' make their way unhindered and unquestioned to the screen – one thinks of Iutkevich's *Lenin in Paris* and Gerasimov's *Tolstoi* as prime examples of this form of vanity publishing – especially when there are urgent communiqués on hand from parts of the body politic formerly denied any place on Soviet screens. But first, there is a reckoning with history.

Appropriately it was a critic, Andrei Plakhov of *Pravda* no less, who led the Union's other main campaign, which has become the most dramatic manifestation of *glasnost'* in Soviet cinema. This is now universally known, following the conventional Russian phrase, as taking hitherto banned or restricted films 'off the shelf'. The process began soon after May 1986 with the establishment of a 'commission for the resolution of creative conflicts' chaired by Plakhov, which invited film-makers to submit grievances for independent reassessment. This soon brought to light a long list of complaints against the bureaucrats of Goskino, the State Committee for Cinematography, who, under the Brezhnev-appointed minister Filip Ermash, had exercised not only stringent 'ideological' censorship, but also highly personal and on occasion incomprehensible vendettas.[13]

The whole issue of 'unshelving' has loomed so large since mid-1986 that already it is vital to distinguish reality from myth. First, the number of works involved. Published estimates have varied from twenty-five to several hundred, but the most frequently cited total is 60. This figure was confirmed in a short 1988 article by the distinguished actor and director Rolan Bykov which is worth quoting in full for the light it sheds on less publicised aspects of the whole process:

> The USSR Goskino Collegium has ruled to reinstate 60 films.
> The Collegium's world-wise members shook their heads mournfully – 'What? *Kuban Cossacks* is banned! And *Eugene Onegin* and *Loyal Friends*!
> The long list was read – yes, all these films were banned. In the case of *Kuban Cossacks*, it was because one of the actors, Yuri Lyubimov later went abroad. *Eugene Onegin* was banned because of Galina Vishnevskaya who played Tatyana – and also misbehaved. Aleksandr Galich, a scriptwriter of *Loyal Friends*, was responsible for that film being relegated to the shelf. The stories are similar for all the 60 films. Only the names are different – Gabai, Vladimov, Korchnoi, etc.
> Some films were lucky to get a 'one showing' permit. Others were banned 'temporarily', which meant forever. People thought this was done for political reasons. But art dominated by bureaucrats is always apolitical. The Pope even recommended Catholics to watch Soviet films because they were highly moral and were not revolutionary.
> If a work of art is inseparable from its author, it is also inseparable from the people to whom it belongs. That's why I think that the request of the mediation commission of the USSR Union of Cinema Workers and the collegium's decision are real political acts. These works of art have been reinstated as public, socialist property, which cannot be confiscated.[14]

This account confirms that the relationship of the 'conflict commission' to Goskino is still technically advisory, although so successful has the tide of publicity proved that Goskino has apparently acquiesced to all 'requests' thus far made. Bykov also explains why so many seemingly quite innocuous films were shelved: it was for circumstantial reasons, often to do with the changed status of personnel associated with them, rather than for any intrinsic reasons of subject or style. And finally, he provides evidence of a long-suspected hierarchy of banning, which consigned many films to a limbo existence, where they might be shown briefly and inconveniently within the USSR but withheld from any foreign exhibition.[15]

But if much of the commission's work has amounted to undoing the absurd excesses of Goskino's bureaucracy, there has also been an important element of genuine rehabilitation and discovery. At least five major talents, all virtually unknown outside professional circles and of a calibre which Soviet cinema could ill afford to deny itself, have so far emerged; and perhaps another half dozen 'missing' films by major directors can now be reinserted in their makers' filmographies. With fitting irony, the artists and works in question turn out to be of unimpeachable seriousness, most of them more in tune with the imperatives of ideological exhortation than the bulk of Soviet cinema's normal output.

Consider first the case of Kira Muratova (b. 1934), who began co-directing shorts with her then husband Aleksandr Muratov at the Odessa Studio in 1961. By 1967 she was ready to direct her first solo feature, *Brief Encounters*, in which she had to substitute for the lead actress herself and play opposite the now-legendary actor and song-writer Vladimir Vysotskii. The ecstasy of the relationship, however, lies in the past, while the present is a tug-of-war between personal fulfilment and a demanding job in local government which involves monitoring construction standards. Was it the few scathing scenes in which the heroine is seen rejecting typical Soviet shoddy workmanship that provoked Goskino's ire? Or, more likely, was it the teasing, elliptical rhythm of the film which mingles past and present, and sets Vysotskii at the apex of a triangle, with a simple peasant girl competing for his attention? At any rate, one of the most original and sophisticated of Soviet films from the 1960s was promptly 'shelved'.

Four years later the same fate befell Muratova's second feature, *A Long Farewell* (1971). Here the loss was perhaps even greater, for this acute and painful study of a mother struggling to hold down a job (she is an interpreter in a large industrial concern) and hold on to her increasingly restive teenage son, is surely one of the finest of all modern Soviet films. Again, the film's arresting images and intricate structure closely mirror its themes. The boy is embarrassed by his mother's emotional behaviour and idealises his distant father in Siberia: the almost unbearable tension between the mother and son is expressed in a series of brilliantly oblique, inconclusive sequences of them in public together, and in the territorial arrangement of the single room they share. And the boy's use of a slide projector to create his own fantasy world becomes a powerful visual metaphor for his frustration. Was Muratova's treatment of this familiar social problem too unstereotypical, one wonders? Did it offend by an excess of psychological realism and a failure to offer any affirmative conclusion?[16]

Whatever the reason, Muratova did not direct again until 1979, when *Getting to Know the Wide World* was also shelved. *Among the Grey Stones* (1983) was in fact released, but extensively revised and attributed to the fictitious 'Ivan Sidorov'. Not until the arrival of the 'conflict commission' was the full span of her *oeuvre* revealed and her achievement in the face of her persecution saluted. For Klimov and the union activists, Muratova's example was all the more important because she had refused to compromise, preferring to accept menial work around the studios rather than make her films acceptable to the bureaucrats. Since her 'rehabilitation' in 1986, Muratova has directed one new film, *Change of Fortune*, a remarkable absurdist version of Somerset Maugham's story 'The Letter' – but since the Soviet authorities neglected to clear copyright with the Maugham estate, this remains unseen in the West. However, it is heartening to discover that her own remarkable 'change of fortune' has not blunted Muratova's appetite for innovation and risk. Her transposition of Maugham's steamy melodrama into a series of discrete, often ironic tableaux is overtly feminist and avoids any comparison with Wyler's classic 1940 Bette Davis version. Twenty years after she brought some of the laconic intensity of the French *nouvelle vague* into Soviet cinema (and paid the price), she is now reaching out towards a 'post-modern' selfconsciousness of style which invites comparison with New York independents like Yvonne Rainer or Sheila McLaughlin and places her, along with Sokurov, in the vanguard of Soviet film-makers.[17]

If any precise explanation is still lacking as to why Muratova was so comprehensively 'shelved', there is at least more evidence in the case of Aleksei German (b. 1938). It was in fact the rearguard action of Goskino in trying to withhold German's *My Friend Ivan Lapshin* from would-be foreign buyers even after its domestic release that provoked one of the last such skirmishes before May 1986. And appropriately, one of the symbols of the film-makers' victory was an early television screening of *Lapshin* that same year – too early for the mass audience, as it transpired, since the vast correspondence received ran two to one against the film.[18]

German is the son of the well-known writer Iurii German, on whose semi-autobiographical writings both his first solo feature, *Trial on the Road*,[19] and *Lapshin* were based. After a decade working in theatre in Smolensk and Leningrad, he joined Lenfilm Studio in 1965 and co-directed his first feature (with Grigorii Aronov), *The Seventh Com-*

*panion*, in 1967. Although this does not appear to have been shown in the West, and German states that he played a secondary role in making it, his account is fascinating:

> The story took place in 1918, during the Red Terror, a subject rarely dealt with in our films. This terror was in some ways a response to the White Terror. A little-known decree was published which said: 'Not an eye for an eye, but a thousand eyes for one, a thousand bourgeois eyes for the life of the leader. Long live the Red Terror!' Our film began with this decree. Then we told the story of a Tsarist general who finds himself in jail with prisoners from all classes. They are used as hostages: twenty of them are shot each time a Red is killed. The general turns out to be something of a revolutionary sympathiser, who took a courageous position at the time of the sailors' revolt in 1905. Finally they let him go. But nobody wants him; he doesn't know where to go. They won't take him back into jail; and he doesn't want to serve the Whites, since they are allied with foreign powers. In the end he's killed.[20]

Surprisingly – in the same year that two other challenging Civil War period films, *The Commissar* and *From the Beginning of an Unknown Century*, were shelved – *The Seventh Companion* was released with no trouble. German's explanation is that

> it wasn't a film which showed any talent, that's why they let it be shown. ... While *Trial on the Road* may have dealt with fewer delicate themes – the screenplay posed no problems – it was held up because of the way it was directed.[21]

*Trial on the Road* had been developed by German with his father, who died before the film went into production. It concerns the attitudes of two Red Army officers during the Patriotic War when a sergeant who collaborated under duress with the German invaders tries to rejoin his own side. While the sergeant is welcomed and, after a 'trial' ambush, trusted by one of his captors (played by Rolan Bykov), the Major in command remains hostile and displays a generally paranoid attitude. It is indeed a remarkably austere portrayal of the harsh realities of the war – with the peasants as suspicious of their Red Army 'defenders' as of the Germans and marauding partisans – and a telling microcosm of the still sensitive issue of how returning Soviet prisoners were treated.

Despite a year's struggle by German and the support of influential friends like the writer Konstantin Simonov, it was emphatically banned by Goskino and the studio ordered to pay back the money 'wasted' on its production.[22] Yet such were the paradoxes of Soviet cinema in the 'period' of stagnation' that German was encouraged to continue as a salaried director at Lenfilm because he had 'shown talent'! Five years later, his next film, *Twenty Days Without War*, based on a story by Simonov (who had long been a family friend), penetrated still further into the 'texture' of wartime experience. It followed the almost classic pattern of a combatant's period of leave from the front: in this case, Lopatin is a war correspondent who visits the film studio where a travesty of his war writing is being made. But this debunking of the conventional Soviet 'inspirational' war movie is by no means the film's main focus, which is rather the emotional, psychic impact of war. Here the former circus clown Iurii Nikulin gives a memorably impassive performance as the writer – detached, numbed, yet somehow responsible for witnessing and articulating his fellow-countrymen's experience; and his partner in a brief quasi-romantic interlude is the celebrated actress and singer Liudmila Gurchenko, who registers a similarly low-key presence of great intensity.

*Twenty Days without War* was not exactly banned: it was even shown in the Critics' Week at the 1977 Cannes Festival (although this was later considered an oversight). But Goskino's hostility ensured that it received scant attention or exhibition, despite being one of the most mature contributions to Soviet cinema's generally hackneyed Second World War genre. Working in black-and-white has been an important element of German's aesthetic – he observes in an interview that Bondarchuk's *They Fought for the Motherland* would have been much better had it not been in colour – and his three films to date are distinguished by the remarkably subtle *grisaille* of Valerii Fedosov's monochrome cinematography. He also considers unstaged amateur snapshots, rather than 'organised' official photographs, a vital source for reconstructing the atmosphere of the past.

For his third and most significant work to date, German turned again to his father's writings and entered the decade which in cinema, if not in literature, had long been forbidden territory: the 1930s. The script of *My Friend Ivan Lapshin* was apparently first written in 1969, but permission to film it was not given until 1979, by which time it had been altered considerably: 'the main thing for us was not the detective intrigue, not the love story, but the time itself.'[23] The setting was no longer Leningrad in 1937, but a small provincial town, Unchansk, in

1935. Three shots heard at the beginning of the film while a portrait of Kirov is on-screen refer obliquely to the assassination which inaugurated Stalin's 'terror' and place the film's world with scrupulous precision: it is the lull before the storm. But this is not a *film à clef*; above all it is an evocation of 'atmosphere', of the lived reality of crowded communal apartments, of the joys and sorrows of provincial life centring on a gauche, idealistic bachelor – 'our local Pinkerton' – the local police chief Ivan Lapshin.

Much remains to be said about this elliptical, multi-layered work, with its Wellesian complexity of point-of-view. But perhaps what was most significant for Soviet cinema on the brink of *glasnost'* was that German had succeeded like no other Soviet director, apart from Tarkovskii in *The Mirror*, in linking his own life-history with the turbulent history of the 1930s, which is the crucible of the modern Soviet experience:

> We really tried to wipe out the plot, because for me the important thing is more to feel the vibrations of the country, of people of the apartment, to generalise them, to feel again the story of my father and mother – and of myself too.[24]

Once again, the originality of German's aesthetic provoked bureaucratic fury. The film was shelved for two-and-a-half years and denounced in the Lenfilm Studio newspaper, before becoming a major commercial success in 1985 – and winning the highest number of votes in a poll of Soviet film critics for the 'best Soviet films of all time' (see the Appendix to this chapter). After the eventual release of *Trial on the Road* in January 1986 and publication of several substantial interviews with German, he has become probably the most critically respected of all contemporary directors.

No chronicle, however brief, of the impact of 'unshelving' censored films can ignore two further figures rescued from oblivion, Aleksandr Askol'dov and Aleksandr Sokurov, both more controversial than either Muratova or German. It was at the 1987 Moscow Film Festival, the first since the Film-Makers' Union revolt, that Askol'dov spoke out in a public session at the House of Cinema about the suppression of his solitary film, *The Commissar*, made and promptly shelved in 1967. He made no bones about what he considered to be continuing hostility towards him and his film on the part of the new union leaders; and even during the film's triumphant progress around international film festivals throughout 1988 he has collected a series of apparently dismissive statements by Klimov, Andrei Smirnov and others – while at the time of writing, in October 1988, the film has yet to be released publicly in the Soviet Union.

There can be little doubt that the reason for *The Commissar* being withheld originally, as it appears to be still, is its overt sympathy for Jewish life and characters – something virtually banished from Soviet screens since the suppression of the Yiddish theatre in the 1930s. Based loosely on Vasilii Grossman's story 'In the Town of Berdichev', *The Commissar* also challenges the traditionally heroic image of the Civil War commissar, which dates back to *Chapaev*. This commissar is female, ruthless (we see her summarily execute a deserter in the opening sequence) and *sexual*. Klavdiia Vavilova is pregnant and wants to have her child, knowing that she will have to leave it soon, which brings her to lodge with a Jewish tinker's family. Here she discovers a warmth and tolerance which stand like an island of humanity amid the cross-currents of war. But even apart from the shock of hearing Yiddish spoken in a modern Soviet film and witnessing Rolan Bykov, as Efim, perform an astonishing 'morning dance' that lies somewhere between Chaplin and Chagal, Askol'dov includes two visionary elements that give his film an even wider frame of reference. Klavdiia's giving birth occasions an extended heroic metaphor, as she and her comrades struggle to haul a field-gun through sand, which recalls the passionate poetry of Dovzhenko or even Eisenstein. And after the baby's birth, when Klavdiia and the Magazanik family take shelter during an attack, there is a remarkable 'flash forward' or premonition of the Holocaust, which shows Jews being herded together and Klavdiia following them.

Askol'dov was apparently advised by General Romanov of Goskino that his film could be released if he removed the Holocaust reference and changed the 'ethnic' identity of the family. He refused and it remained 'on the shelf', while he was forced to follow another career in the theatre.[25] Seen today, with no changes other than the re-recording of Alfred Shnitke's magnificent score, *The Commissar* vividly, poignantly, shows what degrees of liberalisation Soviet cinema had already achieved by the mid-1960s, after a decade of de-Stalinisation. But mere beginners like Askol'dov could not hope to outmanoeuvre the bureaucrats of Goskino.

If Askol'dov remains a thorn in the side of both reformers and conservatives, publicly questioning whether much has really changed under *perestroika*, Aleksandr Sokurov has quietly assumed the mantle of Soviet art cinema's 'king across the water', Tarkovskii. Again, his was a wholly subterranean career until the conflict commission intervened, and the published text of the resulting letter is worth quoting in full:

> The secretariat of the board of the Union of Cinematographers of the USSR has looked at your films *The Solitary Voice of a Man*, *The Salute*, *The Allies*, *An Elegy* and *Endurance, Effort*. We have exchanged impressions and come to the conclusion that these are serious creative works, which open up the perspectives of cinematic investigation.
> 
> We have taken the first steps and will make efforts to arrange for your documentary films to be released in cinemas and shown on television and also at international festivals. We shall petition for you to have the opportunity to make a version of *The Solitary Voice of a Man* that can be screened and to make copies for showings in clubs. We also intend to do what we can to assure the inclusion of your new project in the production plan of Lenfilm for 1987 immediately after you finish work on the screen version of Bernard Shaw. It would be desirable for this project to be on a contemporary theme.
> 
> Respected Aleksandr Nikolaevich, we are glad to inform you that the secretariat has voted for your acceptance into the Union of Cinematographers of the USSR!
> 
> We wish you creative success. We thank you for your courage, for refusing to compromise and for sticking to your principles.
> 
> E. G. Klimov
> 
> First Secretary of the Board[26]

Sokurov's very free adaptation of Shaw's *Heartbreak House*, known variously as *Mournful Indifference* or *Anaesthesia Dolorosa*, was the first of his films to be seen abroad.[27] This weirdly surreal fantasy, resembling nothing so much as a Ken Russell dramatised documentary (Shaw appears as a character wandering around Captain Shotover's ark-like house) interspersed with a seemingly autonomous collage of newsreel footage and prewar American songs on the soundtrack, puzzled most viewers at the 1987 Berlin Festival. It was followed by the Platonov adaptation mentioned in the union's letter, *The Solitary Voice of a Man*, shown at the Locarno Festival in the same year. More recently, his new feature, *Days of Eclipse*, was shown along with a selection of the short films at the 1988 Riga Forum, which made possible some assessment of this difficult but outstanding talent.

Sokurov (b. 1951) has had an unusual career for a Soviet filmmaker. He worked as an assistant television producer while studying history at Gor'kii University, then enrolled at VGIK. but 'for reasons beyond him did not graduate'.[27] With support from Tarkovskii, and from the two Leningrad-based directors Il'ia Averbakh and Dinara Asanova,[28] Sokurov nonetheless found work at Lenfilm Studios in 1979 and in particular at the Leningrad Documentary Film Studio, where his 'creative, artistic and civic position, as well as his worldview were respected'.

His film-making is indeed rooted in documentary, but a documentary that is unusually critical, interrogative and reflective. *Maria*, for instance, is a two part study of a 'typical' woman farm-worker, seen first in 1978 with her husband and adolescent daughter. Ten years later (the passage of time signified by an interminable tracking shot along a drab counry road), the film-makers revisit Maria's village to show their original film to those who appeared in it. But Maria is dead and there is a long-standing feud between the remarried husband and daughter, also now married. The former rural idyll now looks hollow, as Sokurov reflects that Maria died longing to have another child in place of the son who was killed by a drunken tractor-driver, but overwork had made her infertile. *Elegy* (1985–6) is another surprising variation on a familiar form. Ostensibly it chronicles the career of the great bass Chaliapin, starting from a visit to Leningrad by his surviving daughters. But amid the familiar commemorative images, Sokurov introduces other discourses – including a pointed reference to Lunacharskii's argument that great Russian artists like Chaliapin must be given enough freedom to enable them to return from abroad.[29] Once again, the result is an exquisitely elegant work which seems both fiercely 'national' and deeply critical.

There is indeed a close link between Sokurov's untypical avantgardism and his aggressive cultural chauvinism. He believes that Soviet cinema, like Soviet society, has followed a disastrously wrong path since the 1920s and that there must now be a drastic purgation of both:

> Russia was where the aesthetics of cinema originated. France may have contributed techniques but it was only in Russia that individual creativity could develop in the 20s. Now those years have

been completely forgotten. Russian cinema thought it had to make the same choices as in other countries: commercial sentimentality, narrative, representation. Apart from Robert Bresson, the aesthetic principle has been completely lost. The strongest influences on me are Eisenstein's *The Strike* and Kozintsev.[30] There is a link between the 20s and the 80s. Our cinema has for too long suffered from the paradox of politics overshadowing aesthetics, which has greatly damaged Soviet culture. The rights of aesthetics must be recognised and we can then draw inspiration from the 20s. . . .[31]

During public debates in both London and Riga in 1988, Sokurov argued vehemently for an aesthetic 'absolute', totally distinct from any political or entertainment imperative.[32] Art, he maintains, can only strive to save the soul of Russia and prepare the individual for death – an apocalyptic view that certainly taps many mystical-cum-religious currents within contemporary Soviet society, while infuriating the rationalist supporters of *perestroika*. It also accords with Tarkovskii's general position on the sacramental role of art, which no doubt explains why Sokurov has been so widely regarded as the 'heir' of Tarkovskii.[33]

But it must be said that, whereas Tarkovskii's increasingly sententious philosophising seemed to hasten the atrophy of his film-making, Sokurov's daring dialectic of images and, especially, sounds offers an exciting prospect for a new Soviet cinema of *art et essai*. His most recent films are the opposite of didactic: they are open, suggestive and boldly experimental. Perhaps the most telling is the 18-minute *Evening Sacrifice* (1987), which simply shows large crowds roaming the streets of Leningrad after a military ceremony. Merely by the choices of framing and lenses, and the mix of sound, Sokurov has here created an intensely moving portrayal of that Soviet cliché, 'the people'. As the Riga programme note aptly put it: 'A patriotic demonstration . . . takes on the appearance of a disturbing mystery play'.[34] And his latest feature film, *Days of Eclipse*, presents an extreme study of alienation as a young doctor living rough in a remote Kazak town desperately seeks some meaning in life. The ambiance and appearance of the film often recall Wenders – there is even an angelic interruption, as an unseen figure suddenly whisks a child away from the doctor and up into the sky – but its acute sense of *distance* from Russia and the West, and the few telling moments of focused narrative, which include a suicide and an exiled Crimean Tatar recalling his wretched childhood, all suggest that Sokurov rejects the European 'progressive' tradition in Russian thought, and is here exploring the lure of an 'Eastern' destiny, of the kind once envisioned by the Futurist Khlebnikov.

While Sokurov's own philosophical and political bearings must remain open to further clarification, there can be little doubt that he has already become a commanding influence on artistically ambitious younger film-makers. To judge from several impressive films by associates shown at Riga – a powerful documentary on the Acmeist poet Gumilev and a suggestive nocturnal 'vox pop' on a sleeper train – this influence will greatly extend the range of subjects and stylistic options in the future.[35] Through Sokurov, the 'secret cinema' of Soviet documentary, much of it already emancipated from the conformism of its fictional counterpart, may yet speed the latter's sophistication. The critic Mikhail Iampol'skii wrote of *Anaesthesia Dolorosa* as, in part

> the parody of an infantile, impotent culture: a parody which includes much of the contemporary cinema, such as the 'metaphysical' epigones of Tarkovskii, or the 'retro' style of Mikhalkov. Sokurov aims to construct his cinema on a completely different basis, explicitly opposing these two styles of excessive eclecticism with a cinematic language which is complex, referential and associative.[36]

Another film-maker whose career has remained virtually unknown until recently is in fact a documentarist, the Armenian Artavazd Peleshian, whose first film to be seen abroad, *The Beginning* (1967), marked him as an inheritor of the mantle of Dziga Vertov, prophet of the 'cine-eye' and pioneer of Soviet propaganda newsreels.[37] Peleshian's fiftieth anniversary celebration of 1917 cuts together familiar and unfamiliar footage of troops, horsemen, trains and planes with rhythmic virtuosity to make the Revolution seem an irresistible force of nature. In his subsequent films, the same shaping skills produce a moving affirmation of Armenian national identity: *We* (1968); a vivid calendar of land and animal husbandry, *The Seasons* (1975), which recalls Kalatozov's 1930 classic *Salt for Svanetia*; and an extraordinary chronicle of man's aspiration to conquer the air and space in *Our Century* (1982). Again, it is ironic that a film-maker so attuned to the original ideals of Soviet documentary should be treated as a pariah. Was it the sheer kinaesthetic force of Peleshian's rhythms that felt dangerously compelling (Vertov had inspired this unease too among the pedestrian)? Or was it his disdain of language, which leaves the films' meaning 'unanchored'? Whichever was the case, both cinema and television authorities have severely inhibited the career of this most 'heroic' of modern Soviet documentarists.

As well as the whole careers of the five film-makers discussed above, a number of isolated films by well-known directors have been brought to light by the Conflict Commission. In most cases these were already known titles, recorded in the film-makers' filmographies, but tantalisingly unavailable. Now, with their release – and with the 'ur-texts' of several major 1960s films not previously known to have been cut against the director's wishes – a wholesale process of revaluation is under way. The past has literally invaded the present, reopening long-forgotten debates and reviving diminished reputations.

As already noted, 1967 can now clearly be seen to be the moment when Goskino, under Ermash, decided to teach defiant film-makers a lesson. In addition to the complete suppression of *The Commissar* and the long rear-guard campaign initiated against Paradzhanov's *The Colour of Pomegranates*, no less than four further casualties have now appeared: Konchalovskii's *The Story of Asia Kliachina*, two of the three completed parts of *The Beginning of an Unknown Century*,[38] Okeev's *The Sky of Our Childhood* from Kirghizia, and Kiisk's *Madness* from Estonia. What then, apart from their considerable intrinsic merits, was at stake in these works?[39]

In the case of Konchalovskii's documentary-style portrayal of life on a collective farm, it was a vernacular realism, derived from shooting on location with only two professional actors among a cast of farm-workers, and using improvisation to cut through the in-grained conventions of scripting. The collective farm has been at the heart of Soviet cinema's mythmaking tradition since the early 1930s: Khrushchev's 'secret speech' to the Twentieth Party Congress in 1956 singled out this area of falsification for special censure.[40] The ostensible focus of concern had been Asia's independent decision to reject both the bullying father of her unborn child *and* an exemplary suitor in the shape of a newly-arrived tractor-driver (shades of the 1930s *kolkhoz* romance!). This led to an imposed change of title, *Asia's Happiness*, but ultimately the film's integral realism must have seemed to official eyes too far removed from a cherished myth – although Vasilii Shukshin was already sketching his equally unidealised view of the village life by this time.[41]

*The Beginning of an Unknown Century* was intended as a major commemoration of the fiftieth anniversary of the Revolution, with four separate episodes commissioned from promising young directors. Larisa Shepit'ko (whose death in 1979 robbed Soviet cinema of one of its boldest talents) turned to the controversial 'primitive' writer Andrei Platonov for a mystical treatment of the coming of electricity to a remote village suffering drought in the early 1920s. *The Homeland of Electricity* recalls the early Dovzhenko in its lyrical intensity, but doubtless its harrowing picture of peasants' resort to religion in the midst of drought was enough to damn the film (although its banning did not deter Shepit'ko from pursuing an increasingly religious quest in *The Ascent* (1977, from Bykov's story, *Sotnikov*) and her planned adaptation of Rasputin's *Farewell to Matera*).[42] The second panel of the film, *Angel*, directed by Andrei Smirnov (now deputising for Klimov as First Secretary of the Film-Makers' Union) took its story of everyday heroism and brutality during the Civil War from another controversial writer, Iurii Olesha. Here again one senses a sharper challenge than was acceptable to an established genre – the Civil War adventure tale – and resistance to the covert rehabilitation of a still suspect writer.[43] Smirnov would go on to direct the sentimental though evocative *Belorussian Station* in 1971, a major commercial and 'official' success (reputedly Brezhnev's favourite film); but his next film, *Autumn* (1973), was shelved.

The problem with Tolomush Okeev's *The Sky of Our Childhood* seems to have lain in the intensity of its commitment to the traditional lifestyle of a nomadic people. To imply that progress is not automatically beneficial, that it might even be destructive and demeaning to the once-proud Kirghiz herdsmen, was clearly not what officials wanted to propagate in the aftermath of what many hardliners already considered the deplorable slackening of discipline that had taken place under Khrushchev. The sheer brilliance of Okeev's soaring mountain landscapes (in widescreen) cannot have helped; as German noted, mediocrity was much more acceptable. Later, in 1976, Otar Ioseliani's gentle portrait of a Georgian village, *Pastorale*, was shelved for no discernible reason other than its refusal to reproduce the banalities of village life. In the case of the Estonian Kiisk's *Madness*, banned in 1968, a more straightforward political interpretation seems in order. The setting is the Nazi occupation of Estonia, during which a Gestapo intelligence officer enters a mental hospital to search out a sheltering English spy and, naturally, falls prey to the prevailing cat-and-mouse lunacy. Clearly this was a film all too susceptible to subversive readings, especially in restive Soviet Estonia.

'Shelving' continued throughout the 1970s, although many film-makers had obviously learned a *modus vivendi* with the censors. According to one veteran of such struggles, there was even an element of game-playing by the early 1980s: film-makers were constantly devising new ways to outwit censors, while the latter sought to impose their increasingly unrealistic code. And as Konchalovskii pointed out in a recent interview, the dearth of even competent scripts meant that promising ones, on however sensitive subjects, would tend to get through the early stages of approval.[44] The most eagerly awaited of the later shelved films has probably been Gleb Panfilov's *The Theme*, finished in 1980, but withdrawn abruptly after several Soviet festival screenings in that year.[45] Although the taboo subject of Jewish emigration makes a brief appearance in this tragi-comedy, when an over-successful writer overhears a furtive conversation between the woman he has been following and her shadowy friend, an unpublished country writer, the film works best as a satire on the superficiality of 'official' culture and the futility of success within its canons, animated by the furious self-destructive energy of that most 'official' actor, Mikhail Ul'ianov.

More revealing, perhaps, has been very recent information about a hitherto unsuspected strand of mid-1960s censorship which demanded heavy cuts in the original versions of two of that decade's key works, Tarkovskii's *Andrei Rublev* and Khutsiev's *I Am Twenty*. Both films were well-known to have had considerable censorship problems: *Rublev*, finished in 1966, has appeared in no less than three versions of different lengths. Now we learn that there is an 'original' version, reputedly some 60 minutes longer than the known 186 minutes. According to those who have seen it (my informant is Andrei Smirnov), there are no substantial new sequences, but rather a completely different rhythm. Equally dramatic is the news of an uncensored version of Marlen Khutsiev's 1964 *I Am Twenty*, one of the key 'youth' films of the Soviet 'new wave', under its original title *The Il'ich Gate*. The film is known to have been criticised by Khrushchev in 1963 as showing a 'false' picture of Soviet youth; and was accordingly re-edited.[46] What disappeared, it now seems, was a fantasy-structure which brought the dead father of one of the young characters back to face his son's question, 'How should one live?'[47]

Unquestionably there will be more revelations, more 'discoveries' of work compromised, buried, neglected over the years before the 'era of stagnation' as well as during it. Already Soviet film historians are reaching back to the Tsarist period, now referred to as 'early Russian cinema', to explore its surviving riches, which were long dismissed on principle as worthless.[48] And the tide of rehabilitation in other fields is offering welcome clues towards the reconsideration of even the most familiar tracts of Soviet cinema history. A recent example was the publication of three film reviews by Osip Mandel'shtam leading to the exhumation of a hitherto unknown Georgian film, *The Forgotten Face*, a Civil War comedy no less, directed by Nikolai Shpikovskii in 1929, which does indeed live up to the poet's praise.[49]

*Glasnost'* has developed a powerful momentum; and the continuing revelations of the Conflict Commission have given the Film-Makers' Union at least a moral authority which has enabled it to step into the near-vacuum created by Goskino's retreat and uncertainty about its future role. Despite the replacement of Ermash as Minister by the more conciliatory figure of Aleksandr Kamshalov (formerly with the Komsomol youth organisation), there are persistent rumours that the separate identity of Goskino is in question, and that it may be merged with the Ministry of Culture or some other appropriate organisation. If this happens, it will symbolically mark the end of cinema's special status as 'the most important art' of the Soviet state, and may indeed free it of the obsessive, largely symbolic, scrutiny and tutelage that has dogged it since the mid-1920s. But before this happens (if it does) there is a painful adjustment to present and future realities under way. Since mid-1986, the main thrust of the union's policy has been to negotiate a long-term guaranteed independence from bureacratic control; and the route chosen is that widely favoured under *perestroika* – self-financing.

To understand what a profound change this would mean, it is necessary to appreciate that the basic structure of Soviet cinema has changed little since Stalin's time. Hitherto, the controlling mechanism has been the ubiquitous annual plan: in the case of production, this is negotiated between Goskino, the union and the studios, with appropriate funds for fixed costs and for the agreed production programme supplied in full by Goskino, supposedly from its box-office revenues. Other than keeping productions within budget, the studios have had little real responsibility for their output, while all production personnel have enjoyed the status of permanent studio employees.[50]

Henceforth it is envisaged that at least all creative personnel will become 'freelance', subject to short-term contracts, and that individual studios should fund their production from the proportion of box-office revenues that will come to them. Studios failing to make ends meet will, we are assured, be allowed to go bankrupt. The most obvious problem with this is that the studios will still have scarcely any input into, let alone control over, the massive national distribution process, which remains the monopoly of Goskino and Glavrepertkom. They are therefore in no position to match expenditure with any vigorous strategy to recover it. And even if Goskino were to commit itself fully to maximising audiences, there is still the awkward fact that cinema admission prices have been kept uneconomically low for so long that the average box-office yield is incommensurate with actual production costs.[51] However, as a strategy to galvanise (or traumatise) the largely inert production elite, introducing unheard-of disciplines into budgeting and scheduling, it may achieve its main purpose, while the new emphasis on meeting public demand – at a time when an unprecedented 50 per cent of Soviet films have been attracting fewer than 5 million admissions – may also help keep the threat of renewed censorship at bay.[52]

Nonetheless, at this crucial juncture, with Klimov at least temporarily returned to film-making, many serious film-makers are openly apprehensive about the changes under way. They fear, understandably, that in the drive to become economically self-sufficient and more competitive with its Western counterpart, Soviet cinema may sacrifice its considerable reserves of outspokenness and artistry for a mess of populism – and may still only succeed in opening the door to a flood of more attractive, and cheaper, imports.

They are also aware that Soviet cinema is technically backward, not only in terms of training, equipment and materials (the notoriously uneven quality of colour film stock was condemned in 1987 by the State Quality Control Commission, resulting in an acute supply crisis), but more crucially in its dramatic and expressive fluency. With very few exceptions, to watch the handling of a musical number or an action sequence in a contemporary Soviet film is to witness not so much a different idiom as an embarrassing ineptitude. The normal 'prose' of Soviet cinema has become flaccid, even-paced, inexpressive – far removed from the dynamism of the 1920s or 1930s; over-reliance on the zoom lens and a lack of sophisticated camera movement have tended to make it one-dimensional; sound-mixing and reproduction are generally of a low standard; and the majority of films are simply too long and too sluggishly edited. The economy and precision of a Raizman (*Your Contemporary, Private Life*), an Abdrashitov (*A Train Has Stopped, Parade of the Planets, Plumbum*), a Muratova, Sokurov or a German is still rare; and some of the most successful *oeuvres* of recent decades have precisely exploited a distinctive vein of primitivism – notably Paradzhanov's and Shukshin's, but also much of Georgian cinema. However, it remains true that the normal run of Soviet film-making falls far short of Western standards of quality and attention to detail – compare, for instance, the plausibility of the Soviet sailors (played by British actors) in the low-budget British production *Letter to Brezhnev* with the totally unconvincing English telegraph operator in Dzhordzhadze's *My English Grandfather* (poorly dubbed by an American).

The leading directors are acutely aware, as are too few in the West, just how much was achieved in spite of censorship and bureaucratic interference during the last thirty years. For it would be a grave mistake to assume that honest, critical film-making only became possible under *glasnost'*. Veterans like Raizman and Kheifits, and their protégés such as Abdrashitov and German, have long dwelt on the yawning gap between propaganda ideal and everyday reality – and it would be difficult to find any indictment of bureaucratic mendacity today more damning than Raizman's 1968 *Your Contemporary*, or any exploration of class difference more subtle than Abdrashitov's *The Turning* of 1978. The makers of films like these, together with leading figures from the republics like the Georgian Rekhviashvili and the Belorussian Rubinchik, strongly supported the general thrust of Gorbachev's *perestroika* but fear its over-hasty application to cinema.

What of the actual course of reform? It is still too early to pass judgement on most of the new developments, but the evidence so far is mixed. Democratic election of the heads of VGIK and Mosfilm Studio has not introduced energetic new talent, while the longstanding management of the export-import agency Sovexportfilm remains unchanged. Apart from the Union's dramatic revolt in May 1986, equally drastic action has only followed at the Film Art Institute VNIIKI, the centre for critical and historical studies, where *perestroika* swept away an old-guard leadership and brought an uncompromised (if unexpected) new director, the Belorussian writer Ales' Adamovich (author of Klimov's *Come and See*). Adamovich appears to be backing both the empirical and the theoretical tendencies among institute staff which were formerly suppressed by a conservative 'ideological' directorate.

The main thrust of reform at the massive Mosfilm Studio is to break this monolith down into more manageable and responsive production units, known as 'associations', which will be responsible for implementing their contrasting policies *and* becoming economically self-sufficient. In place of the previous small number of large groups, there are now eleven associations operating at Mosfilm, with a mixture of veterans, mid-career directors and newcomers at their head.[53] These include Raizman, Vladimir Naumov (former partner of Alov), Sergei Bondarchuk, Georgii Daneliia, Sergei Solov'ev, Vladimir Men'shov (director of the US Academy Award-winning *Moscow Does Not Believe in Tears*), Karen Shakhnazarov (the new cult figure among 'youth' directors, with *A Winter Night in Gagra* and *Messenger Boy*), the actor and director Rolan Bykov (with an association designed to bring production aimed at young people back from the Gor'kii Studio to Mosfilm), the scriptwriters Valentin Chernykh and Iurii Arabov (the latter Sokurov's regular writer, now responsible for the 'Debut' association, which is supported by the Film-Makers' Union, jointly with Smirnov) and Sergei Kolosov (in charge of the television film unit, concerned with both series and one-off dramas). A similar reform has been announced at the second largest studio, Lenfilm, where four associations now operate. Again, emphasis is given to production for television, with Sergei Mikael'ian, director of the most celebrated 'production' film (a genre which re-emerged in the Brezhnev era), *The Bonus*, acting as its artistic director.[54]

The underlying 'collegiate' structure of production has not changed. Each of the new associations appears to have a target of about five films per year, with between five and ten directors attached to the unit on a long-term basis. In addition to the Artistic Director, usually an experienced director, there is the usual Artistic Council, although a number of these now sport unexpected names – such as the celebrated eye surgeon Sviatoslav Fedorov and *Moscow News* editor-in-chief Egor Iakovlev on the council of Men'shov's 'Genre' association. Each association is obviously trying for a balance of tried and trusted directors, with an eye to the box office, as well as riskier new talent. Thus, for example, the 'Rhythm' unit, headed by Daneliia, includes on its roster both the extremely popular comedy director El'dar Riazanov – probably the most 'bankable' of current Soviet film-makers – as well as the young Sergei Bodrov, director of an outstanding recent 'road movie' set in Kazakhstan, *Non-Professionals*; and Gennadii Poloka, now re-starting a career that was aborted by the banning of his flamboyant *Intervention* in 1968 (another fiftieth anniversary commission shelved by nervous censors). Daneliia's prospectus also includes a planned Bulgakov adaptation to be directed by the normally dull Aleksei Sakharov and *The Black Monk*, based on Chekhov's story, scripted by Solov'ev and directed by Ivan Dykhovichnyi. This latter, incidentally, a thoroughly pretentious exercise in costume elegance, tricked out with dated hallucination episodes, shows how little concerned with either topical or cinematically advanced matters are some of the leaders of the reform movement.

When Klimov took over the reins of the Film-Makers' Union he predicted that it would take at least two or three years before any significant change became apparent in what he called the 'pig-iron cart' of Soviet cinema. On the whole, his prediction has been confirmed. Film-makers have been slow to exercise and explore their new freedoms, and the corresponding responsibility to present a positive image of *glasnost'* and *perestroika*. Much of the new ground, understandably, has been broken by documentary-makers – with Podnieks and the 'Baltic school' which produced him, led by Herz Frank, to the fore – but there are now frequent complaints that these films are not shown.[55] In fiction, some established directors have simply incorporated Gorbachev-era themes into their normal procedures: as in Riazanov's *Forgotten Melody for the Flute*, about the private life of a censorious bureaucrat; or Aleksandr Proshkin's *Cold Summer of '53*, which uses Beriia's unleashing of criminal bands after the death of Stalin as the basis for a tough Peckinpah-style *plein air* thriller. While Shakhnazarov's 'youth films' appear relatively anodyne, as does Solov'ev's *Assa*, there is clearly great scope for the belated development of new youth genres. Ogorodnikov's *The Burglar* is one promising model: Bodrov's *Non-Professionals*, incorporating a more sophisticated aesthetic of obliqueness and understatement, is another.

If there is any single rallying point for the Soviet film community at present, it is probably the respect felt for Tarkovskii's achievement and the sense that his early death in exile was a grievous loss. But whereas Sokurov seems to have inherited Tarkovskii's mantle without succumbing to stylistic imitation, or even agreement with his aesthetic, others have not been so circumspect. Konstantin Lopushanskii worked on the production of *Stalker* while still a student and, unsurprisingly, his graduation film, *Solo* (1981?) shows clear signs of influence. Set in a surreal Leningrad under siege during the last war, it ingeniously occupies the space between rehearsal and performance as a wretched orchestral player traverses the ruins of his city and life (the director trained as a musician before turning to cinema). But this ambitious and highly promising film has since been followed by Lopushanskii's debut feature, the widely-publicised *Letters from a Dead Man* (1986), a post-nuclear catastrophe tract released only a month before Chernobyl which, for all its timeliness and noble sentiment, seems almost to parody Tarkovskian apocalyptic motifs – although perhaps no more so than Tarkovskii did himself in *The Sacrifice*. Another Tarkovskii disciple, the actor turned director Aleksandr Kaidanovskii (who played the Stalker), seems also to be in danger of falling into sub-Tarkovskian mannerism in his *An Ordinary Death* and *The Guest*, although these have elements of real cinematic distinction amid their pretensions.

In an industry which has produced few real individualists in recent decades, the rapid decline of Sergei Ovcharov must be reckoned a sad disappointment. By all accounts, Ovcharov's first two sub-feature films were riotously amusing folk comedies, one about a missing lorry-load of vodka bearing some resemblance to *Whiskey Galore*. His first feature to be widely seen, *Tall Tales* (1983), was certainly a novelty: a series of improbable folk-tales visualised literally to produce something both fantastic and touching. Comparisons with the deadpan humour and faux-naif artistry of Medvedkin seemed entirely proper. But something went terribly wrong with Ovcharov's subsequent prestige project, an adaptation of Leskov's classic fantasy *Lefthander* (1986). Here, everything that was charming before has congealed into coyness; and stylisation has run riot to produce a *beriozka*-style folksiness. It may be too soon to pass judgement on Ovcharov, but indications are that he has fallen into the familiar Soviet film-maker's trap of *folie de grandeur*.

Meanwhile, the unusually candid family drama Vasilii Pichul's *Little Vera* is widely regarded (and debated) as a benchmark for liberalisation. Too much attention has already been paid to its modest sexual frankness: more important is its utterly unromantic portrayal of lives circumscribed by appetite and tribal custom in a typical Soviet industrial city (actually Zhdanov in the Crimea). Here, almost for the first time, is the authentic tang of *byt* prose in the cinema as *Little Vera* points one important way forward for Soviet film-making, beyond cosmetic 'socialist realism'.

Perhaps the first true comedy of *perestroika* is Iurii Mamin's *The Fountain* (1988), which follows his satire on tourist folklore in the short *Neptune's Feast*. This new film follows the pattern of an Ealing comedy, with escalating chaos and fantasy as the entire fabric of life collapses for the inhabitants of a Leningrad apartment block, eventually driving them out to dance around a tribal bonfire. Mamin and, in a very different fashion, Sokurov are two directors who clearly find the new climate congenial to their interests. And in the space between these extremes of vulgarity and refinement (both pessimistic in their diagnosis of the current Soviet scene) there is much to look forward to with optimism. However, for the stalwarts of the 'era of stagnation', such as Abdrashitov and Mindadze, Panfilov (still at work on a long-promised 'revisionist' version of Gor'kii's *The Mother*) perhaps Klimov himself, there is a discernible feeling that *perestroika* and artistry do not go easily together. The pressure to modernise, to expose and to anatomise the current dilemmas of Soviet society is felt by many film-makers to be inconsistent with the demands of Art – a view which most Western film-makers and audiences would find incomprehensible.

Many, of course, realise that the future of Soviet cinema lies less in the hands of the film-makers than the economists and planners who control the rate of development of television and video – precisely the same equation as in the West. No one appears to know just how low the rate of Soviet cinema attendance has fallen, but informal soundings indicate that many regular attenders have now gone over almost entirely to video. Although the supply of VCRs and new tapes is still far below demand, the rapid growth of a network of video libraries and 'salons' (like that on Moscow's Arbat) is bridging the gap.[56] A recent report on one such library in the Moscow dormitory suburb of Businovo describes a stock of 500 tapes, housed in two adjoining flats taken over for the purpose, with a staff of five catering for about a hundred regular customers.[57] The library charges couples who come to view on the premises an average of four rubles, and the sample list of titles suggests that such libraries are catering as much for specialised tastes (Muratova's *Brief Encounters*, Buñuel's *The Discreet Charm of the Bourgeoisie*) as for more mainstream demand (*The Man from the Boulevard des Capuchines*).

With television now scheduling a much greater range of cinema films than ever before (cinema authorities complain of highly unfavourable competition and unfavourable financial terms) and producing more attractive documentaries and drama series, cinema can only expect to lose audience share. The potential of trans-national DBS has also still to be explored, which may further stimulate domestic consumption. The monolith of Stalin's (and Shumiatskii's) Soviet cinema cannot be expected to survive but, as the 1988 Riga International Film Forum triumphantly demonstrated, in its place we can look forward to a lively, contentious culture of the moving image, embracing history, education, participation, entertainment and, yes, Art – the history of which, as Shklovskii observed, more often proceeds by 'knight's moves' than in straight lines.

**Notes**

1. This remark was quoted in Boris Berman's report on the Baku Festival, *Moscow News* 1988, 19, p. 12.
2. According to foreign sales figures reported in *Soviet Film*, 1988, 8, *Repentance* was sold to over three times more countries – 84 against 23 – than its nearest rival, a thriller entitled *The Man from the Boulevard des Capuchines*. This figure should, however, be viewed with caution, since the bulk of worldwide rights to *Repentance* were sold directly to the Cannon group, which ensured its wide (if commercially disappointing) circulation.
3. Western attitudes to early Soviet cinema of the 1920s and 1930s parallel this mythmaking. See the introduction to R. Taylor and I. Christie (eds), *The Film Factory: Russian and Soviet Cinema in Documents 1896–1939* (London and Cambridge, Mass.: 1988), pp. 1–17.
4. *Soiuz kinematografistov* translates literally as 'Union of Cinematographers', but its elite membership of about 6500 includes members of all the 'creative' cinema professions, such as directors, scriptwriters, cinematographers, composers, as well as critics and historians. The Union was launched officially in 1965 after an organising committee had been formed in 1957. It is thus very much a product of the post-Stalin period in Soviet film-making.
5. Nathalie Laurent, 'La "Transparence" à l'épreuve: l'exemple du VGIK', *L'Autre Europe*, 14, 1987, pp. 81–84. I am indebted for documentation of this and some other important matters to Julian Graffy's paper 'Recent Soviet Cinema: salvaged films, salvaged careers', *Slovo, A Journal of contemporary Soviet and East European Affairs*, London, 1, 1988, pp. 40–47.
6. See Ian Christie, '*Perestroika* in Person', *Sight and Sound*, 56, 1987, 3, p. 156; 'Unauthorised Persons Enter Here; the Career of Elem Klimov', *Monthly Film Bulletin*, July 1987, p. 199.
7. See, for instance, the entry on Kulidzhanov in Galina Dolmativskaya and Irina Shilova, *Who's Who in the Soviet Cinema* (Moscow: 1979), pp. 151–59.
8. According to Klimov, it was only Khrushchev's appreciation of the film's humour that secured its release. Ian Christie, 'Unauthorised Persons Enter Here', loc. cit.
9. Ian Christie, '*Perestroika* in Person', loc. cit.
10. Ibid.
11. Started by Valerii Kichin in the face of widespread hostility, according to an interview with the author, September 1988. The chart which

appears as an appendix to this article is a more ambitious consequence of Kichin's initiative.

12. See, for instance, Sergei Muratov, 'Documentaries You Can't See', *Moscow News* 1988, 28, p. 10; and a letter from a doctor reporting a severely truncated version of *Repentance* seen in a provincial town, *Ogonek*, 1988, 13, p. 4 (quoted in Graffy, loc. cit).

13. Sources on the work of the 'conflict commission' and unshelving are mostly journalistic, fragmentary and often contradictory. One of the earliest accounts to appear in the West was a brief report from Moscow in the *New York Times*, 'Soviet Union to Review Censored Films' (21 June 86). Fuller accounts were provided by Deborah Young in *Variety*, 'Soviet Filmers Abolish States' [sic] Censor System' (1 October 86), and David Robinson in *The Times*, 'Films that came in from the cold' (1 December 1986). The fruits of 'unshelving' began to be seen at the Berlin, Cannes and Moscow festivals in 1987, with extensive coverage in the trade press accompanying these.

14. Rolan Bykov, 'Plus Sixty', *Moscow News,* 1988, 29, p. 15.

15. I have had some personal experience of such cat-and-mouse games during negotiations with Goskino for programmes to be shown at the British Film Institute's cinemas. In 1983, I was 'allowed' to see *Farewell* on the explicit understanding that I would not request it for a National Film Theatre Soviet Film Week.

16. Natal'ia Riazantseva, the film's scenarist, has recently chronicled the obstacles placed in the way of its production in a preface to the screenplay published in *Kinostsenarii: literaturno-khudozhestvennyi al'manakh,* 1988, 1 (information kindly supplied by Clare Kitson).

17. Information on Muratova comes from interviews with her by the author in London, July 1988, and with Klimov in May 1987. *Change of Fortune* was viewed at the Arsenal International Film Forum, Riga, September 1988.

18. I first saw *Lapshin* at a Moscow cinema in July 1985, during the Moscow Film Festival, where it was not even present in the film market, despite widespread Western demand. German told of the television response in an interview with Emmanuel Decaux and Bruno Villien, 'Du côté de Guerman', *Cinématographe*, 124, November 1986, p. 56.

19. *Proverka na dorogakh* (1971), has also been variously known in English as *Operation 'Happy New Year'* (its original title), *Checkpoint, Roadcheck*, and *Trial on the Run.*

20. Vincent Amiel and Eric Derobert, 'Entretien avec Alexei German', *Positif*, 310, December 1986, p. 42. Part-translated in the catalogue of the 1987 San Francisco International Film Festival.

21. Loc. cit., p. 43.

22. Decaux and Villien, interview, loc. cit., p. 54. The vicissitudes of German's career have now been extensively discussed and documented in various Soviet publications: see, for example, Aleksandr Lipkov, 'Proverka ... na dorogakh'. *Novyi mir*, 1987, 2, pp. 202–25.

23. Information from the Lipkov interview, parts of which are quoted in translation by Graffy, loc. cit.

24. Amiel and Derobert interview, loc. cit., p. 45. (This transcription unfortunately contains some serious errors, such as 'Skirov' for 'Kirov', '1937' instead of '1917', and so on.
25. Information from two interviews with Askol'dov by the author: February 1988, Berlin; September 1988, Toronto. Also from William Wolf and Anne Williamson, 'Askoldov! The Man Who Made "Comissar"', *Film Comment*, 24, 1988, 3.
26. *Iunost'*, 1987, 2, p. 13; translated in Graffy, loc. cit.
27. This phrase come from a biographical note clearly incorporating Sokurov's own words in the 1988 Riga International Film Forum catalogue, p. 64.
28. Both of whom died suddenly and recently. Averbakh (1934–86) was a respected mainstay of Lenfilm, best known for *Other People's Letters* (1976) and *Declaration of Love* (1978), and married to the scriptwriter Natal'ia Riazantseva. Asanova (1945–85) was of Kirghizian origin and worked at Lenfilm for ten years, specialising in unsentimental films about young people, such as the outstanding *Tough Kids* (1983).
29. The commentary of *Elegia* quotes from a letter by Lunacharskii recommending that special financial allowances should be made for Chaliapin, but notes that the letter was not posted.
30. Grigorii Kozintsev (1905–73), co-founder with Leonid Trauberg of the Factory of the Eccentric Actor (FEKS), an experimental theatre, in Petrograd in 1922. Collaborated with Trauberg on a series of lively and provocative silent films, culminating with *New Babylon* (1929). Sound films included the highly successful 'Maskim trilogy' (1935–39). From 1947, Kozintsev worked alone and his solo career climaxed with three notable literary adaptations: *Don Quixote* (1957), *Hamlet* (1964) and *King Lear* (1972).
31. François Albéra, 'Voyage dans un cinéma en mutation', *Cahiers du cinéma*, May–June 1987, p. 103 (my translation).
32. Sokurov took part in a discussion with Muratova and Andrei Smirnov at the National Film Theatre, London, on 3 July, at which he disagreed violently with the position put forward by Smirnov; at the Riga Forum in September 1988, Sokurov's press conference also proved highly controversial. The views cited here are paraphrased from the latter occasion.
33. Sokurov did not work with Tarkovskii, but was close to him and helped by him. As a result, he was commissioned by the Film-Makers' Union to make a memorial film, *Moscow Elegy*, shown at Dom Kino in Moscow on 4 April (Tarkovskii's birthday) 1988.
34. 1988 Riga Forum Catalogue, p. 64.
35. *Shooting in Africa* (1988) directed by Igor' Alimpiev; and *Public Railway* (1988) directed by Viktor Semeniuk.
36. Quoted in Albéra, loc. cit., p. 104. Compare M. Iampol'skii, 'Kovcheg, plyvushchii iz proshlogo', *Iskusstvo kino*, 1987, 9, pp. 38–45 (this passage, p. 42).
37. Peleshian's four films mentioned here were first seen in the West at the Pesaro Festival in 1986 and the San Francisco Festival in 1987. Subseqeuently prints promised for the National Film Theatre in July

1988 and the 1988 Toronto Festival of Festivals did not arrive. On Peleshian's work, see: Serge Daney, 'A la recherche d'Artavazd Peleshian', *Libération*, 8 November 1983; Fabrice Revault d'Allones, 'Le cousin arménien de Vertov', *Cahiers du cinéma*, March 1980; and also Peleshian's own article 'Montage at a distance', *Voprosy iskusstva*, 1973.

38. Only three parts of what was originally conceived as a four-part film were actually made. The third, not yet seen, was directed by Gabai, who later emigrated.
39. See National Film Theatre programme 'Shelf Life', July 1988, for details of the latter two films. *The Sky of Our Children* appears to have had some limited release before 1986, while *Madness* actually dates from 1968.
40. Jay Leyda, *Kino: A History of the Russian and Soviet Film* (London: 1960) p. 401.
41. Shukshin's *There Lived a Lad* (1964) mocked crass attempts to bring urban 'culture' to the *kolkhoz*, while his *Your Son and Brother* (1966) revealed much of the bitterness between villagers who stay and those who drift to the cities. See Ian Christie, 'Holidays for the Soul', *Sight and Sound*, 55, 1986, 4, pp. 261–63.
42. Taken over by her husband, Elem Klimov, after her death in an accident in 1979 and completed in 1981 as *The Farewell*.
43. Iurii Olesha (1899–1960). Journalist, poet, short-story writer, playwright, political agitator and occasional scriptwriter. His career went into sharp decline in the early 1930s, partly due to the scandal of *The Severe Young Man*, (1936) written by Olesha and directed by Abram Room, and effectively still banned. The story *Angel* has not been published in full in the Soviet Union.
44. Michael Ciment, 'Pour saluer *Pastorale* et *Le Bonheur d'Assia*' (interview with Konchalovskii), *Positif*, 206, May 1978, p. 37.
45. See Ian Christie, 'Russians', *Sight and Sound*, 52, 1983, 3, p. 179.
46. Jean-Loup Passek, *Le Cinéma russe et sovietique* (Paris: 1981), p. 244.
47. Tamara Verina, 'The artist and his life' (Interview with Khutsiev), *Culture and Life*, 1988, 6, p. 7.
48. A pioneering course on early Russian cinema is planned for VGIK, and the 1989 Pordenone Festival of silent cinema will include a major early Russian retrospective.
49. 'Osip Mandel'shtam i kinematograf', publ. S.V. Vasilenko, B.S. Miagkov and Iu.L. Freidin, *Pamir*, Dushanbe, 1986, 10, pp. 162–73. Freidin first published 'Shpigun', the review of *The Forgotten Face*, in the western journal *Russian Literature*, Amsterdam, 5, 1977, pp. 177–80.
50. This applies even when their film is deemed unreleasable, as we know from the history of German's *Trial on the Road*. For this Lenfilm was severely censured and forced to pay back the cost of the production (1 million roubles), its director was demoted – and German continued as a salaried director on the studio's staff because he had 'shown talent'! See Decaux and Villien, loc. cit., p. 54.
51. Admission prices range from 35 to 45 copecks in provincial cinemas to about 1 rouble in larger prestige city cinemas. But the matter is further

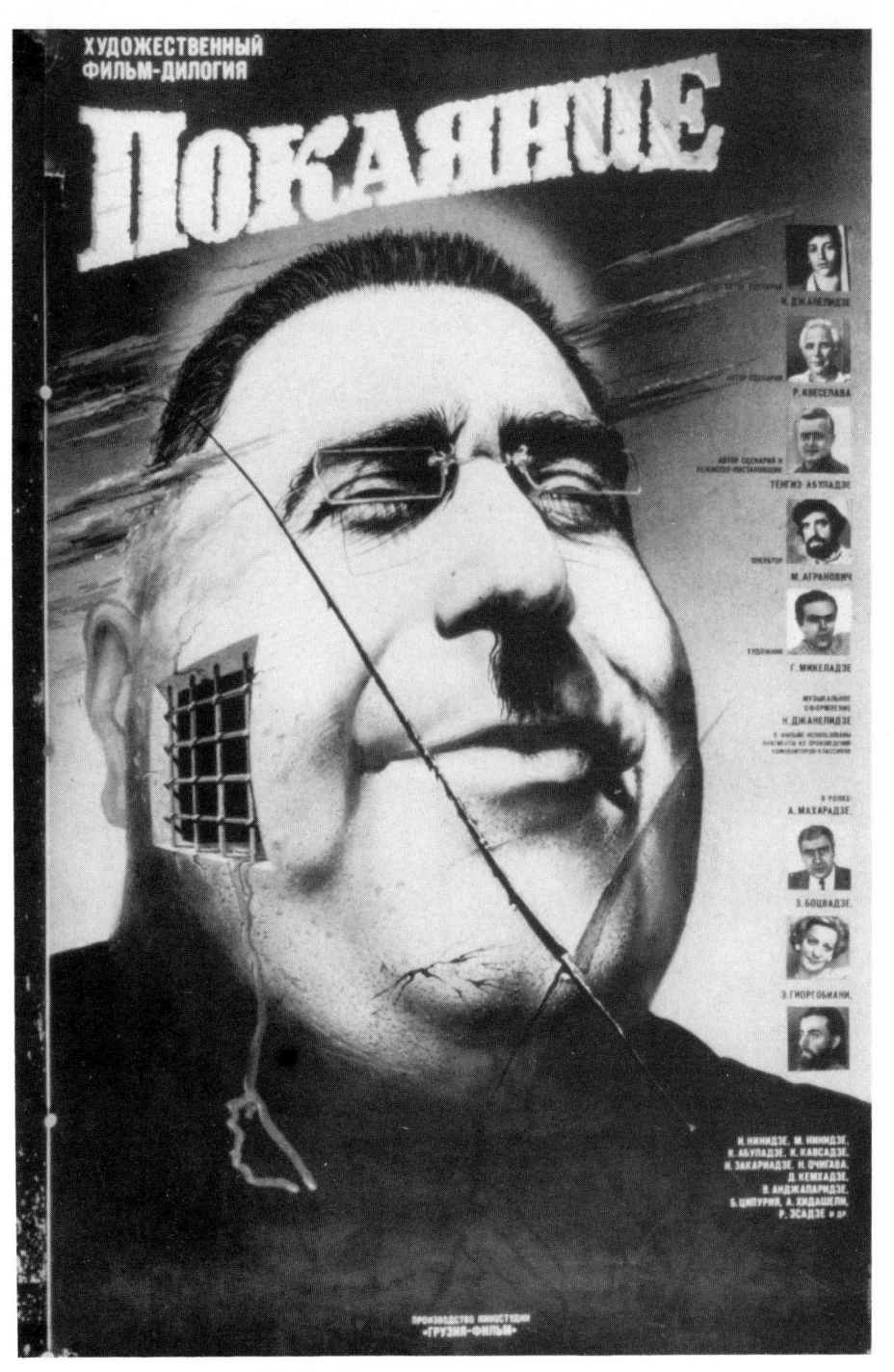

1. Poster for Tengiz Abuladze's film *Repentance*.

2. Zeinab Botsvadze as Ketevan Barateli in *Repentance*.

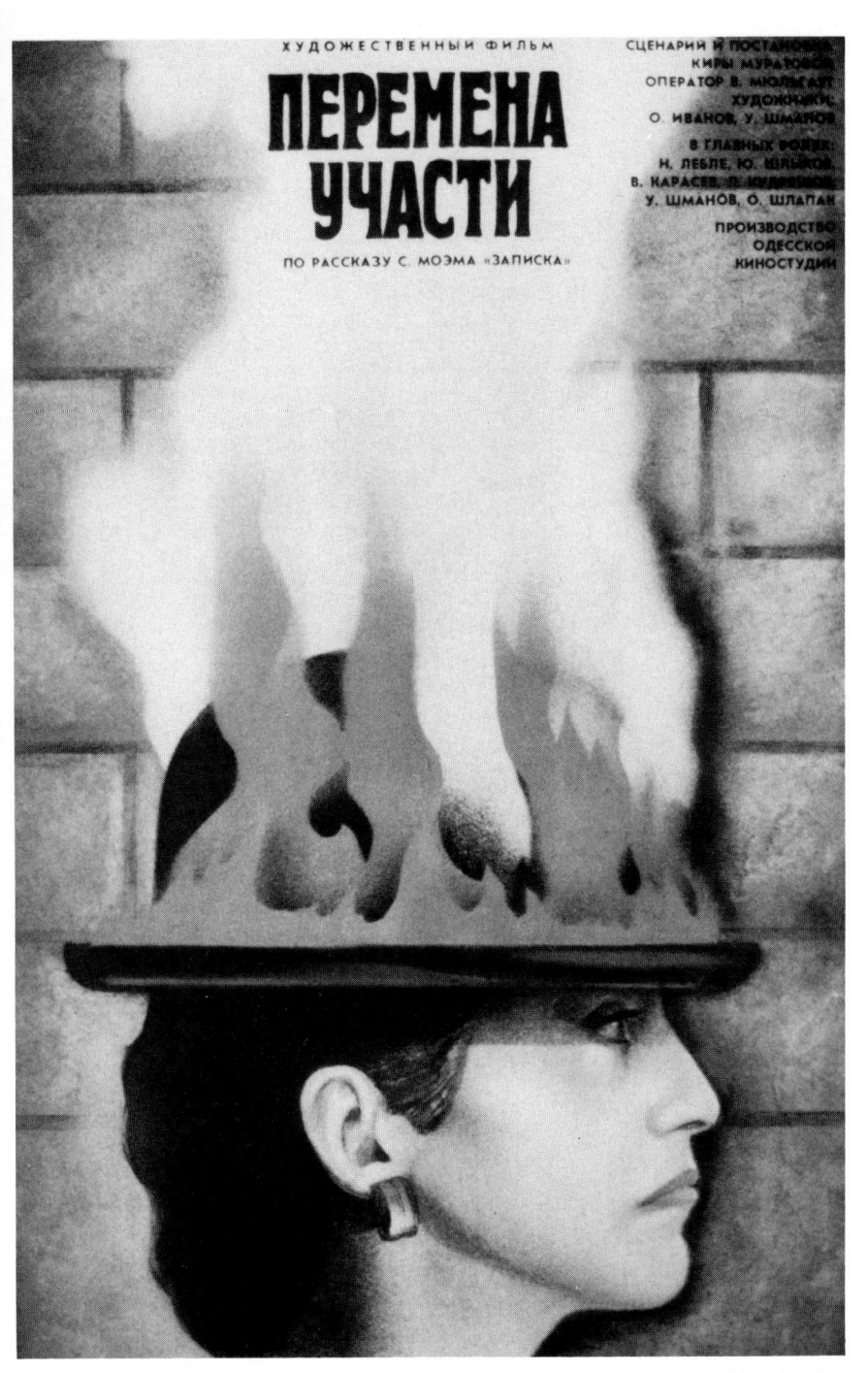

3. Poster for Kira Muratova's film *Change of Fortune*, based on Somerset Maugham's story *The Letter*.

4. Andrei Boltnev as Lapshin and Andrei Mironov as Khanin in Aleksei German's film *My Friend Ivan Lapshin*.

5. Andrei Gradov as Nikita in Aleksandr Sokurov's *The Solitary Voice of Man*.

6. A scene from Larisa Shepit'ko's *The Homeland of Electricity*, the first episode in the collective film *The Beginning of an Unknown Century*.

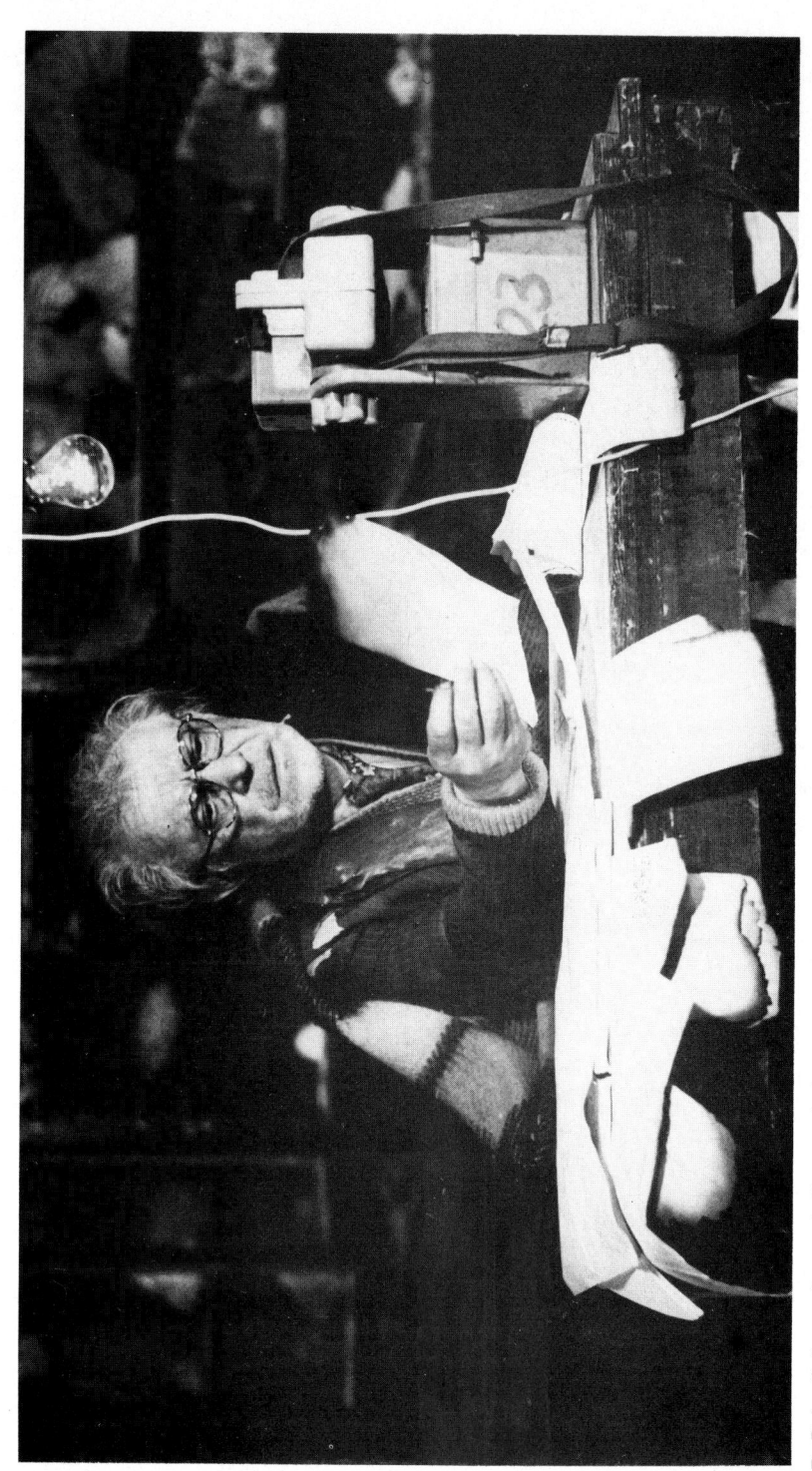

7. Rolan Bykov as Larsen in Konstantin Lopushanskii's film *Letters from a Dead Man*.

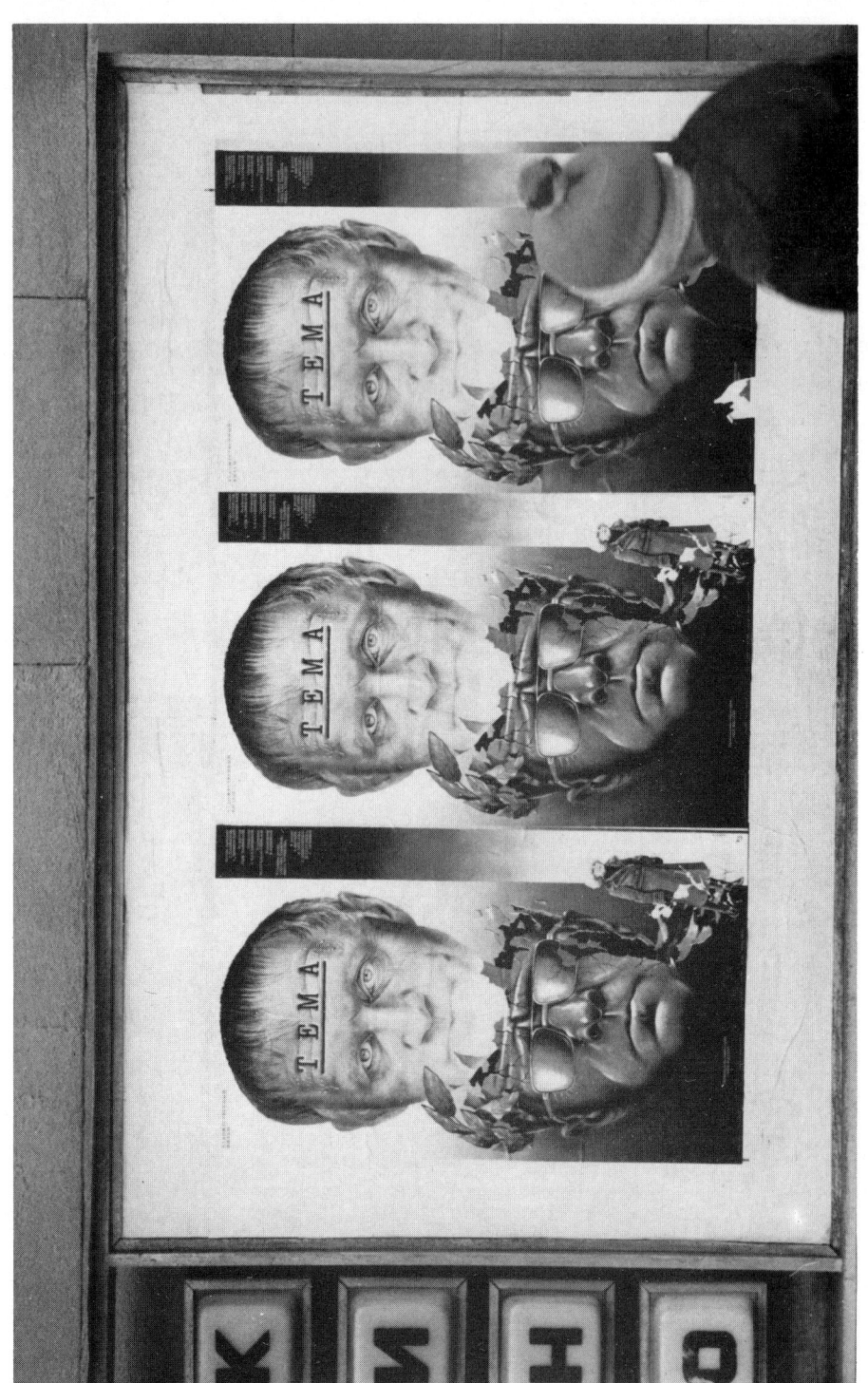

8. Poster for Gleb Panfilov's film *The Theme*.

complicated because the cinemas return only a small percentage of receipts to the distribution agency (as little as 20 per cent) – and attendances have been falling steadily. Albéra reports (loc. cit., p. 100) that film production has received 78 million roubles in the last year to make good the deficit.
52. Albéra, loc. cit., p. 100.
53. Brief statements and outline programmes by each of the associations' Artistic Directors appear in *Soviet Film*, 1988, 5, pp. 8–9.
54. Lenfilm's reform is reported in *Soviet Film*, 1988, 8, pp. 12–17.
55. Sergei Muratov, 'Documentaries You Can't See', *Moscow News*, 1988, 28, p. 10.
56. 'Video in the USSR Today and Tomorrow', *Soviet Film*, 1988, 7, pp. 26–27.
57. 'Modest Charm of a Video Library', *Soviet Film*, 1988, 8, pp. 26–27.

# APPENDIX

The following chart, based on lists of the 'ten best Soviet films of all time' from twelve prominent Soviet critics, first appeared in the Moscow weekly *Nedelia* 1987, 44, p. 18. Thanks are due to Clare Kitson for bringing it to my attention and to Richard Taylor for first transcribing it in this tabular form. The dates of films given in the Russian version have been largely retained, although these are often slightly different from the conventional Western dating of particular films (several obvious errors have however been corrected). I have added the totals of votes cast for each film, which show German's *My Friend Ivan Lapshin* in the lead with nine votes, while seven films tie for joint second, each with six votes. Altogether, the chart records a remarkable change in Soviet critical taste – a snapshot of cultural *perestroika* in action.

|  | IuB | ViD | VlD | VI | VK | VM | AP | KR | IR | IS | MT | MI |  |
|---|---|---|---|---|---|---|---|---|---|---|---|---|---|
| *The Strike* Eisenstein (1925) |  |  |  |  | x |  |  |  |  | x |  |  | (2) |
| *The Battleship Potemkin* Eisenstein (1925) |  |  | x |  | x |  |  | x | x | x | x |  | (6) |
| *The Mother* Pudovkin (1926) |  |  |  |  | x |  |  |  |  |  |  |  | (1) |
| *Bed and Sofa* Room (1927) |  |  |  |  |  |  |  | x |  | x |  |  | (2) |

|  | IuB | ViD | VlD | VI | VK | VM | AP | KR | IR | IS | MT | MI |  |
|---|---|---|---|---|---|---|---|---|---|---|---|---|---|
| *S V D* <br> Kozintsev, Trauberg (1927) |  |  |  |  |  |  |  |  | x |  |  |  | (1) |
| *October* <br> Eisenstein (1927) | x |  | x |  |  |  |  |  |  |  |  |  | (2) |
| *Zvenigora* <br> Dovzhenko (1928) |  |  |  |  |  |  | x |  |  |  |  |  | (1) |
| *The Heir of Gengis Khan* <br> Pudovkin (1928) |  | x |  |  |  |  |  |  |  |  |  |  | (1) |
| *Arsenal* <br> Dovzhenko (1929) |  | x |  |  |  |  |  |  |  |  |  |  | (1) |
| *The Man With a Movie Camera* <br> Vertov (1929) |  | x |  |  |  | x |  |  |  |  | x |  | (3) |
| *New Babylon* <br> Kozintsev/Trauberg (1929) |  | x |  |  |  |  |  |  |  |  | x |  | (2) |
| *The Earth* <br> Dovzhenko (1930) |  | x | x |  | x | x |  | x |  |  | x |  | (6) |
| *Salt for Svanetia* <br> Kalatozov (1930) |  |  |  |  |  |  |  |  | x |  |  |  | (1) |
| *Outskirts* <br> Barnet (1933) | x | x |  |  | x | x | x | x |  |  |  |  | (6) |
| *Jolly Fellows* [Jazz Comedy] <br> Aleksandrov (1934) | x |  |  | x |  | x |  |  |  |  |  |  | (3) |
| *Chapaev* <br> Vasil'ev (1934) |  |  |  |  |  |  |  |  | x |  |  |  | (1) |
| *Happiness* <br> Medvedkin (1935) |  | x |  |  |  |  |  |  |  |  |  |  | (1) |

|  | IuB | ViD | VlD | VI | VK | VM | AP | KR | IR | IS | MT | MI |  |
|---|---|---|---|---|---|---|---|---|---|---|---|---|---|
| *Peter I* <br> Petrov (1938) |  |  |  | x |  |  |  |  |  |  |  |  | (1) |
| *A Great Citizen* <br> Ermler (1939) |  |  | x |  |  |  |  |  |  |  |  |  | (1) |
| *Mashenka* <br> Raizman (1942) |  |  |  | x |  |  |  |  | x |  |  |  | (2) |
| *The Dream* <br> Romm (1943) |  |  |  | x |  |  |  |  |  |  |  |  | (1) |
| *Ivan the Terrible* <br> Eisenstein (1945) | x |  |  |  | x | x |  | x |  | x |  | x | (6) |
| *The Fall of Berlin* <br> Chiaureli (1950) |  |  | x |  |  |  |  |  |  |  |  |  | (1) |
| *The Cranes are Flying* <br> Kalatozov (1957) |  |  | x | x |  | x | x |  | x |  | x |  | (6) |
| *The Ballad of a Soldier* <br> Chukhrai (1959) |  |  |  |  | x |  | x |  |  | x |  |  | (3) |
| *The Destiny of a Man* <br> Bondarchuk (1959) |  |  |  | x |  |  |  |  |  |  |  |  | (1) |
| *Nine Days of One Year* <br> Romm (1962) |  |  |  |  | x |  |  |  |  |  |  |  | (1) |
| *Ivan's Childhood* <br> Tarkovskii (1962) |  |  |  |  |  | x |  |  | x |  |  |  | (2) |
| *The Shadows of Our Forgotten Ancestors* <br> Paradzhanov (1965) |  | x |  |  |  | x |  |  |  |  | x |  | (3) |
| *I Am 20* [*The Il'ich Gate*] <br> Khutsiev (1965) | x |  |  | x |  |  |  |  | x | x |  |  | (4) |

|  | IuB | ViD | VlD | VI | VK | VM | AP | KR | IR | IS | MT | MI |  |
|---|---|---|---|---|---|---|---|---|---|---|---|---|---|
| *July Rain* Khutsiev (1966) |  |  | x |  |  |  |  |  | x |  |  |  | (2) |
| *Wings* Shepit'ko (1966) |  |  |  |  |  |  | x |  |  |  |  |  | (1) |
| *Asia's Happiness* Mikhalkov-Konchalovskii (1967) |  |  |  |  |  |  |  | x |  |  |  |  | (1) |
| *Andrei Rublev* Tarkovskii (1967) |  | x | x | x |  |  |  |  | x | x |  |  | (5) |
| *Brief Encounters* Muratova (1967) | x |  |  |  |  |  |  |  |  |  |  |  | (1) |
| *The Beginning* Panfilov (1970) |  |  |  | x |  |  |  |  |  |  |  |  | (1) |
| *Once There was a Blackbird* Ioseliani (1971) | x |  | x |  | x | x |  | x | x |  |  |  | (6) |
| *The Red Snowball Tree* Shukshin (1974) |  |  |  |  |  | x |  |  |  |  |  |  | (1) |
| *The Mirror* Tarkovskii (1975) |  |  |  | x | x | x | x |  | x |  | x |  | (6) |
| *The Seasons of the Year* Peleshian (1975) |  |  |  |  |  |  |  |  |  |  | x |  | (1) |
| *The Irony of Fate* Riazanov (1975) |  |  |  |  |  | x |  |  |  |  |  |  | (1) |
| *Unfinished Piece for Mechanical Piano* Mikhalkov (1977) |  |  |  | x |  |  |  |  |  |  |  |  | (1) |
| *Twenty Days Without War* German (1977) |  |  |  |  | x |  |  |  |  |  |  |  | (1) |

|  | IuB | ViD | VlD | VI | VK | VM | AP | KR | IR | IS | MT | MI |  |
|---|---|---|---|---|---|---|---|---|---|---|---|---|---|
| *The Ascent*<br>Shepit'ko (1977) | x |  |  |  |  |  |  |  |  |  |  |  | (1) |
| *Five Evenings*<br>Mikhalkov (1979) | x |  |  |  |  |  |  |  |  |  |  |  | (1) |
| *The Tale of Tales*<br>Norstein (1979) Animation |  |  |  |  |  |  |  | x |  |  | x |  | (2) |
| *Stalker*<br>Tarkovskii (1980) | x |  |  |  |  |  |  |  |  |  |  |  | (1) |
| *Agonia*<br>Klimov (1981) |  |  |  |  |  |  |  | x |  |  |  |  | (1) |
| *Flights in Dreams and Reality*<br>Balaian (1983) |  |  |  | x |  |  |  |  |  |  |  |  | (1) |
| *Go and See*<br>Klimov (1984) |  |  | x |  |  |  |  |  |  |  |  |  | (1) |
| *My Friend Ivan Lapshin*<br>German (1984) | x | x | x | x |  | x | x |  | x |  | x | x | (9) |
| *Repentance*<br>Abuladze (1986) | x |  |  |  | x |  |  |  | x |  |  |  | (3) |

Critics taking part:

| | | | | |
|---|---|---|---|---|
| IuB | Iurii Bogomolov | | AP | Andrei Plakhov |
| ViD | Viktor Demin | | KR | Kirill Razlogov |
| VlD | Vladimir Dmitriev | | IR | Irina Rubanova |
| VI | Valentina Ivanova | | IS | Inna Solov'eva |
| VK | Valerii Kichin | | MT | Maiia Turovskaia |
| VM | Valentin Mikhalkovich | | MI | Mikhail Iampol'skii |

# 5 Soviet Theatre: *Glasnost'* in Action – with Difficulty

## MICHAEL GLENNY

To appreciate fully the changes and reforms that have occurred – and are still occurring – in the Soviet theatre since the 'Gorbachev era' began in 1985, some knowledge of its previous state, in particular the legacy of Stalinism, is essential. Under Stalin's rule the innovative, avant-garde brilliance of the 1920s quickly faded into total extinction. Stalin's method of controlling – or rather manipulating – the arts and sciences was to set up one person who represented his own views as his 'dictator' over each particular field, usually an elderly, respected but conservative figure, and the theatre was no exception. Because Stalin's tastes were firmly middlebrow and Moscow Arts Theatre productions were his idea of what plays should be like, in 1934 Stanislavskii became Stalin's appointed 'dictator' of theatrical art in the USSR. This had three main effects: first, the rapid disappearance of the Expressionist, non-realistic theatre of which the most brilliant exponent was Meierkhol'd, who was arrested in 1938 and imprisoned in a labour camp, where he died in 1940; second, the imposition of the Stanislavskii method as the only school of acting allowed throughout the USSR and of Moscow Arts Theatre naturalism as the obligatory style in all theatres, resulting in a uniformity and a stifling of all creative experiment that produced twenty years of what Soviet theatre veterans now recall with a shudder as 'grey realism'. The third effect was more constructive: every theatre was made into a permanent repertory company, giving actors security of employment, allowing companies to develop a cohesion that favoured good ensemble playing and enabling management to plan their repertoires over the long term instead of cobbling them together on a season-to-season basis. It was Stanislavskii's advocacy of the virtues of this system that brought about its adoption throughout the USSR in 1939.

Despite its undoubted virtues, however, this organisational structure has disadvantages that have become very apparent and are now, after fifty years, being subjected to radical scrutiny by the theatrical profession. Guaranteed employment and a nationwide, fixed salary scale have had undesirable effects on professional standards. Theatre companies, for instance, have tended to become static and constipated. All the places at the top of the salary-scale (reached by seniority rather than ability) fill up with ageing actors who cling to their positions like limpets and often have to be cast in parts for which they are too old; it is virtually impossible to sack them until they are 65, the system does not allow for early retirement (except on pressing medical grounds), and in any case there are always a few – but not enough! – parts requiring older actors. Except by growing older and by stepping into dead men's shoes it is very difficult for an actor to be promoted up the scale, even when he or she may deserve it on grounds of natural talent or the increased skill that comes with experience. This is because the planners at the Ministry of Culture fix not only each theatre's overall salary budget but the number of 'personnel units' within each salary grade, and as long as the grades of its personnel establishment were full, a theatre company had the greatest difficulty in promoting talented actors or recruiting new ones to ensure an adequate and healthy infusion of new blood.

Despite such structural problems, and the stultifying effects of the system of censorship and control of the arts instituted by Stalin – only slightly relaxed during the Second World War but made much more stringent from 1946 until his death in 1953 – the Soviet theatre still had sufficient vitality to manage a very convincing renaissance in the years of the 'Khrushchev Thaw', which dated roughly from 1956 and persisted after Khrushchev's fall in 1964 into the early years of the Brezhnev–Kosygin duumvirate. It was in these years that the major plays of Mikhail Bulgakov, Soviet Russia's greatest playwright, were revived (*The Days of the Turbins,* alias *The White Guard*) or given their first performance (*Flight*; the dramatisation of the novel *The Master and Margarita*) and three outstanding directors came to the fore: Georgii Tovstonogov at the Gor'kii Theatre in Leningrad; Anatolii Efros and Iurii Liubimov at the Malaia Bronnaia and Taganka theatres respectively in Moscow. Liubimov in particular had the talent and drive to make the Taganka into a truly innovative, avant-garde theatre, until he could no longer stand the strain of constant battles with the censorship and the restrictive pressures of the Ministry of Culture, and defected during his visit to London in 1983. British audiences then had an opportunity to see two of his Taganka productions based on adaptations from Dostoevskii – *Crime and Punishment* and *The Possessed*. After peregrinations around

Europe and the USA, Liubimov has settled in Tel Aviv, perhaps because Israel has the largest Russian-speaking audience outside the USSR. A striking indication of Gorbachev's new and more liberal approach to cultural politics is the fact that Liubimov was invited back to Moscow in May 1988; there he was able to conduct the final rehearsals of his previously banned production of Pushkin's *Boris Godunov* and to receive a twenty-minute standing ovation from his faithful audience at the Taganka Theatre, who chorused in rhythmic unison: 'Come back home!' Negotiations over his return did indeed take place, but it appears that even under Gorbachev's more liberal dispensation the Soviet authorities were unable to accept Liubimov's terms – namely that for at least six months in a year he should be free to come and go, without having to ask permission, in order to direct plays and operas abroad.

Liubimov's return (albeit temporary) is only one aspect of the Soviet government's radically changed attitudes to the media and the arts.

In the eighteen months between January 1986 and mid-1988, the number of theatres in Moscow increased by 50 per cent – from thirty to forty-five, and that figure does not take account of the considerable number of clubs and 'Houses of Culture' (attached to factories, and so on), which provide auditoria where amateur, semi-professional and *ad hoc* professional groups are able to perform. In principle – and often in practice – this is a welcome development; the expansion of theatrical potential and the legislation that enabled it to occur have, however, created almost as many problems as opportunities. The 50 per cent increase in plays, with a consequently wider choice of genres, styles, etc., available to audiences has meant that the public can be – and is quickly becoming – more discriminating. This is neatly illustrated by a change that has occurred in a typically Russian phenomenon, namely the crowd of hopefuls who in the past were almost always to be found on the pavement outside theatre entrances during the hour before curtain-up and who would ask each person entering: 'You wouldn't have a spare ticket to sell, would you?' Now they are only to be found outside certain theatres, and as often as not they are not trying to buy but to *sell* spare tickets – and strictly at box-office prices.

Even in the bad old days of the Brezhnev regime, each season would produce a crop of new productions which drew full houses and raised the prestige of this or that theatre, making it equally a matter of 'prestige' or *blat* ('pull' or good connections) to get a ticket to such shows. It was frequently impossible to get into such theatres as the Sovremennik ('Contemporary'), the Taganka, the Komsomol, the Satire, a Efremov production at the Moscow Arts or an Efros production at the Malaia Bronnaia. Naturally much of this popularity was due to the reverse effect of repressive behaviour by the Ministry of Culture or narrow-minded Party officials: it was enough for rumours to start circulating that this or that production was threatened with being banned for the whole of Moscow to start scrambling for tickets and to see 'subversive' implications in a play where neither author nor director had ever had any such intention (or so they would claim!).

Alongside those which did take political or artistic risks, a majority of theatres never clashed with the authorities and put on only thoroughly 'safe' plays, with the result that they regularly played to half-empty houses – and still survived quite as well as, if not better than their bolder brethren. This was because all theatres received state subsidies under Ministry of Culture ratings calculated on purely quantitative criteria: fulfilment of the planned number of productions per year; observance of the laid-down ratio between classics, modern Soviet plays and foreign plays; actors' salaries paid strictly according to the Ministry's fixed scale of grades based on seniority. The *quality* of a theatre's productions could not be fitted into this Procrustean bed and was therefore ignored.

Much has changed since the control of theatres was removed from the Ministry of Culture and handed over to the newly-formed and independent Union of Theatre Workers, which in 1986 replaced the former theatre union, the now defunct All-Russian Theatrical Society. The new Union's statute was aimed above all at freeing theatres from the close, pettifogging tutelage of the Ministry, from rigid control 'from above', so enabling theatre companies themselves to take all the essential decisions and manage their own affairs. Perhaps most important, the founding congress of the Union dealt with the urgent need to dismantle the single, across-the-board system of subsidies, proposing instead that alongside a certain number of state-subsidised theatres, other theatres, troupes and fringe companies could be formed that were to be self-financing. There would be no formal restrictions on the creation of such new theatres; their survival or failure would depend on their ability to find premises, to attract audiences and to make a profit.

The first of January 1987 saw the entry into force of a Ministry of Culture directive which started an experiment due to last two years.

This prescribed a full-scale democratisation of the management structure of theatres. Major decisions were to be taken by the whole company on the basis of 'one man, one vote', the franchise extending down to stagehands, ushers and cleaners; the chief director and other directors were to be similarly elected; absolute independence for the company was permitted in the choice of repertoire, without the need for Ministry approval and complete autonomy of decision on the distribution of profits; companies gained the freedom to set their own ticket prices; actors were to be hired and fired according to need and without reference to the fixed manning-scales formerly laid down by the Ministry. By this ordinance, the Ministry of Culture was obliged largely to divest itself of its administrative hold over much of the Soviet theatre.

Not all theatres are affected by this experiment: in the USSR as a whole it has been applied to slightly more than four-fifths of them, and in Moscow to rather less than half the theatres. Its basic aims were to raise professional standards, to improve staff morale and shake up managements through democratisation, and to liberate previously stultified forces of energy and creativity. One thing, however, was not allowed for by the initiators of these revolutionary reforms: the widespread unwillingness of directors and managers to put them into effect. For it can no longer be denied that many of them found the old system thoroughly congenial: free of any need to worry about half-empty houses, they could manage very well with a minimum of thought, originality and creative exertion; their subsidies and salaries were always paid, irrespective of whether or not anyone actually came to see their plays. At the same time they could even acquire a spurious reputation as something of a 'dissident' by grumbling loudly about the impossibility of putting on a politically risky play or of hiring a talented, original but unpredictable young director.

Then suddenly – all was permitted! The censorship was abolished and theatres were given the responsibilities that go with free choice and at least a partial exposure to market forces: subsidies would still be provided, but in direct ratio to the theatre's box-office takings. For the first time, therefore, Soviet managements were faced with the imperative that rules their confrères in the capitalist world: get bums on seats! Artistic directors long conditioned to doing nothing but to obey orders from above were appalled, and in almost all the country's theatres, instead of enthusiasm the reforms initially gave rise to some most unedifying behaviour, reminiscent of civil war: vicious in-fighting between hostile factions, enforced resignations and struggles for leadership within companies conducted with a virulence that occasionally spilled over, like red-hot larva, into the pages of the press. This state of affairs lasted for well over a year, during which that holy of holies of Russian theatrical tradition, the Moscow Arts Theatre, was split down the middle and broke apart, one half staying in its new, technically up-to-date but visually rather hideous theatre, while the younger half of the company, led by the artistic director of the previously united Arts Theatre, Oleg Efremov, migrated back to the old but much-loved building that was designed to the requirements of its founders, Stanislavskii and Nemirovich-Danchenko. Similar titanic quarrels caused the departure and replacement of the artistic directors of seven of Moscow's leading theatres, while a number of others still have no artistic directors, the democratised companies having been unable to agree on replacements for those who resigned. Such, indeed, were the upheavals during 1987 that it was a marvel that Moscow's theatregoers were able to see any plays at all.

Taken overall, the first effects of the reform have been paradoxical. In past decades, when theatre directors were always complaining bitterly that their hands were kept tied by the Ministry in choosing the repertoire, they somehow managed to stage new production after new production, among which were not a few examples of truly talented and original work. Yet as soon as they were given absolute freedom of choice, many theatres in the past eighteen months or so have not produced a single play worthy of serious attention, and some have simply not put on any new productions at all (the Moscow Arts Theatre being one of the most glaring offenders) despite the challenge to be bold, innovative and experimental that is inherent in the reforms. On the other hand, the companies which have come through this turmoil unscathed or with enhanced reputations are those which have obstinately insisted on continuing to work hard and creatively, not chasing after sensation and not afraid of possible flops, companies in which the chief director and his colleagues have kept a clear set of aims in view, and are concerned to keep their whole troupe as fully occupied as possible, attempting to ensure that every actor is given the maximum work compatible with his or her personal talents. For as everyone in the theatre has long known, troubles start brewing in a permanent company only when the actors have too little to do: the harder actors are made to work, the more parts they are given, the happier they are. This, too, might seem paradoxical but it is true, particularly in the Soviet Union, where the trend in the past has been for companies to be overmanned; this leads to featherbedding of actors, and their consequent under-exertion shows up in slack acting.

In attempting to draw up a balance-sheet of the 1987–8 season it is, of course, always possible to use the method employed by the critic and theatre historian A. Smelianskii, who optimistically listed all the playwrights produced on the Moscow stage over that period, including Shakespeare. The resulting picture looked impressive, but bore no relation to the professional quality and artistic worth of the productions themselves, and did not, in consequence, reveal the true state of affairs.

If, however, one takes a harder and more realistic look at the situation, it becomes clear that in the first stage of the USSR's theatrical *perestroika* there have been depressingly few striking or even promising new productions. Instead, each one reflected in varying degrees the situation within the theatre in question, which was often shaky in the extreme, and this has subsequently been admitted in the press and at the last plenary meeting of the Union of Theatre Workers. The few bright flashes of originality and boldness have, if anything, served only to emphasise the surrounding mediocrity. Among these were an increased number of foreign plays, ranging from the first Russian production of Pirandello's *Six Characters in Search of an Author* to Michael Frayn's brilliant farce *Noises Off*; the script of the latter was inevitably a paraphrase rather than a translation, but it nevertheless succeeded in generating a creditable equivalent to the frantic comic lunacy of the original, and gave a much-needed jolt to the Soviet playwriting fraternity, who in recent decades have singularly failed to write any really funny plays. In general, it seems that only a few theatres are yet in a fit state to grasp and exploit the audience-pulling potential of the new relaxation of control and censorship; those that have are finding that it does wonders for the box-office takings. One of the best examples of the rewards of boldness is Aleksandr Galin's play *Stars in the Morning Sky*, which after a long and successful run at Leningrad's Malyi Dramaticheskii Theatre went abroad and toured Glasgow, London, Toronto and New York in May and June 1988. Not only does the play deal with a hitherto strictly taboo subject, prostitution, but Lev Dodin's production has also given Soviet audiences their first glimpses of nudity on stage.

In the shift of audience loyalties away from the less adventurous theatres, a factor much more important than naked actresses, however, is the legislation of the numerous fringe theatres that have sprung up like mushrooms after rain, welcome sign of a latent vitality in Soviet theatre that has hitherto been suppressed. As might be expected, the need to perform in converted basements, schools or garages means tiny auditoria, cramped acting spaces and a minimum of scenery. These 'fringe' companies also tend to be much bolder and more experimental than the established theatres and they draw their audiences largely by the attraction of the unknown and the unpredictable; the other side of that coin is the wildly variable quality of direction and performance.

Two of the small theatres created under the new dispensation, however, stand out from all the others by their consistently high professional standards and imaginative repertoires; they have, as it were, graduated from 'fringe' status to something more permanent, both now receiving state subsidies. One is the so-called 'School of Dramatic Art', run by the highly talented director Anatolii Vasil'ev. Proposals that he should be given his own theatre have been circulating in the Moscow Theatre world for at least ten years, but only since the start of the 'experiment' has the legislative framework existed for Vasil'ev to form his own troupe, made up of actors with whom he has worked in other theatres for many years. For the time being, it performs in a small and inconvenient basement, but the company achieved such rapid fame that it has spent much of its time touring abroad. As well as being the first to perform Pirandello in the Soviet Union, Vasil'ev also brought a remarkable play, *Cerceau*, by Viktor Slavkin – part-Chekhov, part-Pinter – to London in July 1987, where it ran to full houses at the Riverside Studios and was broadcast by London Weekend Television.

The other leader among the new companies is Oleg Tabakov's Studio Theatre, the nucleus of which consists of students from the graduating class of the Moscow Arts Theatre School, where until 1986 Tabakov taught acting and directing. Since the spring of 1987 the Tabakov Studio has been performing in a modest but well-converted building with a 200-seat auditorium. Using no scenery and only a few basic sticks of furniture, a typically successful production by Tabakov and his troupe of enthusiastic young actors is Bulgakov's *The Crazy Monsieur Jourdain*, an adaptation of Molière's *Le Bourgeois Gentilhomme* which moves at a cracking pace in a hilarious mixture of knockabout farce and high camp. This theatre, we are told, will also soon be touring abroad.

More ambitious than single-company foreign tours was the festival of Soviet plays held in Munich over three weeks of February and March 1988, where nine new productions were given an airing in front of an international audience, something unthinkable three or four years previously. The most prominent Russian playwright to attend this festival was Mikhail Shatrov. Having already written several plays about Lenin, Shatrov is putting into words and actions on stage much of the re-examination of Soviet history and the filling-in of the notorious 'blank-pages', which is an essential element in Gorbachev's drive to exorcise the terrible spectres of the Stalinist past which still haunt Soviet Russia to this day. Shown at Munich (and still enjoying a seemingly endless run at Moscow's Komsomol Theatre) was a recent play by Shatrov, significantly entitled *The Dictatorship of Conscience, or The Trial of Lenin*, a refreshing re-assessment and debunking of much of the mythology that for too long has passed for modern history in the USSR. Bolder still in its breaking of hallowed Stalinist taboos is Shatrov's play *The Peace of Brest-Litovsk* (written in 1962 but allowed on stage only after a 25-year time-lag), in which the author introduces Trotskii as a leading character; those who attended the first night of this production in late November 1987, directed by the Georgian Robert Sturua, have lived to tell the tale and to witness that the theatre was not struck by a thunderbolt.

In his latest play, however, Shatrov seems to have overstepped even the undetermined limits of *glasnost'*: entitled *Onward, Onward, Onward!*, it is a vehicle for the ultimate damnation of Stalin out of the mouth of Lenin, achieved by the device of having the leading participants in the 1917 October Revolution (from both sides of the barricades) meet in some timeless limbo in 'the other world'. There, with the benefit of total hindsight, they thrash out the rights and wrongs of the Bolshevik seizure of power, and, most importantly, of Stalin's subsequent distortion of the aims and ideals of the revolution. Published in the January 1988 number of the literary journal *Znamia*, the text of this play caused an immediate controversy in the Soviet press long before it was put into production. Indeed, only two provincial productions have so far been scheduled; no theatre in either Moscow or Leningrad has put it into the repertoire, which is extraordinary for a playwright of Shatrov's reputation. This is probably because the play cuts too near the bone of Soviet ideology – or mythology – by having Lenin admit on stage, and in so many words, that he was himself responsible, even if only by default, for Stalin's rise to absolute power and his subsequent terrible abuse of that power. These are the lines that are holding up the play's production:

> LENIN: I am unquestionably guilty of failing to carry out my intention of having Stalin removed from his post in 1923 – my accursed illness prevented me. ... but that is no excuse, because I realise that I perceived the true state of affairs too late and I did not reform the system in such a way that Stalin's rule would have been impossible.
> SVERDLOV: Vladimir Il'ich ...
> LENIN: No, you don't have to spare me! I want everyone to know that I entirely accept the guilt and the moral responsibility for what happened. ...

It is indicative of the Soviet theatre's standing as a forum for airing the most burning issues that this question was first raised by a playwright; the real test of *glasnost'* will be whether the play reaches the Moscow stage.

# 6 Soviet Music in the Era of *Perestroika*

## CHRISTOPHER RICE

### THE ORGANISATION OF SOVIET MUSIC[1]

At the highest level, Soviet musical life is overseen by the USSR Ministry of Culture and by the culture and propaganda department of the Central Committee of the CPSU. (Both the then Minister of Culture, P. N. Demichev, and the Central Committee secretary responsible for propaganda, A. N. Iakovlev, attended the Soviet composers' congress in 1986.)

The Union of Soviet Composers (*Soiuz sovetskikh kompozitorov*) controls all professional musical composition and is 'the power behind all musical decisions of the Soviet government'. Only about 70 per cent of members are, in fact, composers; the remainder are musicologists, journalists and critics. There is no Soviet organisation of performing artists. The union distributes commissions for works on subjects of current propaganda interest – in 1985, for example, the *leitmotif* was the fortieth anniversary of the victory over fascism – for music festivals and other special occasions. Its directing board is responsible for the general welfare of members and disposes of communal housing, vacation retreats, medical facilities, and so on. It also influences the awarding of prizes, the publication and recording of compositions and the repertoire policies of opera houses, philharmonia organisations, special festivals, radio, TV and film. Finally, the union decides on which of its members to send on special assignments abroad. The union is financed through the State music fund (*muzfond*). While union membership is not, in theory, compulsory for composers, the unified system of patronage makes it practically impossible to work independently.

The Union of Composers was formed in 1932 as part of a general, Party-decreed reorganisation of artistic and literary associations. At its first nationwide congress, which did not take place until 1948, T. N. Khrennikov was elected First Secretary, a post he still holds. The union's seventh congress met in April 1986. Currently there are about 2500 members in all, originating from every part of the Soviet Union. Affiliate organisations exist for the various republics. The views of the composers are conveyed primarily through the monthly journal *Sovetskaia Muzyka* and the bi-monthly *Muzykal'naia Zhizn'*.

The basic concert-organising agencies in the Soviet Union are the philharmonias (*filarmonii*). These derive historically from the philharmonic societies of the nineteenth century but now have much wider functions and responsibilities. The first post-revolutionary philharmonic organisations were founded in Petrograd in 1921 and in Moscow shortly afterwards. There are presently 169 of them, formed variously at republic or regional level, or in major conurbations and industrial centres. Thus Moscow has its own philharmonia, while concert life in Tbilisi is the preserve of the Georgian State Philharmonia.

The purpose of the philharmonias is to promote, via concerts of all types (jazz and pop included), the best in Soviet, Russian and foreign music and music-making. Also, to oversee the development of young Soviet performers and to help in setting up cultural exchanges with musical organisations at home and abroad. The philharmonias have some additional responsibility for the organisation of concert tours inside the Soviet Union.

Like other Soviet enterprises and organisations the philharmonias are governed by the plan, which assigns the finances and sets out detailed guidelines on concert 'output'. Each philharmonia supports a number of permanent musical ensembles: symphony and chamber orchestras, soloists, choirs, jazz bands and pop groups, besides drawing on the resources of other performers on a contractual basis. The philharmonias vary in size. The establishment of the Khar'kov philharmonia, for example, currently includes a symphony orchestra, soloists, a string ensemble, two string quartets, a brass quartet, a wind quintet and an accordion (*baian*) duo. The Estonian State philharmonia has an establishment of only three collectives (two choirs and a chamber ensemble) but also finds work for eleven variety outfits, including several pop groups. The number of concerts organised by the larger philharmonias almost takes one's breath away. The Moscow philharmonia, for example, claims to organise 14 000–15 000 concerts annually, the smaller Kemerovo philharmonia in Siberia, about 6000. These concerts take place in philharmonic halls, opera houses, Houses of Culture, cinemas, libraries, colleges, and so on. The plan also obliges philharmonias to organise regular performances in neighbouring factories and collective farms (Kemerovo puts on 800 village concerts a year). Additionally, lecture bureaux exist to organise musical 'propaganda' in schools, colleges and Houses of Culture.

Overall management of the philharmonias is in the hands of the director and his (or her) chief cultural assistant. An artistic council advises on rates of pay, repertoire policy, admissions and a variety of other matters. The council consists of artists' representatives plus Party, Komsomol, soviet and trade union officials.

For pop musicians at least, philharmonia membership is not always necessary in order to obtain paid work. 'Amateur' bands are occasionally supported by other official organisations like the Komsomol, trade unions or collective farms, while groups playing to university or college audiences sometimes receive a share of the takings. Joining the philharmonia means a much greater degree of financial security, however, as well as opportunities to appear on radio and television and possible access to recording studios. As always there is a price to be paid for these benefits: every band endorsed by the philharmonia has to submit its material for official approval at regular intervals. In the eyes of many Soviet rock fans, when a band joins the philharmonia it is tantamount to 'selling out'.

In order to receive an advanced musical education in the Soviet Union a child needs to attend one of the specialist primary and secondary music schools. There are, in addition, at least twenty Central Music Schools affiliated to the conservatories which offer high-quality musical training to exceptionally gifted children aged seven to eighteen. At the time of the revolution there were five conservatories: Petersburg (founded 1862), Moscow (1866), Saratov, Kiev and Odessa. By the early 1970s there were 24, distributed throughout the Soviet Union in major centres of population like Riga, Baku, Sverdlovsk, Novosibirsk, Tbilisi and Minsk. The overwhelming majority of students (about 90 per cent of those attending the Moscow conservatory) are trainee performers. Most of the courses last five years, after which a small proportion of students continue with postgraduate work.

## THE CURRENT STATE OF SOVIET MUSIC

In November 1987 the Ministry of Culture newspaper, *Sovetskaia Kul'tura*, reported on a debate organised by its editors and attended by a variety of distinguished musical figures.[1] The subject of the debate was the current state of Soviet music. Those invited included the chairwoman of the recently formed All-Union Musical Society, Irina Arkhipova, the director of the Moscow State Philharmonia, Avangard Fedotov, researchers Nikolai Kiiashchenko and Elena Bogatyreva and performers Igor' Oistrakh, Valerii Klimov, Nikolai Petrov, Aleksei Stavronskii and Maksim Konchalovskii. The discussion was chaired by first deputy chief editor, Oleg Ivanov.

The tone of the discussion (at least as reported) was exceedingly gloomy. Oistrakh spoke in terms of the disappearance of musical culture, Garri Grodberg of catastrophe and of the imminent death of classical music. Bogatyreva lamented the fact that a mere 1 per cent of the population was estimated to be familiar with high culture. Serious shortcomings on the part of those charged with organising Soviet musical life were blamed for much of what had gone wrong. On a recent visit to the city of Tambov, Konchalovskii had encountered people so disgusted with the local philharmonia that they could not bear to hear the word. S. Usanov asserted that 90 per cent of philharmonia time was wasted on trivialities. Others argued that the philharmonias had failed to attract able and committed directors prepared to publicise and promote new talent. As Fedotov (Moscow philharmonia) was quick to point out, however, organising concert life is anything but plain sailing when the capital's premier concert venue, the Tchaikovsky Hall, is in desperate need of structural repairs. According to Bogatyreva, 75 per cent of concerts in the country at large now take place outside proper halls and the performances are frequently spoiled by poor acoustics, badly-tuned pianos and uncomfortable surroundings. Touring arrangements were also criticised at the meeting. Oistrakh cited the experience of the violinist, Viktor Pikaizen, who, finding himself sharing a room while on tour in Khabarovsk and asking to be moved to a single one, was told to take the matter up with Moscow. Why is it, Usanov wondered, that while Soviet sportsmen are feted and treated with kid gloves, the nation's artists are ignored or undervalued?

In fact, the debate revealed nothing new. Since 1986 at least, the cultural press has been active in exposing the not-inconsiderable shortcomings of the Soviet musical establishment. So let us take full advantage of the new climate of *glasnost'* and examine the situation in greater detail.

**The officials**

A number of highly-placed officials have come in for unwelcome public scrutiny recently. At the 1986 congress of the composers' union.[3] Rodion Shchedrin, chairman of the RSFSR branch, singled out deputy Minister of Culture, G. Ivanov, for allegedly mishandling relations with the Bol'shoi. He appears to have been dismissed. Shchedrin was also scathing about another ministry official, V. F. Grenkov, whom he referred to as the 'champion of unanswered letters'. Grenkov's subsequent fate has not been revealed. A number of leading philharmonia officials have been attacked openly in the press. The director of the Kiev philharmonia, A. I. Starostin, was lambasted for making a shambles of a major music festival and the leader of the Saratov philharmonia, G. I. Korotkova, was accused of financial profligacy. The artistic head of the Saratov philharmonia also received a reprimand.[4]

Party officials too have not gone unscathed. The Party secretary of the Azerbaidzhan Opera Theatre in Baku was criticised for stacking the cards against the company's chief conductor, regional Party officials in Kazan' have been accused of exercising undue influence in the appointment of officials to the composer's union, a clique of Party members and officials at the USSR State Academic Russian Choir in Moscow was denounced for conspiring to prevent the appointment of a new conductor approved by the Ministry of Culture – and so on.[5]

**The composers**

During 1986 a number of artistic unions held congresses and there were some remarkable, not to say unprecedented developments. The radical film director, Elem Klimov, was appointed first secretary of the cinema workers' union and immediately ordered a re-examination of previously banned films. The Union of Writers elected a former camp inmate, Vladimir Karpov, as its new president, and controversy began to enliven previously sterile debate. In December the theatre workers met to form a union organisation of their own and immediately proceeded to introduce a major new reform. In this context, the seventh congress of the Union of Composers, which convened in April 1986, turned out to be something of a damp squib. Tikhon Khrennikov, First Secretary since 1948, one-time scourge of Prokofiev, Shostakovich, Khachaturian, et al. and aged 73, was still at the helm at the final session. According to one observer, the debates were conducted in a 'skilfully organised atmosphere of general tranquility'.[6] So much for *glasnost*'.

Khrennikov's keynote address was predictably anodyne.[7] Self-criticism was couched in the most general terms, Khrennikov drawing the attention of members to what he saw as a 'lowering of criteria for entry to membership of the union of composers' and calling for 'more open exchange of opinions in our sessions' without obviously setting the tone himself. The First Secretary praised the patriotism and 'civic sense' of many of the works commissioned to mark the fortieth anniversary of the end of the Great Patriotic War, while admitting that some were less worthy of the occasion than others. He claimed to be active in seeking the greater involvement of young composers and musicologists in the life of the union (the average age of members is said to be about 60) but immediately reverted to the stock vocabulary of attacks on 'formalism', accusing some composers of seeking 'cheap sensation' through Western fads and fashions, rather than adhering to the tried and tested principles of the Russian classical tradition. Khrennikov admitted that many theatres were empty as a result of 'routine, drabness and provincialism' but refused to accept that much in contemporary Soviet opera and ballet was little to the taste of the public. He conceded that concert life was in need of 'fundamental restructuring' but seemed content to leave the work to others. As for the light entertainment sector, increasingly the preserve of the long-despised rock bands, Khrennikov rallied the troops with a ringing denunciation of the 'bourgeois commercial show-business machine'.

Having begun his address with some remarks in the Gorbachevian mould, on the need for independent thought and so on, the First Secretary reverted to form by ending with the traditional, self-congratulatory paean of praise for modern Soviet music: 'The eighties have been a period of powerful upsurge in the world authority of Soviet music. Listeners from different continents and professional musicians are increasingly drawn to our culture.'

To be fair, some vigorous and less inhibited criticism was voiced at the seventh congress, though much of it was levelled at others, not the composers themselves. The head of the RSFSR union, Rodion Shchedrin, blamed Komsomol leaders for promoting the 'cult of mindless enertainment' by publishing articles on rock music in their newspaper at the expense of the classics. He contrasted the poor state of Soviet concert halls with those emerging in East European cities like Leipzig and Berlin. And he attacked specific officials in the Ministry of Culture, as well as the general tendency for cultural questions to be 'resolved' by financial experts. There was little self-criticism in his address, however, at least as it was reported.[8] Other delegates bemoaned empty concert halls, poor facilities, low standards of musical training, the inroads made by pop music, the shortcomings of philharmonia organisations, and so on.

If any doubts remained about the *need* for reform in the Union of Composers, these were rudely dispersed by a savage attack on the organisation which appeared in a March 1987 issue of *Izvestiia*, about a year, that is, after the seventh congress.[9] The author, the composer V. Dashkevich, accused the union leadership of complacency and bureaucratic inertia. Eighty to ninety per cent of compositions bought by Ministry of Culture purchasing commissions, he alleged, would be rarely if ever performed, owing to their indifferent quality. On the other hand, creative and forward-looking works by the likes of Al'fred Shnitke, Edison Denisov and Sofiia Gubaidulina had been criticised for showing 'formalism'. Shnitke, for example, had suffered unexplained cancellations of his concerts and, it was implied, his achievements were better appreciated by other cultural organisations, such as the film-workers' union. There were other, more embarrassing revelations: that a former secretary of the Union of Composers had been sacked for plagiarism, while a one-time Director of the Bureau for the Propagation of Soviet Music had been moved on after a financial probe.

Dashkevich also put his finger on fundamental weaknesses in the light music sector. Most composers turned their backs on popular music and deliberately disparaged those involved in it, like the author of the highly successful rock opera *Juno and Avos*. The Union, it was alleged, had made no effort to finance a properly equipped sound laboratory, stocked with synthesisers and other modern equipment, yet relied increasingly for its own funding on revenues from the record sales and performances of rock and variety entertainers, whose activities it spurned to such a high degree.

This no-holds barred attack on the Union leadership, though described as 'polemical' and therefore not necessarily representing the views of the editors, was indicative nevertheless of a growing impatience with the failure of the musicians to match words with deeds in the nationwide struggle for 'restructuring'. Furthermore, many of its criticisms have been echoed by subsequent reports in the press. For example, Aleksei Machavariani, a leading figure in the Georgian branch of the composers' union, has written of the preponderance of 'grey, faceless works' composed exclusively for 'a narrow circle of professionals'.[10] He was particularly concerned by the fate of younger composers in Georgia, whose output is allegedly being ignored by the 'clannishness' of the older generation, representatives of whom effectively control the union, the philharmonia, local opera, radio and TV. They are further hindered by the attitudes of orchestras who 'don't trouble themselves with new works', by Melodiia which is apparently reluctant to record their compositions and by the indifference of the philharmonia which is said to have become the 'exclusive mouthpiece of pop groups'.

While the Georgian composers' union has denied some of these criticisms,[11] particularly that of 'clannism', similar complaints have been heard elsewhere. For example, the Moscow philharmonia has echoed the criticism concerning the quality of modern compositions; a prominent official in the Belorussian composers' union has rebuked his colleagues for being 'unvocal' in response to *glasnost'* and expressed frustration at the few opportunities for local composers to gain a hearing; and a member of the board of the RSFSR union has revealed a scene of quite breathtaking decay at the once esteemed Kazan' conservatory.[12]

The most recent all-union plenum was held in the Siberian city of Kemerovo in September 1987.[13] Moscow Radio revealed that a commission had been set up to draft a new union constitution, with the aim of 'strengthening its social nature and the principle of self-government'. According to the same source, the meeting was in agreement that the union's work was in need of 'resolute restructuring'. However, an English-language report on Moscow's world service spoke of 'clashes of opinion' at the plenum and referred to the 'public's lack of interest in serious contemporary music'.

Since then, the calls for change have not abated. In June 1988, for example, the Union of Composers was treated to yet another candid assessment, this time by Mikael Tariverdiev in *Sovetskaia Kul'tura*.[14] The author, a union member and former official of the RSFSR branch, concluded by calling for bold structural changes which would introduce more democracy and accountability into the union and encourage more artistic toleration: 'the time for "bourgeois" and "proletarian" styles is past'. These included direct elections by all members to union posts in a secret ballot, election for single terms only (starting with first secretaries) and the abolition of sinecure payments, the money to go instead to scholarships for young composers.

**The philharmonias**

The philharmonias have come in for some particularly savage criticism since Mr Gorbachev came to power in 1985. The situation in

Khar'kov, as revealed in an article in *Sovetskaia Muzyka* in December 1986, is extreme in some respects but does illustrate the kind of problems all philharmonias are currently facing.[15]

In 1984 Khar'kov's main concert hall was closed for repairs and the philharmonia took up temporary residence in the local House of Culture. Unfortunately, facilities there left much to be desired. The hall was poorly heated and had bad acoustics. Latecomers habitually disrupted performances by entering through the main doors, while the orchestra had to compete with the strains of disco music invading from neighbouring rooms and corridors. The combination of naughty children, pounding rock rhythms and banging doors was too much for some performers, who were forced to abort their programmes. The philharmonia was still operating from the House of Culture at the end of 1986. A new concert hall was scheduled to open on the premises of the former Uspenskii Cathedral some time during 1987; so far, however, it has not materialised.

Even perfect facilities will not guarantee an improvement in the hitherto wretched attendance figures for philharmonia concerts in Khar'kov. Some performances have been cancelled because there is no audience at all while the majority bring in only 30 or 40 people. The fault does not appear to lie with the orchestra, which carries on gamely in spite of a shortage of reeds, strings and rosin! The programmes too, though unremarkable, are not devoid of interest. The 1985–6 season included performances of the Verdi *Requiem*, the Bach *Magnificat*, a concert version of Gluck's *Orfeo ed Euridice*, some Stravinsky and Richard Strauss as well as works by a local composer, V. Bibik. (Mahler's third symphony could not be performed because the orchestra lacked some of the instruments required by the score.) Why then do audiences fail to materialise? Sometimes, it would appear, because they were unaware that a concert is taking place. The philharmonia has access to a single printing press which can produce only a fraction of the publicity needed, while local newspapers rarely carry information on philharmonia events. It is the philharmonia management which is responsible for repertoire policy, however, and this has been criticised for being generally unimaginative. Hence the failure of the 1986 Khar'kov festival which was devoted to Soviet music. The philharmonia has also come under fire for failing to promote music more effectively in local schools.

Much of what has been said about Khar'kov might equally well apply to philharmonias elsewhere. The Moscow philharmonia, for example, has complained about inadequate facilities; the Tchaikovsky Hall is sorely in need of structural repairs while the great hall of the Conservatory must be shared with other organisations. As a result, the philharmonia orchestra is so under-rehearsed that it has apparently broken down during concerts. Publicity is a problem here too. The print works can guarantee to produce only one-third of the required monthly volume of posters, leaflets and programme notes; consequently, many concerts and recitals go unadvertised. Meanwhile, the educational work of the philharmonia is hampered, it is said, by the miserly funds allocated by the State for the concert-lecture programme. On the other hand, the philharmonia administration is itself far from blameless. Concert subscribers, for example, have complained about the shoddy treatment they have received at its hands in recent years: last minute re-scheduling of concerts, lack of information, mix-ups over seat allocation, and so on.

The Saratov philharmonia still awaits a modern concert hall. Local opera is said to be 'dying' because of the external state of the theatres: shoddy decor, sets, costumes, etc. The chorus lacks proper professional training. Local orchestras suffer because of the poor quality of Soviet-manufactured instruments and there are shortages even of these. There is the now-familiar problem of publicity. At the same time, however, the philharmonia directors have been attacked for gross financial mismanagement: in the space of two years they are said to have run up a debt of around 300 000 roubles, yet plan to celebrate the philharmonia's fiftieth birthday by staging two concerts, costing an estimated 130 000 roubles, in – Moscow! Overall Director G. I. Korotkova has also been blamed for the collapse of several home-grown pop groups which have been starved of funding for such essentials as the purchase and repair of equipment, new costumes, sets for new shows, and so on. Even the best of them, the once highly successful band *Integral*, has seen its profits fall from 245 000r in 1981 to just 84 000r in 1986. The philharmonia organisation has also been criticised for inefficiency and for undersold subscription concerts. Overspending in some areas is covered by retrenchment in the philharmonia's educational work.[17]

To redress the balance a little at this point, it should be said that a number of philharmonias have been praised recently for imaginative work and responsible management. These include Leningrad, Riga, Tallin, Sverdlovsk, Novosibirsk and Kemerovo. The reasons for their success vary. Leningrad, of course, has been blessed with a distinguished musical tradition, as well as one or two world class ensembles like the Kirov opera and the Leningrad Philharmonic; the

Estonian philharmonia at Tallin is a comparatively small and compact organisation, while that of the Siberian city of Kemerovo is relatively new, as is the city itself.[18]

**The performing artists**

Here one must make a distinction between artists who are already, or are on the way to becoming, internationally known – the likes of the pianist Sviatoslav Richter, the violinist David Oistrakh, singers Elena Obraztsova and Vladimir Atlantov, conductors Iurii Temirkanov and Mariss Iansons, the members of the Borodin Quartet – and the rest. Top Soviet artists can expect to make regular trips abroad and receive part of their fees, at least, in foreign currency. As 'titled' artists and prizewinners they enjoy the privileges that, in the Soviet Union, accompany success: rent-free apartments, holiday dachas, places in government sanatoria, and so on. And while Soviet concert fees are hardly princely, even for top artists, they are well in excess of the average working wage. There is one final advantage not to be overlooked – the chance to perform regularly in Moscow and Leningrad to full houses.

The majority of performing artists are not so fortunate, as recent press reports indicate only too clearly. Those lucky enough to study in one of the capitals will pay for the privilege by subsequently being assigned to a lowly provincial centre where the pay is in the region of 150 roubles per month (1978) for performing in 15–20 concerts.[19] Chorus-members of the Bol'shoi are paid at about the same rate. Once appointed, it is difficult to be transferred from one opera house or orchestra to another – very difficult if the artist hopes to move to one of the capitals. At the same time, even gifted performers with one of the leading companies can see their talents wasted or underused. This comes about because of a reluctance to 'loan out' singers and musicians not currently in demand to provincial collectives. It was revealed recently, for example, that a conductor with the Kirov opera, Evgenii Kolobov, was allowed to languish there for years before finally being dismissed. He is currently working as an administrator with the Leningrad concert agency, at a time when provincial opera companies and other ensembles are crying out for experienced musical directors. Unfortunately, the truth may well be that Kolobov would prefer a desk job in Leningrad to 'demotion' to the sticks. However, there are plenty of artists in a similar position who may be prepared to move to a provincial theatre, at least on a temporary basis. Elena Ustinova of the Leningrad Malii theatre, for example, has complained about not being able to get roles which suit her. Elena Svechnikova has languished with the Stanislavskii–Nemirovich Danchenko musical theatre of Moscow at a time when Sverdlosk opera cannot find a Carmen, a role for which she is said to be ideally suited.[20]

All performers spend a considerable amount of time touring the Soviet Union and, by all accounts, this can be a deeply dispiriting experience. According to the great soprano Galina Vishnevskaia, who left permanently for the West in 1974, musicians depart for the provinces armed with suitcases crammed with food, dishes and a thermos so as to avoid using local restaurants. Her reminiscences of other aspects of touring also accord pretty well with the experiences of today's performers. Gruelling schedules, mean accommodation, long journeys on broken-down buses, near-empty concert halls, rude administrators – these are the occupational hazards of the touring artist. To cite just one or two examples: A male voice choir from Estonia, on tour in Central Asia, was due to appear in Tashkent. At the last moment, however, they were told that they would be making a 300-kilometre trip to Samarkand instead. There they gave three concerts; one to a group of children and two to the *same* military unit.[21] Or take the case of the Moscow-based pianist Mikhail Volchok. On tour in the Ukraine, he arrived in Voronezh to give a concert at the local music school. His hotel lacked even the basic conveniences. Worse, no one had thought to advertise his arrival, so he appeared before an audience of a dozen people. Volchok moved on to Tambov where, after a six-hour journey, he gave a forty-minute lecture at the piano to a handful of children. To rub salt into the wound, the local philharmonia was buzzing with excitement over the Tambov appearance of the rock band *Cruise*.[22] The notoriously poor organisation of concert tours within the Soviet Union partly results from the chaotic allocation of responsibilities among various philharmonias and touring agencies like *Roskontsert* and *Soiuzkontsert*.

All hardships can be borne stoically if the performer can look forward to an opportunity to travel abroad. Invitations to Soviet artists from the West, together with the touring arrangements themselves, are handled by the State Concert Agency, *Goskontsert*. This is one of the country's legendary bureaucracies. Western impresarios and concert managers are habitually complaining about the welter of red tape encountered when trying to negotiate a performer out of the

Soviet Union; and about the fact that even when the paperwork is completed there is always the possibility of a last-minute cancellation – or, alternatively, the abrupt replacement of one artist by another. *Goskontsert* has further complicated matters in the past by refusing to allow Soviet performers to be placed with a single manager responsible for a wide geographical area; instead, representation is distributed country by country. Finally, there is a regulation that no Soviet artist may leave the country for more than 90 days in any one year.[23]

Complaints about *Goskontsert* are not restricted to the Western side. The respected Soviet pianist, Boris Eresko, described the agency recently as a 'mysterious, secretive' organisation which had failed to provide him with a single, reliable tour schedule in over twenty years of performing. He went on to accuse the tour administrators of failing to pass on invitations from abroad and blamed them for the 'appalling ignorance' of Western impresarios about performers already well known and respected in the Soviet Union but who remain outside *Goskontsert*'s charmed circle.[24]

**The youth problem**

Put simply, the 'problem' – in its cultural dimension – is this. The overwhelming majority of young people in the Soviet Union are said to be indifferent to 'high culture', serious music in particular. One survey, conducted among 15–30 year-olds in Siberia, found that while 80 per cent of those interviewed were interested in pop music, 94 per cent admitted ignorance of classical music.[25] This trend, long in evidence but only recently acknowledged, has been put down to a number of factors: a lack of suitably qualified teachers, parental indifference, inadequate funding for musical instruments and equipment, failings on the part of Soviet television, new commercial pressures on Melodiia and the insidious influence of Western values. On top of this is the familiar generational dimension. Take the Union of Composers, for example. Their leader is aged 75, the average age of members is around 60. These individuals have long been accustomed, almost conditioned, to rejecting virtually any musical manifestation of the youth sub-culture which began to emerge in the late 1950s and early 1960s. This dismissive attitude is becoming harder to sustain, however, if only because the Soviet state expects its 'official' composers to produce music in the popular as well as serious genres – and music of a kind which will appeal to young people with greater force than that drifting in from the West. In fact, the Union of Composers is failing dismally in this area of its work, losing out to young, 'non-official' composers. Among the union composers, only Raimond Pauls (who apparently collects 15 000 roubles a month in royalties) and the popular singer David Tukhmanov are regularly heard at concerts and discotheques.[26] Many more young, classically-trained musicians are keen to get in on the act. In Belorussia, for example, there are voices calling for rock to be taught at the conservatory and there are plenty of precedents for youngsters wanting to opt out of the official system in order to pursue independent, if hazardous, careers. Members of the bands *Zodiak* and *Copernicus* and Martin Brauns of the Latvian group *Sipoli*, for example, are conservatory-trained, while the singer Alex Gradskii began life as an operatic tenor and Seva Gakkel of the highly successful band *Aquarium* studied 'cello at special music school.[27]

The authorities have tried a variety of approaches in responding to the phenomenal growth in popularity of rock music: studied indifference, selective tolerance, one-off concessions (the 1979 Elton John tour, for example) and repression. According to Soviet rock impresario Art Troitskii, this last-mentioned approach was adopted fairly systematically towards the end of 1983, beginning with an intensive press campaign railing against rock music's alleged 'greyness', 'bad taste' and 'lack of ideals'. It was not only the underground bands who were under attack; the campaign encompassed the vocal-instrumental ensembles (or VIA's); that is, groups operating within the philharmonia system. The press onslaught was accompanied by a resolution of the Ministry of Culture to the effect that, from then on, eighty per cent of the repertory of any rock group had to consist of songs written by members of the Union of Composers. Bands were called to audition before a commission of the Ministry to ensure that this order was complied with. At the same time there was a general clampdown on concerts organised without specific official approval; this seems to have been intended to include the 'independent', technically amateur bands who had been successfully disseminating their work by means of illegal, home-made albums (*magizdat*). One outlet closed to them from now on was to be the discotheque – disc jockeys were provided by the Ministry with a blacklist of recordings which they were not supposed to play.

In the anarchic world of Soviet rock such hamfisted measures were doomed to failure and the draconian approach, designed more than anything to recover the ground lost by the Union of Composers, was quietly dropped after Gorbachev's accession to the Party leadership in March 1985.

Since then the Soviet musical establishment has had to yield more ground to the rock movement, both in the philharmonias and outside. In January 1986, following the earlier example of Riga and Leningrad, Moscow was at last allowed its own rock club – the Rock Lab, operating under the aegis of the cultural department of Moscow City Council. In May of the same year the independent initiative of Soviet rock musicians to stage a concert for the victims of the Chernobyl disaster was approved and accorded organisational *carte-blanche* by officials in the Central Committee, thus effectively bypassing the Ministry of Culture, Komsomol and other interested bodies. The Chernobyl concert brought together big names in the world of unofficial rock and 'official' stars like Alla Pugacheva. At the same time the export-import policies of the Soviet touring agency *Goskontsert* seemed to soften, as Soviet bands like *Autograph* and *Dialogue* were allowed on tour in the West, while Soviet rock fans were able to see the likes of *UB 40* and Billy Bragg. Now, Melodiia is said to have stepped up its recordings of Soviet artists – rumour has it that even the heavy metal band *Cruise* will be on disc, somewhat surprising in that this group's concerts have sometimes been followed by bad behaviour on the part of their fans.

The new, relaxed dispensation seems to be pressurising the Union of Composers into making at least token (if belated) attempts to meet the pop musicians half way. The most remarkable of these overtures took place during the April 1987 plenum and was linked to the Leningrad spring festival.[28] It took the form of a concert-discussion called *vokrug roka* and brought together union members, some of whom had set up a study group called the 'third direction', two pop groups and members of the public. The two bands invited to play were the middle-of-the-road *Aquarium* from Leningrad and the heavy metal band *Cruise* originally from Sverdlovsk. Judging by the tone of the press report *Aquarium*, who performed songs by their lead singer Boris Grebenshchikov, won the grudging approval of the composers – in marked contrast to *Cruise*, who were slammed in print as representing 'negation for the sake of negation' and 'aggression without purpose'. Ears were crushed by the noise level ('decibels, decibels') and eyebrows raised at the lead singer appearing in riding breeches and sporting a Georgian cross on his chest. The playing was described as 'aggressive' and the song 'Separation' as 'gloomy'. The discussion took place during the interval. When asked what they thought, most of the (40–50 year-old) composers and musicologists present were apparently lost for words and dialogue with the youngsters was pronounced 'difficult'. The performers themselves simply refused to take part while their supporters backed them with shouts of 'down with the composers'. The reporter covering the event praised the composers' side (which included David Tukhmanov, Rodion Shchedrin and Alex Rybnikov, author of the music for the highly successful rock opera, *Juno and Avos* to a libretto by the poet Andrei Voznesenskii) for their willingness to listen and their restraint in the face of provocation. Following the performance there was a more general (and apparently more successful) discussion bringing in members of the public. During this session the official composers were criticised for 'elitism'. Comment on the rock music itself was said not to have been very informed.

## *Perestroika* in Soviet music

The Soviet Government has responded to the crisis in music with a number of decrees,[29] the most important of which are:

(a) (April 1986) Decree 'For the Further Improvement of Concert Activity in the Country' (*O merakh po dal'neishemu uluchsheniiu kontsertnoi deiatel'nosti v strane* . . .) This decree introduces a series of proposals for improving concert administration. These have subsequently been incorporated into the (April 1987) Statute for Concert Life in the USSR which was drawn up after unusually wide-ranging consultations involving the Ministry of Culture, the State Committee for Radio and Television, the State Planning Committee (Gosplan), the Ministry of Finance and the Union of Composers. These deliberations, were, however, immediately criticised for leaving the performing artists largely unrepresented. The Statute makes provision for (1) redefining and rationalising the administration of Soviet music; (2) greater autonomy for cultural agencies at the local level; (3) a drastic reduction in the number of plan indicators: from now on maximising attendance figures will be paramount in the planning considerations of administrators, rather than organising a pre-set number of concerts, as previously. The number of concerts will depend on the resources of the individual concert organisation. It is hoped that this reordering of priorities will encourage administrators to plan concerts imaginatively, while at the same time removing or at least reducing the temptation to falsify or distort planning returns. Thus far there has been little feedback on how the Statute is faring, though the initial consensus seems to be that it does not go nearly far enough in overhauling the over-centralised, hierarchical and inflexible structure of the Stalin era. (4) Organisations 'overfulfilling' the planning requirements imposed on them from above will retain the profits themselves, rather than handing them over to the State for general redistribution.

(b) Decree 'On improving the conditions in which the creative unions operate' (*Ob ukreplenii material'noi bazy kul'tury i tvorcheskikh soiuzov*). This piece of legislation, dating from January 1987, allocates substantial sums to the various union organisations for general and specific purposes. In the case of the Union of Composers this will mean more money for the publication of musical scores, additions in the print-run of music magazines, the creation of a museum of folklore, and additional financial support for union activities. For the philharmonias the decree provides for the construction of 40 new concert halls (for example in Vilnius, Kazan' and Cheliabinsk) and 25 houses of culture, including a Palace of Music in Moscow.

(c) *Other innovations*
There is talk of legislation to permit Soviet artists touring abroad to receive a greater share of their foreign currency earnings than at present.

An all-Union Music Society has recently been formed with substantial State help.[30] By July 1987 constituent conferences had been held in the RSFSR, Ukraine, Belorussia, Moldavia, Latvia, Lithuania, Estonia, Kazakhstan and Azerbaidzhan. The aim is to revive interest in music generally, particularly serious music, by increasing contacts and cooperation among professional and amateur performers, teachers, instrument manufacturers, and so on. The society will try to emulate the traditions of nineteenth-century music societies (the traditional philharmonias) in organising and promoting music festivals and competitions, master classes and lectures, exhibitions, conferences and, of course, concerts. Events organised so far by the Society include a conference of music teachers, ballroom dancing and brass band competitions and an exhibition of musical instruments. Contacts will soon be established at international level, journalists in Moscow were told recently.

Western impresarios and concert managers have lately been reporting small, but noticeable improvements in the workings of *Goskont-*

sert.[31] In December 1985 a small group of Western concert agents returned from Moscow after attending an unprecedented, *Goskontsert*-sponsored showcase of some one hundred singers considered worthy of Western exposure. There is talk of a more streamlined look to *Goskontsert*'s administration. A representative of a prominent, London-based concert agency has reported that the traditional ninety-day limit on foreign tours is now being quietly dropped and international artists like the conductors Mariss Iansons and Iurii Temirkanov are now able to negotiate European, even world representation when on tour.

Most noticeable, however, is the great expansion in musical traffic between the Soviet Union and the West. In 1987 alone Britain saw the Kirov Opera, the Leningrad Philharmonic and the Borodin Quartet, as well as the Bol'shoi ballet. The Edinburgh Festival too had a Soviet flavour and Radio 3 put on a month-long tribute to Russian and Soviet music. And the works of a number of modern Soviet composers have been premiered, those of Al'fred Shnitke and Sofiia Gubaidulina, for example. The story is much the same in other countries and in view of the current Soviet–Western rapprochement the future, in this respect at least, looks bright.

# Notes

1. For background on Soviet music see the following:
   A. Olkhovsky, *Music Under the Soviets – The Agony of an Art* (New York: 1955). Boris Schwarz, *Musical and Musical Life in Soviet Russia*, Enlarged edition, 1917–81 (Bloomington, Indiana: 1983). On jazz, see S. Frederick Starr, *Red and Hot – The Fate of Jazz in the Soviet Union* (New York: 1983). On pop music, Artemy Troitsky, *Back in the USSR. The True Story of Rock in Russia* (London: 1987).
2. *Sovetskaia Kul'tura* (hereafter *SK*), 17 November 1987.
3. For the proceedings of the composers' congress, see *SK*, 3 April 1986; 5 April 1986. Most of the major speeches also appeared in various issues of *Sovetskaia Muzyka* (hereafter *SM*) during 1986.
4. (Kiev) *SK*, 14 May 1987; (Saratov) *SK*, 26 November 1987.
5. (Baku) *SK*, 26 September 1987; (Kazan') *SK*, 10 October 1987; (Moscow) *SK*, 11 July 1987.
6. *Izvestiia*, 1 March 1987.
7. *SK*, 3 April 1986.
8. Ibid.
9. See note 6 above.
10. *SK*, 7 July 1987. See also editorial comment on the same page.
11. *SK*, 15 October 1987.

12. (Moscow) *SM*, June 1987; (Belorussia) *SK*, 22 September 1987; (Kazan') *SK*, 10 October 1987.
13. *BBC Summary of World Broadcasts*, 19 October 1987. Khrennikov's address to the congress was published in *SM*, November 1987.
14. *SK*, 2 June 1988.
15. *SM*, December 1986.
16. On the Moscow Philharmonia see *SK*, 31 March 1987; *SK*, 16 April 1987; *SK*, 7 May 1987; *SM*, June 1987.
17. On the Saratov Philharmonia see *SK*, 14 March 1987; *SK*, 26 November 1987.
18. (Tallin) *SK*, 5 November 1987; (Kemerovo) *SM*, May 1987, *SK*, 7 January 1988.
19. Background information has been drawn from G. Vishnevskaya, *Galina. A Russian Story* (London: 1985).
20. *SK*, 12 November 1987.
21. *SK*, 5 November 1987.
22. *SK*, 12 May 1987.
23. *Classical Music* 7 November 1987, p. 35.
24. *SK*, 19 March 1987.
25. *SK*, 28 March 1987. For other articles on youth and music, see *SK*, 1 December 1987 and *SM*, June 1987. The journal *V mire knig* began a series 'Kto est' kto v zarubezhnoi Rock (sic) muzyke' ('Who's who in foreign Rock music') in its issue for June 1988. This journal has also been running a series, with music, on Russian guitar poetry under the title 'Pesni bardov' (Songs of the bards) since April 1988. The series has already featured the hitherto banned songs of Aleksandr Galich. The new journal *Rodnik* (Riga) began serialisation of Troitsky's *Back in the USSR* (see note 1) under the slightly amended title 'Rock in the USSR', in its issue for May 1988. Rock music is also featured in the 1987 film, *Vzlomshchik* (The Burglar), directed by Valerii Ogorodnikov and starring Konstantin Kinchev, singer with the Leningrad group, Alisa.
26. The information on Pauls appeared in Martin Walker's book *The Waking Giant. The Soviet Union Under Gorbachev*, Revised edition (London: 1987), p. 170.
27. Much of the background on rock music has been drawn from Artemy Troitsky's book, *Back in the USSR* (see note 1). Also Anne Nightingale, Radio 1 broadcast 28 December 1987; 'Muzyka v SSSR' April/June 1987 (article on Tartu rock festival); S. Frederick Starr, *Red and Hot – The Fate of Jazz in the Soviet Union*, pp. 289–315 (see note 1).
28. *SK*, 28 April 1987.
29. So far I have been unable to get hold of the texts of these decrees. They have been reported on in the following places: *SK*, 26 March 1987; *SK*, 26 May 1987; *SM*, July 1987.
30. *SK*, 14 July 1987; *SM*, January 1987 (article by T. Khrennikov).
31. See note 23 above.

# 7 The Literary Press

## JULIAN GRAFFY

### I

The most remarkable development in Soviet publishing over the last three years has been the breathtaking transformation of the majority of the literary journals. The two currently most exciting journals, *Novy mir* and *Znamia*, have been utterly rejuvenated by their new chief editors. The veteran writer, Sergei Zalygin, has been editor-in-chief of *Novy mir* since the issue for October 1986. At the beginning of 1987 he brought on to the editorial board the journalist and story-writer Anatolii Strelianyi, the poet Oleg Chukhontsev and others. *Novyi mir* (circulation in January 1988 1 150 000, up from 496 100 in December 1987),[1] has published Platonov's *The Foundation Pit* (1987, 6), Bulgakov's *To A Secret Friend* (1987, 8), Bitov's *Pushkin House* (1987, 10–12), Shatrov's *The Peace of Brest-Litovsk* (1987, 4), Brodskii's poetry (1987, 12) and *Doctor Zhivago* (1988, 1–4). Grigorii Baklanov, another writer-editor, in charge at *Znamia* since August 1986, has co-opted Vladimir Lashkin, a key figure on Tvardovskii's editorial board at the old *Novyi mir* and the urban writer Vladimir Makanin to the board. Unlike *Novyi mir*, *Znamia* has no glorious traditions to look back to, and its sudden dynamism has taken readers by surprise. Its 1988 circulation of 500 000 is up from 175 000 in 1985. It has published Alesandr Bek's *A New Assignment* (1986, 10–11), Platonov's *The Juvenile Sea* (1986, 6), Bulgakov's *The Heart of a Dog* (1987, 6), Pil'niak's *The Tale of the Unextinguished Moon* (1987, 12), Shatrov's *Onward ... Onward ... Onward!* (1988, 1) and Zamiatin's *We* (1988, 4–5). It is no coincidence that the two other most consistently exciting publications of the *glasnost'* era, the weekly magazine, *Ogonek*, and the weekly newspaper *Moskovskie novosti/ Moscow News*, also have new editors. Since the summer of 1986 *Ogonek* has been edited by Vitalii Korotich. The circulation in January 1988 rose to 1 770 000, but since subscription has more than doubled from 561 415 to 1 313 349, it seems clear that *Ogonek* could, if allowed, sell far more. Egor Iakovlev took over the editorship of *Moskovskie novosti* in August 1986 from Gennadii Gerasimov. The Russian-language circulation figure in 1987 was 250 000. Both *Moskovskie novosti* and, in particular, *Ogonek* regularly run pieces that are of great interest to literary scholars.

Most of the major Moscow and Leningrad journals are participating eagerly in the process of liberalisation. *Druzhba narodov* (circulation in December 1987, 150 000, in January 1988, 800 000) under its veteran editor Sergei Baruzdin, has published Rybakov's *Children of the Arbat* (1987, 4–6), the Pasternak–Tsvetaeva–Rilke correspondence (1987, 6–9), Platonov's *Chevengur* (1988, 3–4), Nabokov's autobiography *Other Shores* (1988, 5–6) and the correspondence of Pasternak and Ol'ga Freidenberg (1988, 7–10). *Oktiabr'* (edited by Anatolii Anan'ev, circulation in January 1988 250 000), has published Astaf'ev's *A Sad Detective Story* (1986, 1), Bulgakov's letters to the Soviet government and to Stalin (1987, 6) and Grossman's *Life and Fate* (1988, 1–4). The Leningrad journal *Neva*, (edited by Boris Nikol'skii, circulation in January 1988 up from 290 000 to 550 000), has printed Dudintsev's *Robed in White* (1987, 1–4) and Lidiia Chukovskaia's *Sof'ia Petrovna (The Deserted House)* (1988), 2). Other journals with much smaller circulations have managed to create their own publishing sensations. *V mire knig* (In the world of books) with a circulation of 40 400, has begun two ambitious series in 1988. *Songs of the Bards*, running in issues since April 1988, provides the words and music of the work of the most famous Russian guitar poets. *Who's Who in Western Rock Music*, which began in June 1988, describes itself as an 'encyclopedia', and after two issues was still on the letter A. *Literaturnaia ucheba*, a journal of the USSR Writers' Union (circulation 20 000), has published Nabokov's *Mary* (1987, 6) and three chapters from *Ulysses* (1988, 1) while *Literaturnoe obozrenie*, a literary critical monthly, also published by the Writers' Union of the USSR, (circulation 23 875) has included Semen Lipkin's memoirs of Vasilii Grossman (1988, 6–7).

Not all literary critical journals, however, have been reconstructed in the spirit of *glasnost'*. The quarterly *Russkaia literatura* remains a decidedly dull enterprise, while the changes early in 1988 at *Voprosy literatury*, a monthly published by the USSR Writers' Union and The Institute of World Literature in Moscow, were actually a step in the opposite direction. At the beginning of 1988, some interesting pieces were appearing in the journal, but then the chief editor, Mikhail Koz'min, was replaced by Dmitrii Urnov, who followed his 1987 attack on Nabokov with a piece vilifying Pasternak and *Doctor Zhivago* in *Pravda*, 27 April 1988.

Chief among journals intended for young people is *Iunost'* (Youth; chief editor Andrei Dement'ev, circulation 3 100 000). Its most notable publications include Antonov's *Vas'ka* (1987, 3–4) and the Strugatskii Brothers' *Worn down by evil, or forty years later* (1988, 6–7). Other important youth magazines include *Avrora* (Leningrad, circulation 500 000) which has published Nabokov and Shalamov; the magazine intended for young people in the countryside, *Sel'skaia molodezh'*, the first Soviet journal to publish any of Shalamov's *Kolyma Tales* (1987, 7); and *Studencheskii meridian*, which has been running almost every month since October 1987 the absorbing *Vladimir Vysotskii: episodes from a creative life*, a collage–chronicle which, it has already been announced, will continue into 1989.

The main theatrical magazines have also been compulsory reading over the last three years. *Sovremennaia dramaturgiia* has been a lively journal since its inception in 1982, and the competition it has provided has been reflected in *Teatr* and the fortnightly magazine *Teatral'naia zhizn'*. *Sovremennaia dramaturgiia* has printed Erdman's *The Suicide* (1987, 2) and Bulgakov's *Adam and Eve* (1987, 3), to be countered in *Teatr* by Erdman's *The Mandate* (1987, 10), Platonov's *The Barrel-Organ* (1988, 1) and Shatrov's *The Dictatorship of Conscience* (1986, 6).

During the Brezhnev period, provincial and republican journals were occasionally more successful than their Moscow and Leningrad counterparts in publishing controversial material. The critic Arkadii Belinkov managed to get two chapters of his study of Olesha into *Baikal* in 1968 before the door closed on him. Now, in the new openness, provincial and republican journals are playing their part. The second half of Boris Mozhaev's collectivisation novel, *Peasants and their women*, appeared in the Rostov journal *Don* (1987, 1–3), while *Volga* (Saratov) has had Nabokov's *Laughter in the Dark* (1988, 6–8) and *Ural* (Sverdlovsk) his *The Gift* (1988, 3–6). *Pod"em* (Voronezh) has carried Emma Gershtein's study of Mandel'shtam (1988, 6–10) and *Literaturnii Kirgizstan* (Frunze) has included Bulgakov's *Diaboliad* (1987, 4) and *The Fatal Eggs* (1988, 1). *Literaturnaia Gruziia* (Tbilisi) has had unpublished Mandel'shtam, *Literaturnaia Armeniia* (Erevan) Nabokov stories. The most ambitious and important provincial publications at present are both based in Riga. *Daugava*, the longer-established of the two, numbered Nabokov, Akhmatova, Mandel'shtan and Zamiatin among its authors in 1987.

*Rodnik*, founded only at the beginning of 1987, has already won a reputation by running Nabokov's *Invitation to a Beheading* (1987, 8–1988, 2) and by becoming the first Soviet journal to publish Orwell (*Animal Farm*, 1988, 3–6).

Many literary and other newspapers should also be mentioned as the regular source of interesting materials, including *Knizhnoe obozrenie, Literaturnaia gazeta, Literaturnaia Rossiia, Nedelia* and *Sovetskaia kul'tura*. It must be stressed that the publications mentioned give nothing like a full picture of the newspapers and magazines that are showing the effect of the liberalisation of the Soviet press. There is a real sense of competition between journals over important works. In part this is expressed through double publication of, for example, Tvardovskii's *By the Right of Memory* in both *Znamia* (1987, 2) and *Novyi mir* (1987, 3), or Akhmatova's *Requiem in Oktiabr'* (1987, 3) and *Neva* (1987, 6), the latter accompanied by an injured assertion that theirs was the authorised publication. In part it shows itself in the way major coups such as *Doctor Zhivago*, *Life and Fate*, Kafka's *The Castle* and Karamzin's *History of the Russian State* were launched simultaneously by different journals in their first issues for 1988. It will be apparent that most of the works mentioned in this survey were published long ago in the West and have, in consequence, long been known and available to the Muscovite and Leningrad intelligentsia. It is in bringing them to a vast new public, in circulations that are both huge and accessible, that the literary journals are performing their most important educational function.

Not all major journals have ranged themselves unequivocally on the side of *glasnost'*. A journal of the Writers' Union of the Russian Republic, *Moskva* (circulation 683 000), may have published Nabokov's *The Defence* (1986, 12) and Marietta Chudakova's *The Life of Mikhail Bulgakov* (part one, 1987, 6–8; part two, 1988, 11–12). Its editor, Mikhail Alekseev, however, is a man implicated in anti-liberal campaigns both in the 1960s and now.[2] As *Moskva* proves, publication of previously banned texts alone is not proof of a journal's liberal credentials.

The Leningrad journal *Zvezda* (circulation 150 000), on the other hand, seemed until very recently to have decided to sleep through *glasnost'*. This may largely be explained by the longevity of its editor, Georgii Kholopov, who took over the journal in 1955.[3] Finally, in February 1988, *Zvezda* began publication of the memoirs of the returned émigrée, Irina Odoevtseva, *On the Banks of the Neva*.[4] These were published in issues 1988, 2–5 and were followed by their sequel, *On the Banks of the Seine* in issues 1988, 8–12. (In April 1988 serialisation began of Mario Puzo's *The Sicilian*.) In June 1988 Kholopov was replaced as editor by the writer Gennadii Nikolaev.[5]

About the opposition to liberalisation from the journals *Nash sovremennik* and *Molodaia gvardiia* there can be no doubt. *Nash sovremennik*, edited by Sergei Vikulov, has a circulation of 240 000. Notes from a meeting of its editorial board and authors with their readers in December 1987 were recently published in the West.[6] At this meeting Vikulov accused *Novyi mir* of causing a crisis in the paper industry by publishing *Doctor Zhivago*, 'without which there is enough lack of faith anyway'. The author Vasilii Belov complained that the 'medical aspect' and the 'narcotic quality' of rock music were concealed from Russians, and insisted that the demonstrations of Crimean Tartars were organised from the West. The journal has also been accused of having close links with the *Pamiat'* organisation and of racism.[7] Its publication of Viktor Ivanov's *Day of Judgement* (1988, 4–6) which discovers a Jewish Masonic plot against Russia was heavily criticised by *Ogonek*.[8] *Molodaia gvardiia*, edited by Anatolii Ivanov, and with a circulation of 700 000, despite being officially a journal of the central committee of the Komsomol, nevertheless seems quite out of sympathy with the cultural concerns of most Russian young people, going so far as to call rock music 'the religion of evil'. This is merely one manifestation of the journal's strident conservatism. It has demanded the dismissal of the editors of *Moscow News*, *Ogonek* and other pro-*glasnost'* journals[9] and clearly sees itself as the leading mouthpiece for opponents of reform.

As the above survey has shown, the balance among literary journals leans heavily to the side of liberalisation. Western observers have naturally been more interested in seeking out evidence of reform than in reading old-style attacks upon it. It should, however, be pointed out that one reason for the liberals' massing in the literary journals is that another source of literary power and influence, the Unions of Writers both for the Soviet Union as a whole and especially for the Russian republic, remain a stronghold of reaction.[10]

II

A staggering number of writers have benefited from the liberalisation of the literary journals. One major group is the writers whose careers began in the period of Russian modernism at the beginning of the twentieth century. In this context[11] one might mention Akhmatova, Babel', Belyi, Bulgakov, Chaianov, Chukovskii, Erdman, Gumilev, Vsevolod Ivanov, Kharms, Khlebnikov, Kliuev, Kuzmin, Mandel'shtam, Obolduev, Oleinikov, Pasternak, Pil'niak, Platonov, Panteleimon Romanov, Shershenevich, Shvarts, Tsvetaeva, Voloshin, Vvedenskii, Zabolotskii and Zoshchenko. The *Ogonek* series *The twentieth-century Russian muse* has also included several lesser-known poets from this period, and a series in *Knizhnoe obozrenie* has done the same for prose writers. The case of Gumilev is of particular interest, in that he was the first major writer to be put to death by the Soviet regime, when shot for alleged participation in a monarchist plot in 1921. The centenary of his birth, in 1986, saw the beginning of what has been a stream of republications of his poetry. Platonov's novels *The Foundation Pit* (*Novyi mir*, 1987, 6) and *Chevengur* (*Druzhba narodov*, 1988, 3–4) are of major importance. Mikhail Bulgakov is, however, undoubtedly the key figure under this rubric. The publication in Soviet journals of all his plays and short stories, of his correspondence and of Chudakova's biography leaves no doubt that he is now the most genuinely popular writer of the Soviet period.[12] On the other hand, the name of Maksim Gor'kii, who in the years before *glasnost'* was officially promoted as the most 'popular' twentieth-century writer in the Soviet Union, and who is the author of the canonic Socialist Realist novel, *The Mother*, is the most notable absentee from this list. Little attempt has yet been made to dig below the surface of the partial and misleading official version of Gor'kii's life and work, though the literary-critical journal *Literaturnoe obozrenie* published extracts from his *Untimely Thoughts* in its issues for September, October and December 1988.

Writers from the first wave of emigration, including Aldanov, Averchenko, Sasha Chernyi, Zinaida Gippius, Georgii Ivanov, Viacheslav Ivanov, Khodasevich, Merezhkovskii, Nabokov, Osorgin, Otsup, Zhosefina Pasternak, Remizov, Severianin, Zaitsev and Zamiatin, have all been published in journals during the last three years. This is one of the most important ways in which the current liberalisation differs from the 'thaw' of 1956–64, during which the publication of Khodasevich, Nabokov, Zamiatin and others remained unthinkable. The printing of *We* (*Znamia*, 1988, 4–5), of selections of Khodasevich's poetry and prose, and of five Nabokov novels[13] has provoked wide comment in the Soviet press and the beginnings of a reassessment of literary history.

Despite the importance of these literary rediscoveries, and the interest they have aroused in both the Soviet Union and the West, it is not they, but the Soviet writers of the next generation who are the most significant when we attempt to interpret the true concerns of literary *glasnost'*.

Three of the first literary sensations of the new era, Rasputin's *The Fire* (*Nash sovremennik*, 1985, 7), Astaf'ev's *A Sad Detective Story* (*Oktiabr'*, 1986, 1) and Aitmatov's *The Executioner's Block* (*Novyi mir*, 1986, 6, 8 and 9) were all works by 'conservative' writers set in the present and lamenting the ways of modern Soviet society.[14] As such they seemed to set a trend of what has been called *novaia publitsistika* (new journalistic fiction), and to imply that critical writing about the Soviet present would be a major element in the fiction of *glasnost'*. By mid-1988 these works and others like them no longer occupy such a central position.[15] Soviet history has, at least for now, definitively replaced the Soviet present as the central concern of the literary journals and the subject of a large number of the most significant novels and stories they are publishing.

This process began in 1986 with the appearance of Aleksandr Bek's novel *The New assignment* (*Znamia*, 1986, 10–11),[16] Trifonov's story 'A Short stay in the Torture Chamber' (*Znamia*, 1986, 12), Okudzhava's autobiographical story 'The girl of my dreams' (*Druzhba narodov*, 1986, 10), and Shatrov's play *The Dictatorship of Conscience* (*Teatr*, 1986, 6). These were followed in 1987 by Rybakov's *Children of the Arbat* (*Druzhba narodov*, 1987, 4–6), Trifonov's *The Disappearance* (ibid, 1987, 1), Daniil Granin's *The Buffalo* (*Novyi mir*, 1987, 1–2), Pristavkin's *A Golden Cloud at Night* (*Znamia*, 1987, 3–4), Dudintsev's *Robed in White* (*Neva*, 1987, 1–4), Mozhaev's *Peasants and their Women* (*Don*, 1987, 1–3) and Antonov's *Vas'ka* (*Iunost'*, 1987, 3–4);[17] Shukshin's *The Liubavins*, Book 2 (*Druzhba narodov*, 1987, 1–4); Belov's *The Eves*, part 3 (*Novyi mir*, 1987, 8);[18] Shatrov's play *The Peace of Brest-Litovsk* (*Novyi mir*, 1987, 4); and Tvardovskii's long poem on the consequences of collectivisation, *By the Right of Memory* (*Znamia'* 1987, 2 and *Novyi mir*, 1987, 3).[19]

In 1988, the journals have already published Vasilii Grossman's *Life and Fate* (*Oktiabr'*, 1988, 1–4); Antonov's *The Ravines* (*Druzhba narodov*, 1988, 1–2); Azhaev's *The Wagon* (*Druzhba narodov*, 1988, 6–

8); Chukovskaia's 'Sof'ia Petrovna' (*Neva*, 1988, 2); Dombrovskii's *The Faculty of Unnecessary Things* (*Novyi mir*, 1988, 8–11); four stories by Tendriakov on collectivisation and the war (*Novyi mir*, 1988, 3);[20] major extracts from Iskander's *Sandro from Chegem* as yet unknown to Soviet readers (*Znamia*, 1988, 9–10);[21] Anatolii Zhigulin's story *Black Stones* (*Znamia*, 1988, 7–8);[22] Shatrov's play *Onward ... Onward ... Onward!* (*Znamia*, 1988, 1); and poems by Okudzhava that address themselves to the purges with new directness.[23] Chapters from *1935 and other years*, Rybakov's sequel to *Children of the Arbat*, in *Ogonek*, were followed by book one of the novel in *Druzhba narodov*,[24] and a chapter from Bek's novel on Stalin, '*The Following Day*' appeared in *Nedelia* (1988, 31).[25] Shalamov's *Kolyma Tales* have now appeared in a number of journals.[26] Together with works by writers of an older generation, with *Doctor Zhivago* (*Novyi mir*, 1988, 1–4), *Requiem* (*Oktiabr'*, 1987, 3 and *Neva* 1987, 6), Kliuev's collectivisation poem *Pogorel'shchina* (*Novyi mir*, 1987, 7), Pil'niak's *The Tale of the Unextinguished Moon* (*Znamia*, 1987, 12) and the hitherto unpublished prose of Platonov,[27] these writings cover the range of Soviet history from the revolution to the 1950s, recalling the collectivisation and the events of the 1930s with particular attention. Such a concentration of experience and reflection will radically alter the Soviet reader's awareness and understanding of his country's history. As Iurii Kariakin has put it: 'In short: the last two or three years (and probably the next few) are unprecedented in the entire history of our literature. Never yet in such a short space has there appeared – and all at once! – so much, and of such quality, from different times, but, in essence, all about the same thing. Never before has there been such a socio-artistic panorama, such a crossing of rays from different times, such a polyphony of voices, belonging to the living and the dead. A whole epoch of our recent history is portrayed in these works. A real "second reality" of this epoch is arising, that is to say, its realistic artistic image.'[28]

The readiness of the literary journals to tackle questions of Soviet history, the mass of material that writers and editors had been trying, in some cases for decades, to publish in them, and the contrasting drabness of historical journals gave rise to anguished reflection among leading historians.[29]

Other established Soviet writers have found (some of them posthumously) that they are now able to publish work written long ago. There have been several publications of poetry by Slutskii (d. 1986), Ol'ga Berggol'ts (d. 1975) and Arsenii Tarkovskii (b. 1907). Semen

Lipkin and Inna Lisnianskaia, who left the Union of Writers after the *Metropol'* affair, have been widely published since being reinstated in the autumn of 1986. Journals (and publishing houses) now compete with each other to publish poems and songs by Vladimir Vysotskii, and his *Novel about Girls* appeared in *Neva* (1988, 1). Andrei Bitov's *The Pushkin House* was in *Novyi mir* (1987, 10–12).

What role, it is often asked, are new writers playing in the burgeoning of the literary magazines? Various factors make it difficult to give a clear answer to this question. In the first place, young writers need time to make themselves a reputation. Secondly, some of the writers being newly published in the journals are not young at all, but have been artificially kept out of Soviet print until now for a variety of reasons (often being forced to publish their work in the West). Thirdly, even with the new openness, most literary editors (all of them men of the older literary generation) have their gaze trained firmly upon the past and are both aesthetically and thematically out of sympathy with many young writers. In addition, by contrast with the 1950s and 1960s, the number of new journalistic outlets is very small.[30]

It is nevertheless possible to identify various groups of new writers whose work is, to a greater or lesser degree, finding its way into the journals.

One important group is that of writers who had earlier been either imprisoned or expelled from the writers' union. Iulii Daniel', sentenced with Andrei Siniavskii in 1966 for sending his work abroad, has seen small selections of his poetry appear in *Ogonek* (1988, 29), *Novy mir* (1988, 7) and *Druzhba narodov* (1988, 9). Later *Iunost'* (1988, 11) published the story 'Atonement', one of those deemed anti-Soviet in 1966. Equally remarkable is the case of Leonid Borodin, who was not released from imprisonment until the summer of 1987. His story, 'Barguzin' appeared in *Literaturnaia Rossiia* (1988, 19). In this context one should also mention the return to print of Vladimir Kornilov[31] and Lidiia Chukovskaia.[32] The short story writer Evgenii Popov (b. 1946) had hardly begun to be published in Soviet journals when his participation in the *Metropol'* collection caused his expulsion from the Union of Writers. He was reinstated in late 1986, and his stories have now appeared in *Iunost'* (1986, 11), *Znamia* (1987, 5) *Novyi mir* (1987, 10), *Iunost'* (1988, 9) and *Volga* (1988, 10).[33] Evgenii Kharitonov, who published three stories abroad in the *Katalog* collection (1981) has had his first, posthumous, Soviet publication, the story 'Dzyn'' in *Iskusstvo kino* (1988, 6). An extract from Venedikt Erofeev's *Moscow – Petushki*, long admired in the West (where it is translated both as *Moscow Circles* and as *Moscow to the End of the Line*), was published in *Nedelia* (1988, 36). The whole novel is apparently to appear in 1989 (see below, note 167).

The most talked-about new prose writer of the last few years is Tat'iana Tolstaia (b. 1951). Her stories have appeared widely in journals and have been collected as *Na zolotom kryl'tse sideli* (Moscow 1987).[34] Despite the attention paid to her work, Tolstaia was refused entry to the Union of Writers early in 1988.[35] In a recent interview she said of the fate of young writers: 'They have nowhere to publish!' Speaking of the response from editors, she added wryly. 'They no longer say "It's awful! Take it away!" Now they say, "It'll be published later." But when later?'[36] An older and more established writer who has suddenly reached a new level of popularity is Vladimir Makanin (b. 1937).[37] Sergei Kaledin's story set among urban gravediggers, 'A humble cemetery' (*Novyi mir*, 1987, 5) has been widely praised.[38] Both the economist Nikolai Shmelev and the journalist Anatolii Strelianyi have also published several short stories.[39] In November 1987 *Iunost'* carried a story called 'One hundred days till demobilisation' by Iurii Poliakov, which offers a graphic description of institutionalised bullying in the Soviet army. It provoked a stream of readers' letters to *Iunost'* (1988, 5) and led to a wide debate on army bullying in the Soviet press.[40] Other new prose writers who have been greeted with enthusiasm include Viacheslav P'etsukh ('The Ticket' and 'The New Factory', *Novyi mir*, 1987, 6; 'The War between Central and Ermolaevo', *Ogonek*, 1988, 3); Mikhail Chulaki ('Farewell, green Pryazhka', *Neva*, 1987, 6–7; 'Mamin Sibiriak', *Nauka i religiia*, 1988, 8–11); Oleg Bazunov ('The Seafarer', *Novyi mir*, 1987, 6–7); and M. Kuraev ('Captain Dikshtein', a story of the Kronstadt uprising, *Novyi mir*, 1987, 9)[41]

Poets who have up till now managed to publish their poetry only in the West are beginning to appear in Soviet journals. Gennadii Aigi has had poems in *Druzhba narodov* (1988, 2) and *V mire knig* (1988, 3) and has been interviewed in *Literaturnaia Rossiia* (1988, 7). The enterprising *Rodnik* has already published Elena Shvarts (1988, 5) and Stratanovskii (1988, 6) and intends to publish Krivulin.[42] Five short poems by the conceptualist Dmitrii Prigov have appeared in *Iunost'* (1988, 1). These are, admittedly, small beginnings, but the literary critic Mikhail Epshtein has managed to write widely in the official press about the new poetry.[43] Several plays by Vladimir Arro and

Liudmila Petrushevskaia have appeared in the theatrical journals, which have also published Slavkin's *Serso* and Galin's *Stars in the Morning Sky*. Petrushevskaia has also published some virtuoso stories.[44] The first issue of *Ural* for 1988 was entirely devoted to the work of new writers. All in all there is enough evidence to refute charges that the literary journals have turned into literary museums.

It was always clear that editors would approach the question of publishing émigrés of the third wave with the utmost caution. Publishing first wave émigrés like Zamiatin and Khodasevich was relatively easy. Their provocative and embarrassing views could be safely placed in 'historical context', their love of Russia and nostalgic melancholy in Western exile emphasised. They were no longer around to cast a quizzical eye on *glasnost'* and *perestroika*. Living émigrés, on the other hand, could almost be relied upon to bite the Soviet hand that tried to feed them. Nevertheless it was also clear that the publication of living émigrés was seen, both in the Soviet Union and in the West, as a kind of touchstone. Publication of their work would be construed as a real sign of literary, political and psychological normalisation – it would mean that leaving your country to live abroad was no longer viewed as a criminal act, as 'betrayal of the motherland'. Besides, how could an attempt to provide a truer picture of the literary past succeed without including Solzhenitsyn and Voinovich, Aksenov and Vladimov, Maksimov and Nekrasov?

Signs of a more open-minded attitude to émigrés and their views appeared during 1987. In March 1987 ten eminent émigrés, Aksenov, Vladimir Bukovskii, Eduard Kuznetsov, Liubimov, Maksimov, Ernst Neizvestnyi, Iurii Orlov, Leonid Pliushch and Aleksandr and Ol'ga Zinov'ev published in western newspapers an article sceptical as to how much the Soviet Union had really changed. It ended 'As for people in the West, they should not so readily applaud Gorbachev for promising conditions that *they* would not tolerate for one moment.' To general surprise this letter was almost immediately republished in *Moskovskie novosti*, which went on in the next two weeks to publish its readers' responses.[45] The death of the writer Viktor Nekrasov in Parisian exile on 3 September 1987 was quickly followed by a sympathetic obituary in the same newspaper.[46] The films of Andrei Tarkovskii were shown in Moscow in the summer of 1987.[47]

Any hopes that living émigré writers were immediately going to be published in Soviet journals were quickly dashed, however. In March 1987 Vladimir Voinovich, ex-*Novyi mir* author, now living near

Munich, decided to test (or, maybe, to muddy) the waters of *glasnost'* by writing to Sergei Zalygin, offering his *By mutual correspondence*, which *Novyi mir* had first set in type twenty years previously. Zalygin's reply was not encouraging. 'Respected Vladimir Nikolaevich!', it began, 'It seems to me that you have formed the impression that *Novyi mir* is now publishing everything which was at some time in some place or for some reason turned down and not published. This is far from being the case.' Zalygin then made tactless remarks about exceptions being made only for 'a few works of the highest artistic quality', the correspondence degenerated into predictable mutual insult, and it was duly published in the émigré press.[48]

The situation was unchanged in late 1987, when suddenly, on 22 October, the émigré poet Iosif Brodskii was awarded the Nobel Prize for Literature.[49] It is greatly to the credit of the editorial board of *Novyi mir* that they had by then decided to publish a selection of poems from Brodskii's collections *A Part of Speech* and *Urania* in their issue for December 1987.[50]

In January 1988, *Inostrannaia literatura* reviewed Brodskii's collection of essays, *Less than One*.[51] It soon became clear, however, that not everyone in the Soviet Union was delighted at the way things were going.[52] On 19 March 1988, the newspaper *Komsomol'skaia pravda* carried an article by P. Gorelov which found it 'difficult to understand' why the Nobel Prize had been awarded to Brodskii, and which was accompanied by dispatches from Paris, New York and Bonn quoting the similar incomprehension of alleged Western 'specialists'.[53] This article was roundly condemned in *Moskovskie Novosti* and *Ogonek*.[54]

In March 1988, *Neva* published another collection of Brodskii's poems, with an afterword by the poet Aleksandr Kushner. Kushner describes Brodskii's arrest for 'parasitism' in 1964 and his forced emigration in 1972. Of this emigration he writes that it would not have been better if the authorities had relented 'It was a question of saving his life and saving his poetic gift.' Kushner ends by speaking of the return of Brodskii's poetry to his native land within his lifetime as a triumph for justice. In June 1988 *Knizhnoe obozrenie* published Brodskii's speech on his reception of the Nobel Prize, and appended a list of all previous Nobel laureates.[55] During the summer of 1988 other journals published selections of Brodskii's poetry.[56]

The next émigré writer to be published was Vasilii Aksenov, an extract from whose *In Search of Melancholy Baby* was published in the first issue of *Krokodil* for 1988. But both the place of publication and the mocking tone of the anonymous editorial introduction, showed that Aksenov was not another prodigal being welcomed back with open arms.[57]

The poet and songwriter, Aleksandr Galich, who emigrated in 1974 and died in 1977, had begun to be mentioned favourably in the Soviet press in 1987. A selection of his work was published in *Oktiabr'* in April 1988, with a sympathetic introduction by Stanislav Rassadin. As with the case of Brodskii, this first publication was followed by several others.[58] On 12 May 1988 Galich was posthumously reinstated in the Union of Cinema Workers, and in July he was readmitted to the Union of Writers. His play, *Matrosskaia Tishina*, which was to have had its premiere at the Sovremennik theatre in 1957, finally opened at the Moscow Arts Theatre Studio School in June 1988 (as *The Big Land*).

Throughout 1988, articles continued to appear calling for a new objectivity in the treatment of émigrés. In January, A. Bocharov called for the republication at least of works by émigré authors officially published before their emigration.[59] In April, A. Suetnov bemoaned the loss caused to literary scholarship by the removal from libraries of critical studies by Siniavskii, Etkind and Belinkov.[60] In June, the film director El'dar Riazanov spoke of his attempts to make a film of Voinovich's *The Life and Extraordinary Adventures of Private Ivan Chonkin*, and suggested that it was time 'to return Soviet citizenship to those who were deprived of it by arbitrariness, lawlessness, because of the petty tyranny of bureaucrats, and great power conceit and arrogance'. He quotes a letter which Voinovich wrote him giving details of his fate at the hands of the Soviet authorities.[61] In August, Evgenii Popov named Sokolov, Tsvetkov, Limonov and Kublanovskii as losses for Soviet readers.[62] In the summer of 1988, Nekrasov, Korzhavin and Sokolov were all published by Soviet journals.[63]

Throughout the last two years the émigré writer whose chances of being republished in the Soviet Union have caused the most heated speculation is the symbolic figure of Aleksandr Solzhenitsyn. In March 1987 western newspapers ran stories announcing that Soviet journals were about to publish *The Cancer Ward* and *The Gulag Archipelago*. These stories, apparently emerging from an interview given by Sergei Zalygin to a Danish journalist were quickly denied.[64] In the autumn of that year the western and émigré press carried the transcript of exchanges between Anatolii Strelianyi, a member of the *Novyi mir* editorial board, and the *Komsomol aktiv* of Moscow

University on 15 May 1987. Asked whether they intended to publish Solzhenitsyn, he replied, 'If we don't publish Solzhenitsyn in *Novyi mir*, then other journals will.' He insisted that *Novy mir*'s slogan must be 'Print what nobody else is printing'.[65] By November the name of Strelianyi had disappeared from the journal's editorial board.[66]

On 27 June 1988, the first secretary of the Union of Writers of the USSR, Vladimir Karpov, said at a press conference, 'It is possible that his novels will be published, I have heard that *Novyi mir* intends to publish *The Cancer Ward*'.[67] Next day *The Scotsman* quoted an alleged spokeswoman for the journal as saying that 'Everything should be clear in about ten days. . . . We are in the middle of bilateral discussions.' On 15 July 1988 a startling report was carried by the German radio station Bayerische Rundfunk and taken up by Associated Press. It affirmed that Solzhenitsyn had received two handwritten letters from Mikhail Gorbachev; that all his writings, including *The Gulag Archipelago*, were to be published in the Soviet Union; that homesickness made him unable to write; and that he and his wife would visit the Soviet Union for four or five weeks at the end of 1988. This report was widely carried in the Western press,[68] but was categorically denied in a press statement by Natal'ia Solzhenitsyna of 20 July 1988. There had been no letters from Mr Gorbachev, she insisted, and no proposals to publish any of Solzhenitsyn's books in the USSR.[69] Nevertheless, Soviet journals continued to call for the republication of Solzhenitsyn's works.[70] This process reached new heights in August 1988, when the newspaper *Knizhnoe obozrenie* carried materials on Solzhenitsyn in three consecutive issues. The first, under the provocative title 'Give Solzhenitsyn back his Soviet citizenship', gives a detailed and sympathetic account of the 'persecution and slander' he endured from the Soviet authorities, and informs its readers that in his letter to the secretariat of the Union of Writers of the USSR of 12 November 1969, Solzhenitsyn had asked for 'Glasnost', full and honest glasnost''.[71]

### III

Some remarks should be made about the way all these works have been published. Very often, *Novyi mir* and other journals had made valiant but abortive attempts to publish them in the 1950s, 1960s and 1970s. In many cases they were in fact first published abroad. This information has not always been revealed to Soviet readers. Sometimes, when they did finally make their way into Soviet print, works appeared with cuts, either acknowledged or unacknowledged. Some publications, such as Brodskii's poems in *Novyi mir* or Chukovskaia's *Sof'ia Petrovna* in *Neva*, seemed almost shockingly surreptitious. The émigré press showed no hesitation in drawing the attention of its readers to these shortcomings.[72] Nevertheless, the liberal Soviet literary press seems to be displaying far greater confidence and daring now than it did in the first years of *glasnost'*. Mandel'shtam's 'Fourth Prose', a text so unmentionable that it was not even included in the bibliography of Mandel'shtam's prose collection *Slovo i kultura* (Moscow, 1987), has now had almost simultaneous publication in *Raduga* (Tallinn), 1988, 3 and *Rodnik* (Riga), 1988, 6. The *Raduga* publication includes the full text of Mandel'shtam's Stalin poem, of which, in September 1987, *Iunost'* felt able to publish only the beginning, and that in a footnote.[73] Tat'iana Bek has written to *Znamia* complaining about Mikhail Alekseev's recent false explanation of *Moskva*'s refusal to publish Aleksandr Bek's *A New Assignment* in 1969.[74] The old Bolshevik G. A. Terekhov was sufficiently incensed by the articles by Evgenii Evtushenko and Vladimir Karpov accompanying 1986 selections of Gumilev's poetry to write to *Novyi mir*. He revealed that he had read all the papers of the Gumilev affair, for professional reasons, and stated categorically that Gumilev had not been a member of a monarchist conspiracy. He had been tried for failure to denounce others who were.[75] These cases, and the cases of such writers as Iskander, Zhigulin, Chukovskaia, Brodskii and Solzhenitsyn, show a notable increase in frankness with the passage of time.

One unexpected consequence of *glasnost'* has been the revitalising of the émigré press. The Paris-based newspaper *Russkaia mysl'* and such journals as *Kontinent*, *Sintaksis*, *Vremia i my*, *Strelets*, *Strana i mir* and *Forum* are publishing responses to individual publications in Soviet journals, and general assessments of the evolving literary and political situations.[76] Interviews with Soviet writers visiting the West are also frequently carried.[77] The greater mutual awareness of the Soviet and émigré press is paralleled by a remarkable increase in the warmth with which the two sides speak to and of each other at international gatherings. A conference organised outside Copenhagen in March 1988 brought together émigrés such as Aksenov, Etkind and Siniavskii and a Soviet delegation including Iurii Afanas'ev, the critic Galina Belaia, the editor of *Znamia*, Grigorii Baklanov, Vladimir

Dudintsev, the film director, Aleksei German, Fazil' Iskander and Mikhail Shatrov to discuss their perceptions of each other. Assessments of the conference appeared in both the Western and the Soviet press.[78] A similar conference took place in Amsterdam in May–June 1988, and Soviet and émigré writers also met in Lisbon in May and in Barcelona in October. Soviet publications are also opening their pages to Western scholars.[79]

Like their émigré counterparts, *samizdat* publications within the Soviet Union have flourished unexpectedly in the period of *glasnost'*. Meetings of their editors took place in Leningrad in October 1987 and in Moscow in May 1988.[80] Some, such as *Glasnost'* and *Referendum*, though they are not literary journals, regularly publish materials on cultural questions. Others, such as the Leningrad journals *Chasy*, *37*, *Obvodnii kanal*, *Mitin zhurnal* and *Predlog* are explicitly devoted to literature. Their taste is considerably more adventurous than that of the official press. *Mitin zhurnal*, for example, named after its editor, Dmitrii Volchek, has appeared about six times a year, in issues of 300 pages, since 1986. Its range includes the new Soviet *avant-garde*, archival materials and translations. It was one of the first Russian journals to publish Beckett, Borges, Bruno Schultz, Hesse, Lem, Vian and Marguerite Duras. *Predlog*, the journal of the translators' section of *Club-81*, had published 13 130-page issues and 14 supplementary volumes of longer works by the spring of 1987. Its authors included Pound, Pinter, Lacan, Maurice Blanchot, Hans Küng, Orwell, Robbe-Grillet, Tolkien, Woody Allen, Barthes – the lists are dazzling.[81]

IV

It is the custom of the literary journals to review the prose and poetry that have been published by their rivals. Gradually, through these publications, readers' perceptions of Soviet literary history have been altered. As new authors and new works are given central positions in the canon, so the reputations of 'Soviet classics' are re-assessed, a point made forcefully by A. Bocharov. The 263 works awarded the Stalin prize between 1941 and 1952 have all, he insists, 'harmlessly fallen out (of the canon) like milk-teeth in growing children'. The journal *Sovetskaia bibliografiia* has recently made its own contribution to the re-education of readers by providing bibliographies of a trio of erstwhile outcasts, Vysotskii, Shalamov and Bukharin.[82]

A concentrated effort is being made to fill in the 'blank spots' of Soviet literary history.[83] In 1988 *Ogonek* carried a succession of pieces casting light into dark literary corners. Its fourth issue for 1988 carried a letter from a man wounded in the Second World War, drawing attention to the continuing scandal of Leonid Brezhnev's 'memoir' *Malaia zemlia* remaining in libraries and war museums: 'The aim of this publication was to glorify Brezhnev and to support the cult of his personality. ... Everyone knows that Brezhnev was not its author and consequently was never a distinguished writer. I cannot understand how he could have been awarded a Lenin prize for this work. How could he become a member of the Union of Writers when in daily life he couldn't greet his fellow workers without a crib in his hands?'[84] Later in the year, the literary efforts of Brezhnev's protégé, the Uzbek party chief, Rashidov, came under the journal's mocking gaze. He, too, is revealed not to have been the true author of his 'writings' (the word 'writings' is always in inverted commas with reference to both Brezhnev and Rashidov), and his corrupt links with the Muscovite literary establishment are exposed. The text is accompanied by a picture of Brezhnev and Rashidov executing what Aleksandr Zinov'ev in *The Yawning Heights* calls 'the greatest contribution of Ibansk to world culture', the 'ceremony of the triple kiss'.[85] In a piece entitled 'Ivanovo Samizdat', Dmitrii Gubin remembers events in the town of Ivanovo in the winter of 1978–9. When the December 1978 issue of the journal *Avrora* was found to contain a poem by Evtushenko which the local party secretary deemed insulting to the town's self-esteem, the issue was promptly banned. Copies of the poem, and of an anonymous 'Answer to Evgenii Evtushenko', then began to circulate, to the excitement of local young people. It was only later that arrests began. ...[86] *Ogonek* also printed a reader's letter giving details of the *Metropol'* affair of 1979 and pointing out that several of its contributors are now the bestsellers of *glasnost'*.[87]

A succession of articles expose the appalling treatment meted out to individual writers and directors. Konstantin Rudnitskii describes in detail how the net closed around Meierkhol'd in the 1930s, and how later Eisenstein came into possession of the Meierkhol'd archives which his family had saved with extraordinary courage.[88] Details of Meierkhol'd's torture after his arrest are related by Arkadii Vaksberg in his article on the show trials of writers.[89]

An extensive publication on the sufferings of Mikhail Zoshchenko tells the story of Zhdanov's 1946 attack on him and Akhmatova, includes Zoshchenko's letters to Stalin, Fadeev and Malenkov, and reports on the meeting of Leningrad writers held to censure him in June 1954 after he had told a group of visiting English students that he did not agree with Zhdanov's characterisation of his writings.[90] Daniil Granin provides an eye-witness report of this meeting.[91] Readers have also been given Nikolai Zabolotskii's account of his imprisonment, and learnt of the persecution of Pasternak, Siniavskii and Daniel', and Brodskii.[92] Veniamin Smekhov has catalogued the troubled history of Iurii Liubimov and the Taganka theatre.[93]

An article in *Znamia* by the literary critic and philosopher Iurii Kariakin has caused an understandable sensation Beginning as a response to a letter denouncing Boris Mozhaev for his novel, *Peasants and their women*, Kariakin's fiery polemic widens its scope to address all the earlier campaigns of denunciation against writers. It discusses Zhdanov's treatment of Akhmatova and Zoshchenko, and the campaigns against Tsvetaeva, Pasternak, Dudintsev, Tvardovskii, Vysotskii and others. Kariakin reminds us that now is not 1937, 1946 or 1956, that times have changed. He begins and ends with a crucial question addressed to all the writers of anonymous letters: 'What is your attitude to *glasnost*'?'[94]

Most light of all on Soviet literary mores, past and present, has been shed by a fascinating series of articles concerning Tvardovskii's attempts to publish his poem, 'By the right of memory' in *Novyi mir* in 1969. These materials are of symbolic importance because of the role of *Novyi mir* in the liberalisation of the 1950s and early 1960s. Nevertheless, as the discussion has gone on, and more and more players have been drawn into it, most of them participants both in the events of the 1960s and in present literary struggles, the relevance of this debate has widened and widened. The battles of the present are being waged through a reassessment of those of the past.

It was the publication in late 1986 of Trifonov's memoirs of his relationship with Tvardovskii in the 1960s which revealed to Soviet readers the first details of the campaign against *Novyi mir* that reached its peak in the summer of 1969 and culminated in Tvardovskii's resignation in February 1970.[95] In the first half of 1987 both *Znamia* and *Novyi mir* published *By the Right of Memory*.[96] In August 1987 *Oktiabr'* published an article by Iurii Burtin, who had been provoked by lacunae in Trifonov's story into providing a fuller version of events of the 1960s at *Novyi mir*, something Burtin, who was head of the literary-critical section of the journal at the time, was well qualified to do.[97] He stressed the symbolic significance of Tvardovskii's poem, a work addressed to the question of memory at a time of 'organised forgetting'. He made the first recent mention of what was later to become notorious as the 'letter of the eleven', an article in *Ogonek* of July 1969 entitled 'What is *Novyi mir* against?' More importantly, and for this reason Burtin's article, like Kariakin's, has became a key document of the *glastnost'* epoch, he widens his scope to consider the moral image of the Brezhnev period, the return to half-truth and silence, to lying about Stalin, and the solitary resistance of *Novyi mir*, which he describes as an 'opposition journal'. In the most famous passage in his article he writes: 'The turning of a part – and, let us stress, the best part – of the democratic movement of the time into an opposition movement and of the energy of positive social transformation into the energy of protest, is a sad and dramatic page in our history. For a significant number of people this led to a loss of faith in socialism; the fates of the majority of those whom their inability to express their disagreement with the new official line directly and openly pushed into illegal forms of political self-expression, were shattered. Some were forced into leaving their native land, others had to endure punishment "with all the law's severity" ... The aim was achieved fully.... The desired reign of silence arrived.... And after a decade and a half of living like this we see the truly terrible result we have arrived at. ... A society that seems to be bereft of an intelligentsia, if we understand by that term not simply people working in particular professions, but what it has always been in Russia since the time of Fonvizin and Radishchev – the brain and conscience of the nation.'[98]

In December 1987, *Oktiabr'* published a selection of readers' letters about Burtin's article, and Burtin's reply.[99] This time Burtin produced a calendar of events leading up to February 1970, including the enforced removal of Tvardovskii's closest collaborators and Tvardovskii's unanswered letter to Brezhnev, and for the first time since that period he named the names of those who had signed the infamous *Ogonek* letter.[100] Now it became abundantly clear to readers that the fight for the past is a fight for the present, for eight of the eleven are still prominent in Soviet literature today, including Mikhail Alekseev, Sergei Vikulov and Anatolii Ivanov, editors of the reactionary journals *Moskva*, *Nash sovremennik* and *Molodaia gvardiia*, and the powerful leading member of the Union of Writers of the RSFSR, Petr Proskurin.

Further fuel was added to the flames very early in 1988 by another veteran *Novyi mir* contributor, Nataliia Il'ina, writing in *Ogonek*.[101] Il'ina also named the eleven tormentors of Tvardovskii, and insisted that *Molodaia gvardiia*'s behaviour had not changed over the last twenty years. She broadened the debate further by provocatively attacking members of the old guard by name, and by revealing the network of privilege and corruption that has blighted Soviet publishing. She reminded her readers that the Soviet Union of Writers has 10 000 members, with an average age of 60, and that 820 of them have been honoured with the publication of their collected works during the period of the twelfth five-year plan. Il'ina's article provoked *Pravda* into a sharp attack on *Ogonek*.[102] Throughout 1988 the polemics have continued, ranging *Oktiabr'*, *Znamia*, *V mire knig*, *Ogonek*, *Iunost'*, *Daugava*, *Sovetskaia kul'tura* and *Moskovskie novosti* against *Molodaia gvardiia*, *Nash sovremennik*, *Moskva* and *Literaturnaia Rossiia*.[103] In April 1988 Tvardovskii's widow wrote to *Ogonek*, protesting at the appointment of Proskurin to the commission set up to choose a memorial to her husband's poetic hero, Vasilii Terkin.[104] In June, Burtin returned to the fray, this time in *Daugava*, telling of Alekseev's lies about Tvardovskii in 1979 and his own frustrated attempts to expose them. This sense of the 'impotence of the truth' and of the absence of the 'possibility to make objections' led Burtin to a demand for radical changes in the way the Soviet press is run.[105] In August, Vladimir Lakshin, another close associate of Tvardovskii, provided his own detailed chronicle of the attacks on *Novyi mir* throughout the 1960s.[106]

The examples of Kariakin, Burtin and Il'ina, all of whose studies proceed from the detail of literary life to questions of the current moral state of society, provide eloquent evidence of the uses that 'literary criticism' is being put to in the contemporary Soviet press. Yet literary scholars have been working in extremely difficult conditions, as a number of recent articles have made apparent. At the end of 1987, the leading Bulgakov scholar, Marietta Chudakova, complained vociferously in *Literaturnaia gazeta* of obstruction to her work by those in charge of the Bulgakov archive in the Lenin Library in Moscow.[107] Later, Chudakova widened her attack to deplore the level of competence of many literary scholars, and the 'lies and obfuscations' of the prefaces and afterwords to some recent publications.[108] Lev Gudkov and Boris Dubin have written of the appalling stagnation in Soviet public libraries. Up to 70 per cent of books are not on open access, and librarians hand them out to those they favour. On the other hand, between 30 and 50 per cent of the books on the open shelves have never been taken out, or only once in several years.[109] The recent disastrous fire in the library of the Academy of Sciences of the USSR in Leningrad, and the parlous state of several other academic libraries have also been amply described.[110] Some steps are being taken. In particular, the books previously held for reasons of censorship in the so-called *spetsfondy*, the closed collections of libraries, are now being reviewed by a commission similar to the famous 'conflict commission' for looking at shelved films. The majority of these books were either published abroad or had become politically sensitive through the vicissitudes of Soviet history. Most of them are now being returned to the main collections.[111] The State Public History Library of the RSFSR in Moscow has recently held an exhibition of 'Rehabilitated books' including John Reed's *Ten Days that Shook the World* and a 1928 edition of the Soviet Constitution.[112]

V

It should be stressed that the literary journals are not exclusively concerned with literature. Their engagement with historical issues, for example, is not only through the writings of novelists and poets. They are also directly examining the Russian and Soviet pasts (of which the very title of a newly established journal, *Nashe nasledie*, Our heritage, is another eloquent indication. Most of the major journals have carried articles on the millennium of Russian Christianity.[113] *Moskva* has been serialising Karamzin's *History of the Russian State*.[114]

Unsurprisingly, the journals are compulsively interested in Soviet history.[115] There have been pieces on the fate of Stalin's son, Iakov Dzhugashvili, and on the destruction of Soviet genetics, and memoirs of the 'anti-cosmopolitan campaign' and the 'Doctors' plot'.[116] Here too the standard-bearers have been *Novyi mir*, *Znamia* and *Oktiabr'*, which have run a series of major articles by economists and historians tracing the historical roots of the present crisis. In 1987, in a study called 'Advances and debts', the leading economist Nikolai Shmelev offered *Novyi mir* readers a shattering analysis of the Soviet economy. In a second article in 1988, 'New alarms', he analyses the successes and failures of restructuring in what he concludes is a 'truly revolutionary situation. The "bosses" ["verkhi"] can no longer run things, and those they are running ["*nizy*"] no longer wish to live in the old way'.[117] Another economist, Vasilii Seliunin, in an article revealingly entitled 'Sources', traces the political and economic mistakes of Russian and Soviet history. This study is remarkable for including Lenin as well as Stalin among those whose policies are soberly assessed and soberly found wanting.[118] In an earlier piece Seliunin and Grigorii Khanin had exposed the flaws of the USSR Central Statistical Administration.[119] Andrei Nuikin conducts a survey of the current press to assess the state of *perestroika* and the degree and sources of resistance to it.[120] In his 'Which Road Leads to the Church [*khram*]?' (an echo of the ending of Abuladze's film *Repentance*), Igor' Kliamkin again combines a wide-ranging assessment of the past, of the Westerners and Slavophiles, the *Vekhi*, the three revolutions, the twenties, collectivisation and Stalin, with an elaboration of the needs of the present.[121] In *Oktiabr'*, G. I. Shmelev offers another trenchant analysis of collectivisation; in *Znamia* four economists examine the conditions for Soviet growth.[122] Because of the length at which their contributors have been able to write, the journals have offered perhaps the major intellectual arena for reflection during the past three years. Belatedly there is evidence that the main history journal, *Voprosy istorii*, has undergone its own restructuring and is at last ready to enter the debate. In July 1987, its veteran chief editor, Vladimir Trukhanovskii became an ordinary member of the editorial board. Several months later, in February 1988, a new chief editor, Akhmed Iskenderov, was named and a new editorial board set up, including only four members of the old one. The February issue contained a statement of the journal's new goals and a letter from a reader in Sumgait, complaining that 'So far the breath of *perestroika*, *glasnost'* and democratisation has not been felt on the pages of *Voprosy istorii'*.[123] The March issue carried at length the speeches at a round table on historical studies in the conditions of *perestroika*, which revealed what a crucial role the 'new' history could play and the dangers of leaving 'history' to novelists. For example, Viktor Danilov, head of the sector of the history of the Soviet peasantry and agriculture at the Academy of Sciences Institute of History, had this to say about Mozhaev's *Peasants and their women*: 'A very characteristic – and dangerous – fantasy is the one offered by Mozhaev in his novel *Peasants and their women*, where responsibility for the violence to which the peasants were subjected during collectivization in the winter of 1929–1930 is transferred from the real culprits (Stalin and his close associates, in particular Molotov and Kaganovich), to Trotskii, Zinov'ev, Kamenev, Iakovlev and Kaminskii, the first three of whom had had no connection with the taking of political decisions as early as 1927, and Trotskii was even deported from the USSR in February 1929. None of these fantasies was engendered by *perestroika*. Perestroika and *glasnost'* only brought them into the open.' Danilov goes on to warn against idealisation of the past and the oversimplified apportionment of blame as a refuge from the problems of the present.[124] Most of the issue for June 1988 was devoted to the speeches at a conference held on 27–28 April at which historians, writers and literary scholars had assessed the relative value of historical and fictional elaborations of the Soviet past, in some cases with a frankness unprecedented in the pages of *Voprosy istorii*, and also added their hard-hitting comments on the present. The economist E. A. Ambartsumov derides the argument that 'if the historians had written differently (i.e. the truth?), they would not have been published.' He continues, 'Now that the truthful words by writers are being retrieved from dusty archives or desk drawers and published, let me ask our leading historians: What is there in their desk drawers?' Iurii Burtin quotes a letter in *Pravda* from the secretariat of the Union of Writers which opines that 'During these [three] years, the conception, strategy and tactics of *perestroika* have been collectively elaborated' and adds with characteristic trenchancy, 'We've heard these words several times ... but they just aren't true.'[125]

Individual political reputations are being considered. Konstantin Simonov's reflections on Stalin, dictated just before the writer's death, have been serialised in *Znamia*,[126] which has also carried Aleksei Adzhubei's memoir of the Khrushchev era.[127] Khrushchev is, for obvious reasons, a figure of great interest in a period which is constantly being compared to the thaw. There is an illuminating memoir by the film director Mikhail Romm of Khrushchev's behaviour at the meetings he arranged with leading artists.[128] Iurii Kariakin provides a devastating study of Zhdanov the politician: 'Zhdanov the "pure ideologist" is a myth. He is the most direct organiser of the bloody bacchanalia, no less than Iagoda, Ezhov and Beriia.' This article ranges from Zhdanov to Nina Andreeva's letter and becomes a rhetorically powerful demonstration of the links between the past and the present and a plea for the truth.[129]

Central to the journals' recuperation of true past experience are their publications of memoirs and autobiographies. The writings of Nadezhda Mandel'shtam and Evgeniia Ginzburg were published in Western countries in the 1960s and 1970s and have become classic witnesses of the Stalinist period. In 1988 both these books at last began to appear in the USSR.[130] In 1989 they are to be followed by

Lidiia Chukovskaia's *Notes about Anna Akhmatova*.[131] The second issue of *Ural* for 1988 included Sofiia Shved's memoir of her imprisonment in Tomsk from 1937 to 1943 after the arrest of her husband, and her prison meetings with the wives and sisters of Bukharin, Rykov, Tukhachevskii, Sverdlov and others.[132] Father Pavel Florenskii's autobiography is one of several publications concerning early twentieth-century philosophers including the erstwhile outcasts, Berdiaev and Rozanov.[133] At the other end of the historical scale, veterans recall the Afghan war.[134]

## VI

Other art-forms also provide lively materials. The musical interests of the journals range from Chaliapin through the guitar poets to rock music.[135] The two main Soviet film magazines, *Iskusstvo kino* and *Sovetskii ekran*, were forcibly 'restructured' after the fifth congress of film-makers. They now have new editorial boards and have become considerably more informative.[136] In addition, the literary journals have been the source of several important publications on the cinema. In particular, *Novyi mir* included a long interview with Aleksei German which provides one of the most exhaustive and depressing accounts of how, day by day, bureaucrat by bureaucrat, an artistic career can be blighted.[137] The young film-maker Aleksandr Sokurov laments that VGIK, the main Soviet film school, taught him nothing.[138] There are studies of how Romm was forced to add 630 metres of Stalin into his films *Lenin in October* and *Lenin in 1918*, and how Eisenstein and Kuleshov had to remove Trotskii from *October* and *The Extraordinary Adventures of Mr West in the Land of the Bolsheviks*.[139]

The state of affairs in the contemporary Soviet art world is close in some respects to that in literature. Here too the official Union is predominantly conservative[140] and most liberal activity is taking place elsewhere, in this case through exhibitions and publications. The main art journals, *Iskusstvo* and *Dekorativnoe iskusstvo*, are writing about hitherto ignored artists and including frank reports on, for example, the scandal of the extended and costly restoration of the Tret'iakov Gallery in Moscow, which will keep the gallery closed until at least 1991.[141] But as with the other arts, the general weeklies and the literary journals are also playing their part.

One heartening development is the uncovering of and new pride in the achievements of the early twentieth-century *avant-garde*. There have been exhibitions of Chagal, whose emigration had led to a complete ban on his work until very recently,[142] and of Filonov. The major Filonov exhibition which the Russian Museum in Lenigrad had prepared in 1929 was not allowed to open, and his paintings had not been publicly displayed since 1932. On 30 June 1988 that same Russian Museum began an exhibition of its Filonov holdings.[143] In November 1988 it will have a Malevich exhibition made up of its own pictures and those of the Stedelijk museum in Amsterdam.[144] This will be followed by a survey of the art of the 1920s and 1930s and, in 1989, the first Soviet exhibition of Kandinskii. Moscow has already seen 'Art and Revolution (painting, sculpture and graphic art of the 1920s)' at the New Tret'iakov Gallery[145] and 'Theatrical art of the '20s' at the Bakhrushin museum. One of the most enterprising of these ventures was 'Russian stage design, 1880–1930', which opened at the Pushkin museum in Moscow on 26 February 1988 and then moved to the Leningrad Manège. This was an exhibition of the work of émigré artists, from a private collection built up by members of émigré families, Mr and Mrs Nikita Lobanov-Rostovskii, and organised through the new Soviet Cultural Foundation.[146] In the press, *Ogonek* has been running a well-illustrated series called 'A collection of twentieth-century Russian art', which has included Soviets and émigrés alike (Malevich and Ekster, Larionov and Goncharova, Udal'tsova and Drevin, Somov and Dobuzhinskii among them).

The thick journals have published Chagal's poetry and extracts from his autobiography, memoirs of Filonov and Larionov, and articles on Rodchenko, Malevich and others.[147] All this is contributing to the familiarisation of a new public with a lost *avant-garde*. Soviet scholars have of course long been publishing weighty studies of these painters in the countries of Western and Eastern Europe, and there has been a demand that these books should appear in the USSR too.[148]

The Dali exhibition held at the Pushkin museum in Moscow in April and May 1988, the first time Dali has been shown officially in the Soviet Union, and the Bacon exhibition at the new Tret'iakov gallery in September-November 1988 provide evidence of the new accessibility of modern Western paintings. More recent Western painting, including the work of Julian Schnabel, is discussed in an informative and well-illustrated article in *Rodnik*.[149]

In the area of 'non-official' modern Soviet art, the signs are contradictory, but the period of outright condemnation and abuse seems to have passed. The 'Retrospective exhibition 1960–87', held at the Ermitazh gallery in the Beliaevo area of Moscow from September 1987, for the first time showed works by non-conformist Moscow painters and by émigrés.[150] In the same year there was a posthumous exhibition of the sculptor, Vadim Sidur. The unprecedented Sotheby's auction, held in Moscow on 7 July 1988, contained the works of the new as well as the old *avant-garde*.[151] New cooperative commercial galleries now apparently operate in Moscow. The non-comformist artist Il'ia Kabakov was allowed to write at some length in *Literaturnaia gazeta* about thirty years of attacks on unofficial art and the deleterious effect on public taste of never being able to look at modern paintings. (It is some measure of the state of affairs that this eloquent but extremely moderate and unemotional survey should have caused such a sensation.)[152] On the other hand, recent exhibitions by Kandaurov[153] and Sysoev were closed down. The dizzying turns in the fate of Viacheslav Sysoev are instructive. In 1980 he was expelled from the Moscow branch of the artists' union. He spent the early 1980s in hiding from the authorities, for whom his cartoons of the life of *homo sovieticus* were far too subversive. He was finally sent to a labour camp in 1983. On his release, on 9 February 1985, he was allowed to return to Moscow and reinstated in the Union. In early 1987 he was expelled a second time. On 15 February 1988 he was allowed to have his first official Moscow exhibition. Two days later it was closed down. On 21 February one of his cartoons appeared in *Moscow News*.[154] An attempt in late 1987 by *Ogonek* to publish a round-table discussion on the tribulations of the Muscovite *avant-garde* was thwarted. Vladimir Iankilevskii's memoir of Khrushchev's visit to the Manège on 1st December 1962 appeared instead in Paris ('With regard to art', Khrushchev had told Iankilevskii, 'I'm a Stalinist'). Yet in mid-1988 *Ogonek* carried the very similar memoirs of Mikhail Romm. Similarly, in 1987 *Ogonek* was unable to publish an article it had announced about the situation at the Bol'shoi ballet. But in 1988 *Teatral'naia zhizn'* could publish an article on the émigré dancer Mikhail Baryshnikov.[155]

The 1988 fall in the circulation figures for *Inostrannaia literatura*, the main journal of translated literature, has led some observers to infer that in a time of avid enthusiasm for their own hitherto inaccessible authors Russian readers have lost their curiosity about foreign ones.[156] The regularity with which most journals publish a wide range of translated literature does not bear out such an assessment. The cause of *Inostrannaia literatura's* decline is more likely to have been the stodgy fare its veteran chief editor, Nikolai Fedorenko, was serving up. With his resignation in late 1987, the journal became considerably livelier. The first few months of 1988 saw it running Kafka's *The Castle*, in a translation first commissioned two decades ago, against a different translation of the same book in *Neva*.[157] It followed with Huxley's *Brave New World*, one of a number of anti-utopian works that have appeared in the USSR at the same time as Zamiatin's *We*. *Rodnik* has had Orwell's *Animal Farm*, and *Novyi mir* began serialisation of *1984* in February 1989. *Neva* has given readers Arthur Koestler's *Darkness at Noon*.[158] At the time of writing *Inostrannaia literatura* has followed *The Growing Pains of Adrian Mole* with *The Name of the Rose*.[159] It has also announced its menu for 1989, of which the chief plum is a full translation of *Ulysses*, to last the entire year. There will also be Sartre's *Nausea*, Graham Greene's *Monsignor Quixote*, Mishima, Fowles, *The Long Goodbye*, Ray Connolly's *John Lennon: 1940–1980*, chapters from Ingmar Bergman's autobiography, and Nabokov's *Pnin*. There will defintely be *Yes, Prime Minister*.[160]

Other journals are also providing a steady succession of translated works and studies of foreign writers. At the heavyweight end of the scale there have recently been T. S. Eliot and Virginia Woolf, Lorca, Apollinaire, Artaud and Vian, Borges and cummings. There have been *One Flew over the Cuckoo's Nest* and *Rabbit is Rich*.[161] There have been a clutch of thriller and detective writers ranging from Chandler and Hammett to Le Carré and Mario Puzo. Agatha Christie has long been popular, especially in provincial journals. In 1988 *Don* announced Christie's *Sparkling Cyanide* only to have to revert to her *Dead Man's Folly* when *Volga* poached it from under their nose.[162] A number of major English writers are regularly translated.[163]

## VII

Soviet book publishing has not been transformed to anything like the extent of the literary journals. A succession of articles in *Knizhnoe obozrenie*, the weekly newspaper of the State Committee for Publishing, Printing and the Book Trade, and two major investigations in the journals, provide eloquent evidence of a continuing crisis now officially described under the terms 'book hunger' and 'book deficit'. I. S. Gol'denberg, starting from the paradox that 'there's a sea of books but nothing to buy', solves his own riddle by supplying figures on the enormous print-runs given to unwanted books by writers in whom the public has no interest. (*Poets of Africa* in an edition of 300000 was not apparently a great seller.) He points out that membership of the Soviet Union of Writers doubles every twenty-five years, and that of the 10000 members in 1986, 3000 were poets. Of these maybe thirty have a real following. He concludes that the restructuring of book publishing is entirely feasible: 'we should publish what people read and not what ends up being re-cycled'.[164] Tat'iana Zhuchkova provides damning evidence of the disparity between the vast editions of powerful writers (39 695 000 copies of the works of Sergei Mikhalkov, the chairman of the writers' union of the RSFSR, were printed between 1980 and 1987) and the negligible orders for their works placed by librarians with the central book-buying organisation.[165] In the conditions of Soviet publishing, losses sustained by overprovision are simply written off. Lev Gudkov and Boris Dubin offer a masterly analysis of libraries, book shops, book production and the various sections of the reading public. They show the historical roots of the situation and the extent to which the Soviet Union lags behind Western countries. The range of books on offer to the Soviet reader is apparently not greater than it was in 1913. The professional and intellectual level of editors is extremely low. Changes in print-runs have so far done little to solve the problem of the accessibility of desired books to any but an elite. Without access to more ambitious fare, literary taste cannot develop. The effects on society of the behaviour of publishers are profound and pervasive.[166]

Some faltering steps are being taken. Early in 1987 the planned new cooperative publishing houses provoked high expectations. The first of these, called *Zharki,* was set up in Novosibirsk on 29 July of that year. It lasted forty days. Another, *Vest',* announced by the writers Okudzhava, Iskander and others, has so far come to nothing. Other endeavours in Riga and Georgia soon ran into difficulties. At present this initiative seems to have stalled.[167] So-called 'authorial publishing', by which an author pays to have his book published, has been marginally more successful. The first such book, a chemistry textbook, Iurii Cherkinskii's *Polymerology. A posing of the problem,* appeared in July 1988 in an edition of four hundred at a cost to the author of six hundred roubles. But publishing houses are reluctant to cooperate in such ventures.[168] The first work by a Western Sovietologist, Robert M. Slusser's *Stalin in October: the man who missed the revolution,* is soon to appear.[169] New publishing houses are being set up and established ones are re-assessing current practice and future plans.[170] There has been a great deal of publicity around an initiative called 'express publishing', which aims to bring out the most popular journal publications in book form within a matter of months. Of the twenty-eight titles included in the first programme, for publication in the first six months of 1988, only seven had appeared by early June. Nevertheless a second programme has been announced and more publishing houses have joined the scheme. *Knizhnoe obozrenie* is balloting its readers to establish a list of the hundred books in most demand.[171] Pricing policy is also changing, with popular books appearing at unprecedented 'market' prices. Books in the new 'Literary heritage' series from the *Kniga* publishing house (including works by Nabokov, Zamiatin, and Mandel'shtam) will sell at twenty and twenty-five roubles. There is now another impassioned debate about pricing policy.[172] *Knizhnoe obozrenie* has just published a major discussion document on publishing plans in the new conditions until the year 2005.[173]

## VIII

What is the situation of Soviet publishing in late 1988? The journals are announcing their plans for 1989. The liberal editors are more adventurous than ever. *Oktiabr'* proposes to publish Vasilii Grossman's *Forever Flowing*, a novel which condemns the Leninist heritage of the state. Other journals intend to bring out Roi Medvedev's studies of Stalin, Khrushchev and Brezhnev. Conservative opposition to these endeavours is hardening, on the other hand. There has been a general clarification of position.

Subscriptions to the Soviet press rose by over 18 000 000 in 1988.[174] But in August 1988 it was announced that the print-runs of all 10 000 newspapers and journals published in the Soviet Union, with the exception of *Pravda, Izvestiia, Sovetskaia Rossiia* and five political journals, would be held to 1988 levels. In addition, over forty publications, including *Ogonek, Novyi mir, Znamia, Neva, Iunost'* and *Druzhba narodov*, would have limits set on subscriptions. The reason given was shortage of paper, but liberal journals were quick to imply other motivations.[175] Soviet history has shown that the tap of *glasnost'* can be turned off, that what is allowed today may be banned tomorrow. Perhaps such fears are unfounded. It would be tragic if the attempt by some contributors to the journals to be once again, in Iurii Burtin's words, 'the brain and conscience of the nation', should be curtailed.[176]

## POSTSCRIPT (December 1988)

The autumn 1988 issues of the literary journals gave considerable space to anxious letters from readers, bemoaning the difficulties they were now having in arranging subscriptions for 1989. Evidence of another kind that they were continuing to offer a provocative diet was provided in an illustration in *Znamia* (1988, 10, p. 233) of a threatening letter received by the editor Grigorii Baklanov. The text reads: 'We'll deal with you! Fighters of the patriotic organisation "Pamiat"'. Vengence is inevitable!' According to Baklanov similar letters had been received by several writers and editors.

Among the most remarkable initiatives of the autumn was the serialisation in *V mire knig* of extracts from the New Testament, beginning in the November issue. At the end of 1988 *V mire knig* was carrying four continuing series: Songs of the guitar posts; Who is who in Western Rock Music; the diaries of Catherine the Great; and the New Testament. This eclectic mix must give some idea of what editors perceive their readers to want to read.

Politics and history also continued to fascinate the journals. Dmitrii Volkogonov's 'Triumph and tragedy: a political portrait of I. V. Stalin' appeared in *Oktiabr'* (1988, nos. 10-12). The Khrushchev period was considered by Fedor Burlatskii in 'After Stalin: notes on a political thaw' (*Novyi mir,* 1988, 10, pp. 153-97) and in Anatolii Strelianyi's study of Khrushchev and agriculture 'The last romantic' (*Druzhba narodov,* 1988, 11, pp. 190-228). A. Anan'ev's article 'The Soviet farmer' was in *Oktiabr'* (1988, 11, pp. 3-15). In *Novyi mir* Gennadii Lisichkin published a study entitled 'Myths and reality. Does perestroika need Marx?' (1988, 11, pp. 160-87). For January 1989 *Znamia* announced Roi Medvedev's 'Stalin and Stalinism', and later in the year the same author's *All Stalin's Men* will appear in *Iunost'* and his study of Khrushchev in *Druzhba narodov.*

More émigré writers were welcomed back into the Soviet press. Vladimir Voinovich was interviewed in *Iunost'* (1988, 10, pp. 81-8), and an extract from his *The Life and Adventures of Private Ivan Chonkin* was carried in *Nedelia* (1988, 39, pp. 18-19). The whole novel appeared in *Iunost'* (1988, 12-1989, 2). There were twelve poems by the émigré poet Iurii Kublanovskii in *Znamia* (1988, 11, pp, 106-11). Serialisation of the memoirs of the veteran émigrée writer Nina Berberova began in *Oktiabr'* in October. In an article in *Nedelia* (1988, 42, p. 9) Anatolii Pristavkin spoke warmly of the émigrés Voinovich, Kopelev and Vladimov.

Inevitably, however, the main story of the autumn was of an émigré who was not being published in the journals, Aleksandr Solzhenitsyn. In late October and November the western press carried reports that printing of the October issue of *Novyi mir* had been halted when it was found to list *The Gulag Archipelago* on its back cover among works slated for publication in 1989. Solzhenitsyn was said to have agreed to the publication of his works in *Novyi mir* as long as *The Gulag Archipelago* appeared first. A call 'from the very top' was unexpectedly received at the printers however, stopping publication of the announcement (*Russkaia mysl'*, 3747, 21 October, p. 1; 3750, 11 November, p. 16; *The Independent*, 21 October). Copies of the October issue of *Novyi mir* showed evidence, when they arrived in the west, of having been re-bound.

The October issue had, however, apparently already gone on sale in Kiev before the call was received. This might explain the extraordinary appearance of Solzhenitsyn's 1974 appeal 'Live not by lies' in *Rabochee slovo*, the Kiev published newspaper of the south-western section of the Soviet railway network (18 October 1988, p. 1). It is assumed that the announcement of *The Gulag Archipelago* as forthcoming in *Novyi mir* was taken in Kiev to signify the removal of the ban on publishing him (Martin Dewhirst, 'The second rehabilitation of Alexander Solzhenitsyn?', *Soviet Analyst*, vol. 17, no. 23, 23 November 1988, pp. 5–7).

From then on, however, the opposition to the publication of Solzhenitsyn has become more explicit. According to the samizdat journal *Referendum*, no. 19, *Noyyi mir* then removed Solzhenitsyn's Nobel prize speech from the schedule of its issue for December 1988 (*Russkaia mysl'*, 3748, 28 October, p. 1. It will be recalled that *Novyi mir* began the cycle of re-publication of third wave émigrés by publishing Brodskii poems in its issue for December 1987). The journal *Vek XX i mir* was similarly prevented by a call from the Central Committee from publishing 'Live not by lies' in *its* December issue (*Ekspress-khronika*, 46, 13 November 1988, quoted in *Russkaia mysl'*, 3751, 18 November 1988, p. 16). On 9 November Vadim Medvedev, secretary of the Central Committee, told a group of editors that Solzhenitsyn would not be published in the USSR as long as he continued to be 'inimical to, and therefore unnecessary to Soviet society'. He made similar remarks in Riga, on 12 November, at a meeting of ideological workers, stating:

The Central Committee and the Presidium of the Supreme Soviet of the USSR have recently received many communications about the political and literary rehabilitation of Solzhenitsyn. I have not earlier had cause to read his work, but now I have had to. *Lenin in Zurich* and *The Gulag Archipelago*. Well what can I say? Only one thing, that he is not a fighter against distortions of socialism, against Stalinism and so on. He is a fighter against our system as such. An opponent of Lenin, an opponent of all our ideology ... And after this some people try to portray Solzhenitsyn as a man expressing universal humanitarian values. There's nothing universal and humanitarian about it. It's, how shall I put it, a direct stance of open opposition to our system and out worldview. To everything.

In the face of such vehemence, a letter apparently began to circulate in Moscow in mid-November signed by nineteen 'supporters of perestroika' who considered publication of *The Gulag Archipelago* to be undesirable at the present time because of uncertainty about its possible effect on readers (*Russkaia mysl'*, 3751, 18 November, p. 16; 3752, 25 November, p. 4).

At the end of 1988 the battle over publishing Solzhenitsyn in the USSR was still being waged. (See the Postscript on page 154.)

### Notes and References

1. Circulation figures are taken from *Moscow News*, 1988, 8, p. 2, and from Julia Wishnevsky, 'A guide to some major Soviet journals', *Radio Liberty Research Bulletin*, RL Supplement 2/88, 20 July 1988, an excellent survey of the current state of the literary journals.
2. See Section IV, below.
3. On Kholopov, see Nataliia Il'ina, 'Zdravstvui, plemia mladoe, neznakomoe', *Ogonek*, 1988, 2, pp. 23–26 (p. 26).
4. Odoevtseva's return to the Soviet Union from an emigration that had begun in 1923 was announced by Radio Moscow on 13 April 1987. See Nancy P. Condee and Vladimir Padunov, 'Recharting Soviet Cultural History', *Framework*, 34, 1987, p. 62 and note 8, p. 102.
5. Wishnevsky, 'A guide', op. cit. (note 1) p. 14.
6. 'Vstrecha redkollegii i avtorov zhurnala "Nash sovremennik" s chitateliami, *Russkaia mysl'* (Paris), 3711, 1988, pp. 6–7.
7. Wishnevsky, 'A guide', op. cit. (note 1) pp. 15–16. See also her 'A second "Pamyat'" emerges', *Radio Liberty Research* RL 463/87, and '*Nash Sovremennik* talks to Soviet TV viewers', RL 346/88; and Elena Gessen 'Bitvy "Nashego sovremennika"', *Vremia i my* (New York), 99, 1987, pp. 175–89.
8. 'Eshche raz o proiskakh i zagovorakh', *Ogonek*, 1988, 20, pp. 19.

9. These details are taken from Julia Wishnevsky, 'Molodaya gvardiya: a leading voice of opposition', *Radio Liberty Research*, RL 1/88, an excellent analysis of this journal. See also her 'Anatolii Ivanov: The other side's choice', RL 245/88.
10. On this, see Julia Wishnevsky 'Reactionaries tighten their hold on the writers' union', *Radio Liberty Research*, RL 148/88, and John B. Dunlop, 'Soviet Cultural Politics', *Problems of Communism*, November–December 1987, pp. 34–56 (pp. 40–56), which provides a revealing analysis of the strength of the conservative writers. See also the interview with the émigré writers Vladimir Voinovich and Sergei Iur'enen in *Radio Svoboda: Materialy issledovatel'skogo otdela*, RS 45/88.
11. These subdivisions of writers are of necessity arbitrary. Some writers would fit as appropriately into more than one grouping.
12. Among the most important publications of Bulgakov are a chapter from *The White Guard* and letters (*Novyi mir*, 1987, 2); *Adam and Eve* and the letters to the Soviet government and to Stalin (*Oktiabr'*, 1987, 6); 'To a Secret Friend' and the letter to the government (*Novyi mir*, 1987, 8); 'To a Secret Friend' (*Pamir*, 1987, 4); *The Crimson Island*, (*Druzhba narodov*, 1987, 8); *The Diaboliad* (*Literaturnyi Kirgizstan*, 1987, 4); *The Heart of a Dog* (*Znamia*, 1987, 6); *Notes on the cuffs* and *Bohemia* (*Teatr* 1987, 6); *The Fatal Eggs*, (*Literaturnyi Kirgizstan*, 1988, 1); *Batum*, (*Sovremennaia dramaturgiia*, 1988, 5); and the opera libretto *Peter the Great* (*Sovetskaia muzyka*, 1988, 2).
13. *The Defence* in *Moskva* (1986, 12); *Mary* in *Literaturnaia ucheba* (1987, 6); *Laughter in the Dark* in *Volga* (1988, 6–8); *Invitation to a Beheading* in *Rodnik* (1987, 8–1988, 2) and *The Gift* in *Ural* (1988, 3–6). Nabokov's autobiography, *Other Shores*, is in *Druzhba narodov*, (1988, 5–6), his study of Gogol' in *Novyi mir* (1987, 4), and there have been several publications of stories and poems.
14. On *The Fire*, see M. Nazarov, 'Nado zhit'' *Grani*, 140, 1986, pp. 309–15. On *A Sad Detective Story*, see ibid., 'Borot'sia so zlom–znaia ego prirodu', ibid., 142, 1986, pp. 282–87. On *The Executioner's Block*, see R. Porter, 'Chingiz Aitmatov's *The Execution Block*: Religion, Opium and the People', *Scottish Slavonic Review*, 8, 1987, pp. 75–90; Katerina Clark, *'The Executioner's Block*: a novel of the thaw', *The Times Literary Supplement*, 26 June 1987, p. 696; and R. Pittman, 'Chingiz Aytmatov's *Plakha*: Novel in a time of change', *The Slavonic and East European Review*, 66, 1988, pp. 357–79. Aitmatov himself has apparently suggested that *The Executioner's Block* did not appear in the July 1986 issue of *Novyi mir* because he was simply too busy to check the proofs.
15. Compare Condee and Padunov, 'Recharting', op. cit. (note 4), pp. 72–79 with their later analysis in their 'The frontiers of Soviet Culture: Reaching the Limits?' (*The Harriman Institute Forum*, 1, 1988, 5, pp. 1–8 (p. 3). See also Dunlop, 'Soviet Cultural Politics', op. cit. (note 10), p. 44.
16. *The New Assignment* is the first work specifically sent abroad for publication to appear later in a Soviet journal. For a useful survey of

the fate of this novel, see Mark Kuchment, 'Twenty years later', *Russian Review*, 46, 1987, pp. 433–37.
17. On these seven works, see Geoffrey Hosking, 'At last an exorcism', *The Times Literary Supplement*, 9–15 October 1987, pp. 1111–12. On *Children of the Arbat* see also John Barber, 'Children of the Arbat', *Detente*, 11, 1988, pp. 8–11, 38. On *Peasants and their women*, see also David Gillespie, 'History, politics and the Russian peasant: Boris Mozhaev and the collectivization of agriculture', *Slavonic and East European Review* 67, 1989, pp. 183–210. On *The Buffalo*, see also V. T., 'Pravda i polupravda v novoi knige o sovetskoi nauke', *Russkaia mysl'* 3677, 1978, pp. 11, 14.
18. On the first books of *The Liubavins* (1965) and *The Eves* (1972–76) see Geoffrey Hosking, *Beyond Socialist Realism. Soviet Fiction since Ivan Denisovich*, London, 1980, pp. 168–70, 67–70.
19. On Tvardovskii's unsuccessful attempt to publish *By the Right of Memory* in his own journal, *Novyi mir*, see Iurii Burtin, 'Vam, iz drugogo pokolen'ia ...; *Oktiabr'*, 1987, 8, pp. 191–202, (pp. 201–2); and below, Section IV.
20. On these stories see Ol'ga Martynenko, 'V polnyi golos. Rasskazy Vladimira Tendriakova v "Novom mire"', *Moskovskie novosti*, 1988, 14, p. 15; and Julia Wishnevsky, 'Roy Medvedev's figures on victims of collectivisation cited in *Novyi mir*', *Radio Liberty Research*, RL 155/88.
21. More than half of Iskander's novel, including the chapters on Stalin, had not been published in the Soviet Union until the autumn of 1988. According to Iskander these totalled some 600 pages ('Neizvestnyi Sandro', a conversation between Iskander and Natal'ia Ivanova, *Moskovskie novosti*, 1988, 28, p. 11).
22. The poet Anatolii Zhigulin was arrested in 1949 at the age of 18 as a member of an anti-Stalinist organisation based in Voronezh, the 'Communist Youth Party'. He spent years in the camps of Taishet and Kolyma. The story about these experiences, his first prose work, was written in 1984. *Znamia* first announced that it was to appear in the issue for February 1988. Zhigulin is interviewed about the novel in *Moskovskie novosti*, 1988, 31, p. 12 and in *Knizhnoe obozrenie*, 1988, 34, pp. 4, 15. This second interview includes Zhigulin's correspondence with Solzhenitsyn about Shalamov's Kolyma poems and stories.
23. There is an extremely interesting study of all Shatrov's plays, David Joravsky, 'Glasnost Theater', *The New York Review of Books*, vol. 35, no. 17, 10 November 1988, pp. 34–39. On Okudzhava's new poems, see G. S. Smith, 'Okudzhava marches on', *Slavonic and East European Review*, 66, 1988, pp. 553–63.
24. *Ogonek*, 1988, nos. 30–35. *Druzhba narodov*, 1988, nos. 9–10. Book two will appear in the same journal in 1989.
25. Bek's novel has been announced for publication in 1989 by *Druzhba narodov*.
26. Shalamov's Kolyma stories have appeared in *Sel'skaia molodezh'* (1987, 7), *Literaturnaia Rossiia* (1988, 4 and 31), *Nedel'ia* (1988, 30), *Novyi mir* (1988, 6), *V mire knig* (1988, 8), *Moskva* (1988, 9), and

*Iunost'*, (1988, 10). In his lifetime, Shalamov was able to publish only poetry in his own country.
27. 'The Juvenile Sea' (*Znamia*, 1986, 6), 'For Profit' (*Don*, 1987, 12), 'Doubting Makar', (*Literaturnaia ucheba*, 1987, 4, and *Knizhnoe obozrenie*, 1987, 22); *The Foundation Pit* (*Novyi mir*, 1987, 6) and *Chevengur* (*Druzhba narodov*, 1988, 3–4).
28. Iurii Kariakin, 'Stoit li nastupat' na grabli?', *Znamia*, 1987, 9, p. 210.
29. Iurii Afanas'ev, rector of the State Historical Archive Institute, described Shatrov's plays as a 'bitter reproach to historians' in an interview in *Sovetskaia kul'tura*, 21 March 1987, p. 3. This interview appears in English as 'We are only beginners', in *Socialist Register 1988*, ed. Ralph Miliband et al., London, 1988, pp. 79–89. The historian Iurii Poliakov, interviewed by *Literaturnaia gazeta*, 29 July 1987, p. 10, added: 'Historical scholarship has fallen behind literature, where the appearance of interesting works by Aitmatov, Granin, Rybakov and Dudintsev has revealed negative aspects of the development of our society.'
30. During the 1950s Thaw, several new journals, notably *Iunost'*, a journal directly connected with the new 'young prose' writers, were founded in a short space of time. For an extremely interesting analysis of the current publishing situation for young writers, see the discussion between Evgenii Popov and Sergei Chuprinin in *Literaturnaia gazeta*, 3 August 1988, p. 3. Popov relates the case of a young poet who was told that his poems could certainly be published ... in 1996.
31. Vladimir Kornilov was expelled from the Union of Writers in 1977, after a decade of human rights activities and of sending his work abroad for publication. His poems began to appear again in the Soviet Union at the end of 1986 (*Znamia*, 1986, 11). Kornilov describes his experiences in an interview in *Literaturnaia gazeta*, 1988, 28, p. 7.
32. Lidiia Chukovskaia was expelled from the Writers' Union in January 1974 after her campaigns in support of Siniavskii and Daniel', Solzhenitsyn and Sakharov. She describes her expulsion in her book *Protsess iskliucheniia*, Paris, 1979.
33. By now almost all the *Metropol'* authors have returned to print, notably the poets Lipkin and Lisnianskaia. Evgenii Rein, another *Metropol'* poet, has recently been published in *Novyi mir*, 1988, 2, *Ogonek*, 1988, 1, *Literaturnaia Rossiia*, 1988, 32, *Avrora*, 1988, 5, and *Druzhba narodov*, 1988, 10.
34. On Tolstaia, see Helena Goscillo, 'Tat'iana Tolstaia's "Dome of Many-Coloured Glass": The world refracted through multiple perspectives', *Slavic Review*, 47, 1988, pp. 280–90, which contains, note 2, p. 280, a list of Tolstaia's journal publications.
35. See Natal'ia Ivanova, 'Fal'shivyi Gogol'', *Moskovskie novosti*, 1988, 11, p. 3.
36. *Knizhnoe obozrenie*, 1988, 1, p. 4. The words 'They have nowhere to publish!' are directly echoed in Sergei Chuprinin's insistence 'The young have simply nowhere to publish' in his *Literaturnaia gazeta* conversation with Popov, note 30.

37. Three new sober tales of city life by Makanin were published in 1987: *Loss* (*Novyi mir*, 1987, 2), *A man and a woman* (*Oktiabr'*, 1987, 3) and *The Laggard* (*Znamia*, 1987, 9). The literary-critical journal *Voprosy literatury* devoted a substantial part of its issue for February 1988 to a discussion of Makanin's work. He is now a member of the editorial board of *Znamia*.
38. On Kaledin see Irina Murav'eva, 'Izlechenie pravdoi', *Kontinent*, 55, 1988, pp. 385–93.
39. Shmelev's most important stories are 'The Pashkov house' (*Znamia*, 1987, 3) and 'A play in honour of the Prime Minister' (*Znamia*, 1988, 3). He has been interviewed about his fiction in *Moskovskie novosti*, 1988, 10, p. 11 and in *V mire knig*, 1988, 7, pp. 20–24. In the first of these interviews he reveals that he had one story published by *Moskva* in 1961, but that the editor added a happy ending to it. This apparently put him off the idea of writing fiction for ten years. 'I began seriously regarding myself as a writer in the early 1970s and have been writing regularly ever since.' A collection of Shmelev's fiction, under the title, *A play in honour of the Prime Minister*, is about to appear. Anatolii Strelianyi's sketches about life in his village were published in *Iunost'* and *Druzhba narodov* in the 1970s. His most recent stories are 'A year of personal life (The tale of an old acquaintance)' (*Znamia*, 1988, 8) and 'Shooting on the Wing' (*Druzhba narodov*, 1988, 6).
40. There is a useful survey of the debate in the Soviet military in Stuart Dalrymple, 'Bullying in the Soviet Army', *Radio Liberty Research*, RL 185/88. See also 'Sluzhu Sovetskomu Soiuzu', *Strana i mir*, Munich, 1988, 2, pp. 76–83.
41. Chulaki's 'Farewell, green Priazhka', set in a psychiatric hospital, is discussed by Natal'ia Gorbanevskaia in *Russkaia mysl'*, 3730, *Literaturnoe prilozhenie*, 6, 1988, p. v. Evgenii Popov praises 'The Seafarer' in his conversation with Chuprinin (note 30).
42. These and other new poets were represented in *Krug*, Leningrad, 1985, a selection of the work of the 'Club 81' writers. Krivulin's assessment of this 'concession' by an official publishing house is withering: 'They didn't really publish our work. They murdered it. A subtle form of murder, but murder all the same. They chose our least interesting work, and they published it in a context that was completely alien to it.' (Sally Laird, 'Soviet literature – what has changed?', *Index on Censorship*, 1987, 7, pp. 8–13 (p. 11).
43. M. Epshtein, 'Pokolenie, nashedshee sebia', *Voprosy literatury*, 1986, 5, pp. 40–72; 'Kontsepty ... Metaboly ... O novykh techeniiakh v poezii', *Oktiabr'*, 1988, 4, pp. 194–203; (reprinted as '... Ia by nazval eto – "metabola"'. Zametki o novykh techeniiakh v poezii', *Vzgliad*, comp. A. N. Latynina and S. S. Lesnevskii, Moscow, 1988, pp. 171–96). See also his 'Life after Utopia: new poets in Moscow', *Index on Censorship*, 1988, 1, pp. 12–14.
44. Arro: 'The rut', *Teatr*, 1987, 4. Petrushevskaia: 'Andante' and 'Columbine's flat', *Teatr*, 1988, 2; 'I'm a Sweden Fan', 'Columbine's Flat' and 'A glass of water', *Sovetskii teatr*, 1988, 2; stories in *Neva*, 1987, 7, and

*Novyi mir*, 1988, 1. Slavkin: *Serso, Sovremennaia dramaturgiia*, 1986, 4. Galin: *Stars in the Morning Sky, Teatr*, 1988, 8.
45. This article was published under the title 'Still Waiting for Real Reform' in *The Times*, 16 March 1987 and as 'Is Glasnost' a game of mirrors?' in *The New York Times*, 22 March 1987. It appeared in *Moskovskie novosti*, 1987, 13 (29 March). Readers' letters were published in the issues for 5 and 12 April.
46. *Moskovskie novosti*, 1987, 37 (13 September). The obituary is signed by Grigorii Baklanov, Bulat Okudzhava, Viacheslav Kondrat'ev and Vladimir Lakshin.
47. For a discussion of the evolution of the representation of emigration in such Soviet works of art as Gleb Panfilov's film *The Theme*, see Condee and Padunov 'Recharting', op. cit. (note 4), pp. 61–70.
48. See for example Vladimir Voinovich 'Putem vzaimnoi perepiski', *Novoe russkoe slovo*, 21 June 1987, pp. 5, 7.
49. As has been frequently pointed out, this is by no means the first time that the award of the Nobel Prize to a Russian writer has caused embarrassment in the Soviet Union. In 1933 it went to the émigré, Bunin, in 1958 to Pasternak, who had just published *Doctor Zhivago* abroad and was forced to renounce it, in 1970 to Solzhenitsyn. Only the 1965 award, to Mikhail Sholokhov, could at the time be greeted with unalloyed enthusiasm in official Soviet literary circles, but paradoxically some of them may now be more embarrassed by this award than by any of the others to Russian writers.
50. The footnote which accompanies these poems (*Novyi mir*, 1987, 12, pp. 160–68) suggests that the decision to publish Brodskii was taken before the award of the Nobel Prize. There is nevertheless something surreptitious about the publication. The note reads: 'When this issue with poems by Iosif Brodskii, a Russian poet now living in New York, was already definitively typeset, news came of the award to him of the Nobel Prize for Literature.

The poems are taken from the books *Urania* and *A Part of Speech*. The publication has been approved by the author.'

On the selection and the question of the author's attitude, see *Russkaia mysl'* 3700, p. 11, 3701, p. 9.
51. *Inostrannaia literatura*, 1988, 1, p. 252. This was another surreptitious publication not announced in the issue's table of contents.
52. The editor of *Moskva*, Mikhail Alekseev, had told the British journalist Sally Laird in May 1987 that 'Brodsky is not a poet . . . Also, he is not a Russian' (Sally Laird, 'Soviet Literature – what has changed?', *Index on Censorship*, 1987, 7, p. 10.
53. For a detailed analysis see Julia Wishnevsky, '*Komsomol'skaya pravda* attacks Joseph Brodsky', *Radio Liberty Background Report*, RL, 134/88.
54. Natal'ia Ivanova, *Moskovskie novosti*, 8 May 1988. Letter from Tat'iana Tolstaia and Viktor Erofeev, *Ogonek*, 1988, 18, p. 3.
55. This publication, in *Knizhnoe obozrenie*, 1988, 24, pp. 8–9, 16, omitted the following sentence from the speech: 'Lenin was literate, Stalin was

literate, so were Hitler and Mao Tse Dun, who even wrote poetry.' The sentence was immediately published by *Moskovskie novosti* (1988, 25, p. 2) under the headline 'Absurd! ...'.

56. *Ogonek*, 1988, 30 contains Brodskii's 'Roman Elegies' and an interview in which he names Russian and émigré poets whom he admires. The selection in *Druzhba narodov*, 1988, 8 is followed by a brief survey of Brodskii's poetic career by M. Lotman. There are poems in *Druzhba narodov*, 1988, 8, *Literaturnoe obozrenie*, 1988, 8 and *Iunost'*, 1988, 8; and Brodskii's 'Elegy for John Donne' and his translations of Donne in *Inostrannaia literatura*, 1988, 9. The *Novyi mir* selection of poems is reviewed by I. Vinokurova in *Oktiabr'*, 1988, 7.
57. This impression was confirmed when *Krokodil* published letters from its readers (*Krokodil* 1988, 7, p. 13; 9, pp. 13-14; 11, p. 13). 'I am glad that my country rid itself of yet another parasite of the type, who, along with the Stalinist usurpers, defame the ideals of the Russian revolution' wrote a retired docker (9, p. 14). See also ibid., 19, p. 5.
58. The major publications of Galich's work are in *Oktiabr'* 1988, 4, *Novyi mir*, 1988, 5, *Literaturnyi Kirgizstan*, 1988, 5, *Ogonek*, 1988, 24, *V mire knig*, 1988, 6, *Znamia*, 1988, 6, *Iunost'*, 1988, 6, and *V mire knig*, 1988, 6 and 8.
59. A. Bocharov, 'Pokushenie na mirazhi', *Voprosy literatury*, 1988, 1, pp. 72-73. The examples Bocharov gives are Nekrasov's *Frontline Stalingrad*, Solzhenitsyn's *One Day in the Life of Ivan Denisovich*, Akenov's *A Ticket to the Stars* and Vladimov's *The Big Ore*.
60. A. Suetnov, 'Otkuda berutsia "belye piatna"?', *V mire knig*, 1988, 4, pp. 85-86.
61. E. Riazanov, 'Velikodushie', *Moskovskie novosti*, 1988, 25, p. 12.
62. Popov and Chuprinin (note 30).
63. Viktor Nekrasov, 'Gorodskie progulki', *Iunost'*, 1988, 7; 'Iz tsikla "Malen'kie portrety"', *Druzhba narodov*, 1988, 8. Nine Korzhavin poems, *Oktiabr'*, 1988, 8; his long poem, 'Tan'ka', *Znamia*, 1988, 12; Sokolov, extracts from *The School for Fools*, *Ogonek*, 1988, 33, with an introduction by Tat'iana Tolstaia. Tolstaia had singled out this novel for praise in her *Knizhnoe obozrenie* interview (note 36).
64. *Guardian*, 4 March 1987, *Financial Times*, 4 March 1987, *The Times*, 6 March 1987.
65. See, for example, 'Postepennost' gubit revoliutsii', *Strana i mir*,1987, 4, pp. 36-37, 'An editor preaches "Revolution"', *Encounter*, September-October 1987, pp. 62-64.
66. Strelianyi was among those introduced to the board by Zalygin at the beginning of 1987. For Igor' Vinogradov, who left at the same time as Strelianyi, this was the second departure from *Novyi mir*. He was forced off Tvardovskii's editorial board in February 1970.
67. *Argumenty i fakty*, 1988, 27, p. 8.
68. See, for example, *Guardian*, 16 July 1988.
69. The background to this story is examined in two articles in *Russkaia mysl'*, 'Letiat utki', 3734, 22 July 1988, p. 16 and 'Mezhdunarodnaia dezinformatsiia vokrug imeni A. I. Solzhenitsyna', *ibid.*, 3735, 29 July

1988, p. 16. The latter report contains the text of Natal'ia Solzhenitsyna's press statement.
70. See, for example, A. Bocharov (note 59), and the editorial statement in *Daugava*, 1988, 7, p. 128.
71. Elena Chukovskaia, 'Vernut' Solzhenitsynu grazhdanstvo SSSR', *Knizhnoe obozrenie*, 1988, 32, p. 15. See also *Knizhnoe obozrenie*, 1988, 33, pp. 6–7, for readers' letters unanimously in support of Chukovskaia, and *Knizhnoe obozrenie*, 1988, 34 for Solzhenitsyn's correspondence with Zhigulin (see note 22). See also L. Voskresenskii, 'Zdravstvuite, Ivan Denisovich!', *Moskovskie novosti*, 1988, 32, p. 11, which describes *One Day in the Life of Ivan Denisovich* for the benefit of readers who have not been able to get hold of it.
72. On cuts in Nabokov's *Other Shores*, see *Russkaia mysl'*, 3729, 1988, p. 10. On cuts in Vasilii Grossman's *Life and Fate*, see ibid. 3724, 1988, p. 12. In its issue for September 1988, *Oktiabr'* published a chapter from *Life and Fate* on antisemitism which it had previously omitted. *Ogonek* published Khodasevich's essay 'Koleblemyi trenozhnik' (1987, 6) with the last sentence missing. Of all writers, Khodasevich seems to be the most vulnerable to cuts. Others to have suffered include Zamiatin and Mandel'shtam.
73. *Iunost'*, 1987, 9, p. 74.
74. *Znamia*, 1988, 2, pp. 237–38.
75. *Novyi mir*, 1987, 12, pp. 257–58. On Terekhov, see A. Golovkov, 'Vechnyi isk', *Ogonek*, 1988, pp. 28–31.
76. See, for example, Elena Gessen, 'Kommentarii k kommentariiam', *Strana i mir*, 1987, 6, pp. 133–38; N. Kuznetsova, 'Pokaianie ili preklonenie?', *Russkaia mysl'*, 3697, 1987, pp. 10–11, 14; B. Vail', 'Stalinskoi ulybkoiu sogreta ...', ibid, 3707, 1988, p. 10, all of which are sceptical about the historical accuracy of Rybakov's *Children of the Arbat*. In a hard-hitting piece in *Russkaia mysl'*, Vladimir Maksimov eloquently describes how some of the present supporters of *glasnost'* participated in earlier campaigns against writers ('Dukhovnoe maroderstvo, ili Komu i za chto stydno?, *Russkaia mysl'*, 3710, 1988, p. 11).
77. Obviously, different journals are responding to developments with differing degrees of warmth. For a survey of recent appearances by Soviet cultural figures in different émigré journals, see G. Andreev, 'Vstrechi s deiateliami sovetskoi kul'tury na stranitsakh emigrantskikh gazet i zhurnalov', *Russkaia mysl'*, 3735, 1988, p. 10.
78. See 'O konferentsii v Kopengagene', *Russkaia mysl'*, 3718, 1988, p. 12; Julia Wishnevsky, 'Soviet and émigré academics and writers meet in Denmark', *Radio Liberty Research*, RL 102/88; G. Belaia, 'Dialog vo imia nashei obshchei kul'tury', *Knizhnoe obozrenie*, 1988, 20, p. 4. The conference speeches by Afanas'ev, Cronid Lubarskii, Iskander and Siniavskii are in *Index on Censorship*, 1988, 5, pp. 13–22, 36.
79. On the Lisbon meeting, see *The Times Literary Supplement*, 13–19 May 1988, p. 528. On the Barcelona meeting, see materials in *Russkaia mysl'*, 3752, 1988, pp 12–13. The West German Slavist Wolfgang Kasack was interviewed in *Moskovskie novosti* (1987, 49) about *peres-*

*troika* and literature. The British economist Alec Nove wrote on the problems of radical economic reform in the USSR in *Kommunist* (1988, 12). And the American Slavist John Malmstad discussed Russian literature with a Soviet colleague in *Literaturnoe obozrenie* (1988, 9).

80. See *Russkaia mysl'*, 3697, 1987, p. 2 and ibid 3724, 1988, pp. 1–2, 5. For an assessment of the *samizdat* press, see Boris Kagarlitskii, 'Glasnost, the Soviet press and red greens', *The Times Literary Supplement*, 25–31 December 1987, pp. 1430, 1442, reprinted in his *The Thinking Reed*, London, 1988, pp. 341–47.
81. The information on *Mitin zhurnal* and *Predlog* is taken from 'O leningradskom samizdate', *Russkaia mysl'*, 3715, 1988, p. 10. Materials from *Mitin zhurnal* appeared in *Vestnik russkogo khristianskogo dvizheniia*, Paris, 151, 1987.
82. On the Stalin prizewinners, see A. Bocharov, 'Pokushenie na mirazhi', *Voprosy literatury*, 1988, 1, pp. 40–77, (p. 51). On pages 50, 51, 54 and 55 of his article, Bocharov lists authors and works he would gladly consign to oblivion. For Vysotskii, see *Sovetskaia bibliografiia* 1988, 2, pp. 83–86; for Shalamov, see ibid., 1988, 3, pp. 68–70; for Bukharin, see ibid., pp. 58–60.
83. It should be stressed that in this endeavour Soviet journals are belatedly following in the courageous footsteps of *samizdat* and of émigré publishers, in particular the *Pamiat'* (Memory – the very title is indicative of their aims) and *Minuvshee* volumes. Five issues of *Pamiat'* appeared first in samizdat and then in New York and Paris between 1976 and 1982. Six volumes of *Minuvshee* have appeared in Paris between 1986 and the time of writing. These excellently edited volumes remain the major source for the dark places of Soviet literary (and not only literary) history. On literary history in *Pamiat'*, see J. Graffy, 'Ogosudarstvlenie', *Sbornik*, Leeds, 9, 1983, pp. 97–107.
84. *Ogonek*, 1988, 4, p. 6.
85. Ibid., 1988, 29, pp. 26–29.
86. Ibid., 1988, 24, pp. 28–30.
87. Ibid., 1988, 31, p. 3. The *Metropol'* affair is also discussed by Popov and Chuprinin (note 30). Neither publication reveals that one of the prime movers of *Metropol'* was Vasilii Aksenov.
88. *Ogonek*, 1988, 22, pp. 10–14. Rudnitskii insists that the 'speech of defiance' allegedly made by Meierkhol'd at the All Union Directors' Conference in June 1939 and included by Iurii Elagin as an appendix to his book *Temnii genii* (New York: 1955; second edition, London: 1982) is a fabrication. Meierkhol'd's speech, of which, according to Rudnitskii, there is a signed transcript, abjectly praises the 'wise directions of comrade Stalin'.
89. Arkadii Vaksberg, 'Protsessy', *Literaturnaia gazeta*, 1988, p. 12. 'This study concentrates on the fates of Meierkhol'd, Mikhail Kol'tsov and Babel'. Neither Rudnitskii nor Vaksberg includes certain of the details of Meierkhol'd's torture provided by the young archivist, Dmitrii Iurasov, at a meeting at the Tsentral'nyi dom literatorov in Moscow on 13 April 1987 (see *Russkaia mysl'*, 3675, 1987, pp. 4–5). Iurasov has now written briefly in the Soviet press about the tortures inflicted on

Meierkhol'd, in a short report on documents he encountered while working as an archivist in Moscow ('Vernite pravo na pamiat'!', *Sobesednik*, 1988, 22, p. 5). There is an extremely interesting article on Iurasov and his activities, V. Chalikova, 'Arkhivnyi iunosha', *Neva*, 1988, 10, pp. 152-62; see also *Sovetskaia bibliografia*, 1988, 5, pp. 61-7.

90. ' "... Pisatel' s perepugannoi dushoi – eto uzhe poteria kvalifikatsii" ', *Druzhba narodov*, 1988, 3, pp. 168-89. There is another major documentary study of the fate of Zoshchenko in *Iunost'*, 1988, 8, pp. 69-86.
91. Daniil Granin, 'Mimoletnoe iavlenie', *Ogonek*, 1988, 6, pp. 9-11, 29.
92. Nikolai Zabolotskii, 'Istoriia moego zakliucheniia', *Daugava*, 1988, 3, pp. 105-16. On the Pasternak affair, see V. Kaverin, 'Literator', *Znamia*, 1987, 8, pp. 80-121 (109-21). Vladimir Simonov describes the trial of Siniavskii and Daniel as 'oppressive' in *Moskovskie novosti*, 1987, 8, p. 23. Brodskii's arrest and trial are briefly mentioned in the afterwords to publications of his poems by Aleksandr Kushner, *Neva*, 1988, 3, pp. 109-10 and M. Lotman, *Druzha narodov*, 1988, 8, pp. 184-86; in detail in *Neva*, 1989, 2, pp. 134-66, and *Iunost'*, 1988, 2.
93. V. Smekhov, 'Skripka Mastera', *Teatr*, 1988, 2, pp. 97-124. For reader response to this article, see ibid., 1988, 6, pp, 67-70, 7, pp. 138-40. For the transcript of the discussion of Liubimov's production of *Boris Godunov* in 1982, see *Sovremennaia dramaturgiia*, 1988, 4, pp. 196-223. The present director of the Taganka, Nikolai Gubenko, discusses Liubimov in an interview in *Ogonek*, 1988, 30, pp. 16-19.
94. Iurii Kariakin, 'Stoit li nastupat' na grabli? (Otkrytoe pis'mo odnomu inkognito)', *Znamia*, 1987, 9, pp. 200-24.
95. Iurii Trifonov, 'Vspominaia Tvardovskogo', *Ogonek*, 1986, 44, pp. 21-24.
96. *Znamia*, 1987, 2, pp. 3-14; *Novyi mir*, 1987, 3, pp. 190-203.
97. Iurii Burtin, ' "Vam, iz drugogo pokolen'ia ...", K publikatsii poemy A. Tvardovskogo "Po pravu pamiati" ', *Oktiabr'* 1987, 8, pp. 191-202.
98. Ibid., p. 199.
99. *Oktiabr'*, 1987, 12, pp. 190-205.
100. Ibid., p. 201.
101. Nataliia Il'ina, 'Zdravstvui, plemia mladoe, neznakomoe', *Ogonek*, 1988, 2, pp. 23-26.
102. Anatolii Salutskii, Pogovorim vser'ez', *Pravda*, 29 January 1988, p. 6.
103. Among the most important contributions to this debate are V. Vozdvizhenskii, 'Pozitsiia. "Novyi mir" shestidesiatikh godov', *V mire knig* 1988, 3, pp. 2-5; S. Rassadin, '... Vse rasresheno?', *Ogonek*, 1988, 13, pp. 6-8; A. Sakhnin, 'Ne brosat'sia slovami", V. Lakshin, 'Na tribune i doma. Otvet Arkadiiu Sakhninu', *Moskovskie novosti*, 1988, 17, p. 15; N. Il'ina, 'Moi prodolzhitel'nye uroki', *Ogonek*, 1988, 17, pp. 26-29; A. Ivanov, 'Vysoka tsena istiny', *Literaturnaia Rossiia*, 1988, 18, p. 9; M. Lobanov, 'Posleslovie. Iz vospominanii', *Nash sovremennik*, 1988, 4, pp. 154-59; I. Dement'eva, 'Est' khoroshee narodnoe slovo ...', *Iunost'*, 1988, 7, pp. 83-85; S. Kuniaev, 'Kleveta vse potriasaet ...', *Molodaia gvardiia*, 1988, 7, pp. 247-62. See also B. Zaks, 'Vokrug Tvardovskogo', *Russkaia mysl'*, 3734, 1988, pp. 8-9, for an assessment of Sakhnin.

104. *Ogonek*, 1988, 11, p. 7.
105. Iurii Burtin, 'Vozmohnost' vozrazit'. (Iz lichnogo opyta)', *Daugava*, 1988, 6, pp. 66–79.
106. Vladimir Lakshin, 'Ne vpast' v bespamiatstvo. (Iz khroniki "Novogo mira" vremeni Tvardovskogo)', *Znamia*, 1988, 8, pp. 210–17.
107. M. Chudakova, 'O Bulgakove, i ne tol'ko o nem', *Literaturnaia gazeta*, 1987, 42, p. 6. See also 'Writer Mikhail Bulgakov and the fate of his works', *Moscow News*, 1988, 5, Supplement, pp. 6–7. On recent improvements in access to State archives, see *Argumenty i fakty*, 1988, 38, p. 1.
108. M. Chudakova, 'Vzglianut' v litso', in *Vzgliad. Kritika. Polemika. Publikatsii*, comp. A. Latynina and S. Lesnevskii, Moscow, 1988, pp. 376–404 (especially pp. 400–04). And see her contribution to the debate 'Aktual'nye problemy izucheniia istorii russkoi sovetskoi literatury', *Voprosy literatury*, 1987, 9, pp. 3–78 (Chudakova pp. 10–21).
109. Lev Gudkov and Boris Dubin, 'Literaturnaia kul'tura: protsess i ratsion', *Druzhba narodov*, 1988, 2, pp. 168–88, (pp. 168–71).
110. D. Likhachev, 'Gor'kie mysli posle pozhara', *Knizhnoe obozrenie*, 1988, 12, p. 16; idem, 'Pozhar', *Moskovskie novosti*, 1988, 13, pp. 1, 13; 'Chto vysvetil pozhar?', *Knizhnoe obozrenie*, 1988, 22, p. 5; K. Liasko, 'Kogda rasseialsia dym', ibid., 1988, 29, pp. 4, 15; Iu. Zerchaninov, 'Chto sluchilos' v Leningrade', *Iunost'*, 1988, 7, pp. 71–75.
111. 'Vozvrashcheno iz spetsfondov', *Sovetskaia kul'tura*, 22 March 1988, p. 8. Iu. Maksimov, 'Spetsfondy otkryvaiut dveri', *Nedelia*, 1988, 25, p. 4.
112. G. Kuz'minov, ' "Reabilitirovannie" knigi', *Knizhnoe obozrenie*, 1988, 28, p. 16.
113. See, for example, S. S. Averintsev, 'Vizantiia i Rus': dva tipa dukhovnosti', *Novyi mir*, 1988, 7, pp. 210–20, 9, pp. 227–39. The analysis of the Christian past naturally differs from journal to journal.
114. Nikolai Karamzin, 'Istoriia gosudarstva rossiiskogo', in *Moskva*, all issues from January 1988. On the republication of the nineteenth-century historians Karamzin, Solov'ev and Kliuchevskii, see A. Tsamutali, 'Prava pamiati', *Zvezda*, 1988, 4, pp. 201–7.
115. For excellent surveys of the press debate over Soviet history, see R. W. Davies, 'Soviet History in the Gorbachev revolution', *Socialist Register 1988*, ed. Ralph Miliband et al. (London: 1988), pp. 37–78; Stephen Wheatcroft, 'Unleashing the energy of history', *Australian Slavonic and East European Studies*, 1, 1987, 1, pp. 85–132; idem., 'Steadying the energy of history', ibid., 1, 1987, 2, pp. 57–114.
116. On Stalin's son see Nikolai Dorizo 'Iakov Dzhugashvili, Byl' i legenda. Tragediia', *Moskva*, 1988, 2, pp. 53–62, 3, pp. 27–41. On genetics see 'Chto im trebovalos' dokazat'? Poslednii akt tragedii genetiki', *Teatr*, 1988, 3, pp. 58–80. On the 'anti-cosmopolitan campaigns' see Nataliia Dolinina, 'Pervye uroki', *Neva*, 1988, 1, pp. 37–63 (Dolinina recalls the arrest of her father, the literary scholar Grigorii Gukovskii); and Sergei Iutkevich, 'My s uvlecheniem nachali s"emki', *Iskusstvo kino*, 1988, 2, pp. 94–108. On the 'doctors' plot' see Iakov Rapoport, 'Vospominaniia o "dele vrachei" ', *Druzhba narodov*, 1988, 4, pp. 222–45; Nataliia

Rapoport, 'Pamiat' – eto tozhe meditsina', *Iunost'*, 1988, 4, pp. 76–81; and Aleksandr Shtein, 'I ne tol'ko o nem', *Teatr*, 1988, 1, pp. 171–90; 2, pp. 166–85; 3, pp. 169–90 (on Boris Zbarskii).
117. Nikolai Shmelev, 'Avansy i dolgi', *Novyi mir*, 1987, 6, pp. 142–58; 'Novye trevogi', ibid., 1988, 4, pp. 160–75. On these articles see John Tedstrom, 'Soviet economist sounds the alarm over *Perestroika*', *Radio Liberty Research*, RL 199/88.
118. Vasilii Seliunin, 'Istoki', *Novyi mir*, 1988, 5, pp. 162–89. On Seliunin see Vera Tolz, 'Soviet journalist passes verdict on Russian and Soviet history', *Radio Liberty Research*, RL 244/88.
119. Vasilii Seliunin and Grigorii Khanin, 'Lukavaia tsifra', *Novyi mir*, 1987, 2, pp. 181–201.
120. Andrei Nuikin, 'Idealy ili interesy', ibid., 1988, 1, pp. 190–211; 2, pp. 205–28.
121. Igor' Kliamkin, 'Kakaia ulitsa vedet k khramu?', ibid., 1987, 11, pp. 150–88. For an assessment of Kliamkin's approach see Teodor Shanin, 'Which road leads to the temple?' *Detente*, 11, 1988, pp. 3–6, 38.
122. G. I. Shmelev, ' "Ne smet' komandovat'!" ', *Oktiabr'*, 1988, 2, pp. 3–26; 'Usloviia nashego rosta', *Znamia*, 1988, 7, pp. 155–84. Among other important contributions to the debate are 'Pamiat' i "Pamiat' " ', a debate about history and the present between G. I. Popov and Nikita Adzhubei, ibid., 1988, 1, pp. 188–203; N. Shemelev and V. Popov, 'Anatomiia defitsita', ibid., 1988, 5, pp. 158–83; O. Latsis, 'Perelom', ibid., 1988, 6, pp. 124–78; Anatolii Anan'ev, 'Zemlia', *Oktiabr'*, 1987, 9, pp. 3–14; V. Baliazin, 'Vozvrashchenie', ibid., 1988, 1, pp. 146–71 (a study of the economic theories of A. V. Chaianov).
123. *Voprosy istorii*, 1988, 2, pp. 3–10, p. 174.
124. ' "Kruglyi stol": istoricheskaia nauka v usloviiakh perestroiki', ibid., 1988, 3, pp. 3–57. Danilov's contribution, pp. 21–24, quoted passage, p. 22.
125. 'Istoriki i pisateli o literature i istorii', *Voprosy istorii*, 1988, 6, pp. 3–114. Among the participants are the historians of Afanas'ev and Polikarpov, the writers Astaf'ev, Shatrov and Zalygin and the literary critics Belaia and Burtin. Quotations from Ambartsumov, p. 83, from Burtin, p. 77.
126. Konstantin Simonov, 'Glazami cheloveka moego pokoleniia (Razmyshleniia o I. V. Staline)', *Znamia*, 1988, 3, pp. 3–66; 4, pp. 49–121; 5, pp. 69–96. For a jaundiced reaction see Efim Etkind, 'S chetyrekh storon ogorozhennyi', *Vremia i mir*, 100, 1988, pp. 198–203. See also 'I.V. Stalin glazami ego sovremennikov', *Literaturnyi Kirgizstan*, 1987, 10, pp. 116–34, for extracts from Leon Feuchtwanger's book, *Moscow 1937* and the famous 'Letter to Stalin' of 17 August 1939 by Fedor Raskol'nikov. This version of the letter is far longer than the one in V. Polikarpov, 'Fedor Raskol'nikov', *Ogonek*, 1987, 26, pp. 6–7, but omits the last half sentence (included in the *Ogonek* version) in which Raskol'nikov calls Stalin 'a traitor to socialism and revolution, the chief wrecker, a true enemy of the people, organiser of the famine and the judicial forgeries.' This sentence was restored in the third publication of the letter, in *Nedelia*, 1988, 26, pp. 6–7, which gives the letter in

full. Raskol'nikov's story 'Rasskaz o poteriannom dne' is in *V mire knig*, 1988, 3, pp. 59–63, his 'Bratanie' in *Knizhnoe obozrenie*, 1987, 45, pp. 8–10. See also Riurik Ivnev, 'Sergei Esenin i Fedor Raskol'nikov', *Literaturnyi Kirgizstan*, 1988, 2, pp. 135–38.

127. Aleksei Adzhubei, 'Te desiat' let', *Znamia*, 1988, 6, pp. 81–123; 7, pp. 80–133.
128. Mikhail Romm, 'Chetyre vstrechi s N.S. Khrushchevym', *Ogonek*, 1988, 28, pp. 6–8, 25–26.
129. Iurii Kariakin, ' "Zhdanovskaia zhidkost' " ili protiv ochernitel'stva', *Ogonek*, 1988, 19, pp. 25–27. Other studies of politicians in the journals include S. Parkhomenko, 'Prichina smerti narkoma Rykova', *Teatr*, 1988, 7, pp. 156–65, and V. Amlinskii, ' "Na zabroshennykh grobnitsakh" ', *Iunost'*, 1988, 3, pp. 50–61 (on Bukharin). Bukharin's speech at the first congress of the Union of Soviet Writers in 1934 is in *Pod"em*, 1988, 7, pp. 106–34. In this area the work of the thick journals and such weeklies as *Nedelia*, *Moskovskie novosti*, *Ogonek* and *Literaturnaia gazeta*, which have carried several studies of leading politicians, is thus complementary.
130. Chapters from Nadezhda Mandel'shtam, 'Vospominaniia', *Iunost'*, 1988, 8, pp. 34–61. Chapters covering the Voronezh period will be published in *Pod"em* in 1989. Evgeniia Ginzburg 'Krutoi marshrut. Khronika vremen kul'ta lichnosti', *Daugava*, 1988, 7, pp. 3–58; 8, pp. 9–64; 9, pp. 3–49, 10, pp. 3–50, 11, pp. 3–43 and following. Thirty chapters from this book also appeared in *Iunost'*, 1988, 9, pp. 36–67, making it accessible to an overwhelmingly larger, nationwide readership, and there are extracts in *V mire knig*, 1988, 12.
131. See Alla Latynina, 'Pisat' – eto bylo spasenie ... Vstrecha c Lidiei Chukovskoi', *Moskovskie novosti*, 1988, 17, p. 7. The memoirs are to appear in the journal, *Neva*, and in book form from the *Kniga* publishing house.
132. Sofiia Shved, 'Vospominaniia', *Ural*, 1988, 2, pp. 59–110. Other important memoirs include those of the writer Galina Serebriakova, 'Smerch', *Pod"em*, 1988, 7, pp. 20–72. Evgenii Gnedin, (d. 1983), foreign ministry spokesman from 1937 until his arrest in 1939, recalls the Sukhanovo monastery prison in 'Sebia ne poteriat' ', *Novyi mir*, 1988, 7, pp. 173–209. Ekaterina Meshcherskaia tells how she and her princess mother chose to embrace the revolutionary state, 'Trudovoe kreshchenie', ibid. 1988, 4, pp. 198–242. Bukharin's widow, Anna Larina, recalls her husband in 'Nezabyvaemoe', *Znamia*, 1988, 10, pp. 126–65; 11, pp. 112–80; 12, pp. 93–169.
133. Pavel Florenskii, 'Avtobiografiia', *Nashe nasledie*, 1988, 1, pp. 74–78; idem., 'Vospominaniia', *Literaturnaia ucheba*, 1988, 2, pp. 144–79; idem, 'Vremia i prostranstvo', *Sotsiologicheskie issledovaniia*, 1988, 1, pp. 100–14; idem, 'O literature', *Voprosy literatury*, 1988, 1, pp. 146–76. There are articles by Rozanov in *Literaturnaia ucheba*, 1988, 1, pp. 102–19; *Voprosy literatury*, 1988, 4, pp. 176–200; *Don*, 1988, 6, pp. 151–60 and *Literaturnaia Rossiia*, 1988, 39, pp. 18–19. Chapters from Nikolai Berdiaev's 'Mirosozertsanie Dostoevskogo' are in *Volga*, 1988,

10, pp. 146–63. On Berdiaev, see the interview with Iu.P. Azarov and extracts from Azarov's novel about him, in *Sovetskaia bibliografiia*, 1988, 2, pp. 66–80. In its issue for June 1988, *Voprosy filosofii* announced the forthcoming publication of the émigré philosophers Frank, Trubetskoi and Shestov. There is to be a two-volume edition of Vladimir Solov'ev (*Novye knigi*, 1988, 28, no. 6a).

134. 'Rasskazyvaiut byvshie voiny', *Znamia*, 1988, 7, pp. 185–219. A. Nikishin, 'V gostiakh – "Afgantsy" ', *ibid*, 10, pp. 235–37.
135. Chapters from Chaliapin's 'Maska i dusha' are in *Novyi mir*, 1988, 5, pp. 199–217; 6, pp. 182–204. The songs of the guitar poets have been appearing with music, as 'Pesni bardov' in issues of *V mire knig* from April 1988. The same journal began its 'Who is who in Western Rock Music' series in the issue for June 1988. For extracts from Artem Troitskii's 'Rock in the USSR', see *Rodnik*, 1988, 5, pp. 48–51; 6, pp. 48–51, etc. See also S. Dobrotvorskii, 'Pod zvukom shestistrunnoi liry', ibid., 1988, 6, pp. 42–46 on the 'rock poets'.
136. See pp. 36–39 of Dunlop 'Soviet Cultural Politics', op. cit. (note 10).
137. Aleksandr Lipkov, 'Proverka . . . na dorogakh', *Novyi mir*, 1987, 2, pp. 202–25. See also idem, 'Pervye uroki', *Rodnik*, 1988, 3, pp. 49–51; and 'Kino proizrastaet iz poezii', *Voprosy literatury*, 1986, 12, pp. 124–56, in which German talks to T. Iensen.
138. E. Bokshitskaia, 'Pouchitel'naia istoriia studenta VGIKa, a vposledstvii kinorezhissera tret'ei kategorii Aleksandra Sokurova', *Iunost'*, 1987, 2, pp. 9–13. For an interview with the new rector of VGIK, A. V. Novikov, see 'Kino nachinaetsia s? . . .', *Rodnik*, 1988, 3, pp. 40–41.
139. A. Bernshtein, 'Dva fil'ma i 630 metrov "kul'ta" ', *Ogonek*, 1988, 25, pp. 10–11; Iurii Tsiv'ian, 'Istoricheskii fil'm i dinamika vlasti: Trotskii i Stalin v sovetskom kino', *Daugava*, 1988, 4, pp. 98–101. For Romm's lectures see *Moskva*, 1987, 11, pp. 163–71; 12, pp. 169–74.
140. On the Union of Soviet Artists see Julia Wishnevsky, 'On the eve of the seventh congress of Soviet artists', *Radio Liberty Research*, RL 14/88, and Julia Wishnevsky, 'Andrei Vasnetsov, new head of the USSR artists' Union', RL 42/88.
141. 'Tret'iakovka segodnia', *Dekorativnoe iskusstvo*, 1988, 7, pp. 17–18. See also N. Semenova, 'Chto zhe proiskhodit s Tret'iakovkoi?', *Literaturnaia Rossiia*, 1988, 38, pp. 16–17.
142. On the Chagal exhibition see 'Vozvrashchenie Rodine', *Sovetskaia muzyka*, 1988, 3, pp. 73–76.
143. On the Filonov exhibition see *Pavel Nikolaevich Filonov. Zhivopis'. Grafika. Iz sobraniia Gosudarstvennogo Russkogo muzeia. Katalog vystavki* (Leningrad: 1988); and S. D. 'Filonovskaia vystavka v Leningrade', *Russkaia mysl'*, 3734, 1988, p. 13.
144. On the Malevich exhibition see Viktor Tsoffka, 'Suprematist Kazimir Malevich,' *Moskovskie novosti*, 1988, 9, p. 16; and A. Pistunova, 'Povesim kover kumachevyi . . .', *Literaturnaia Rossiia*, 1988, 49, pp. 19–20.
145. See A. Gracheva, 'Cherez gody zabveniia. Razdum'ia na vystavke v Tret'iakovke', ibid., 1988, 4, p. 13.

146. See *Russkoe teatral'no-dekorativnoe iskusstvo 1880–1930 iz kollektsii Nikity i Niny Lobanovykh-Rostovskikh. Katalog vystavki* (Moscow: 1988).
147. M. Shagal, 'Stikhi', *Inostrannaia literatura*, 1988, 5, pp. 34–40; idem 'Moia zhizn'', *Iunost'*, 1987, 12, pp. 62–66; 'O Marke Shagale', *V mire knig*, 1987, 12, pp. 57–64; 1988, 1, pp. 36–37, 57–63. On Filonov, see E. N. Glebova, 'Vospominaniia o brate', *Neva*, 1986, 10, pp. 148–76 and N. Troepol'skaia, 'Formula liubvi', *V mire knig*, 1987, 2, pp. 30–35; on Larionov, S. M. Romanovich, 'Vospominaniia o M. F. Larionove', *Pod"em*, 1988, 6, pp. 124–31; on Rodchenko, N. Troepol'skaia, '"Nevedomyi" Rodchenko', *V mire knig*, 1987, 11, pp. 38–43, 69; on Malevich, S. Bychkov, 'Iz otriada solntseliubov', *Iunost'*, 1988, 7, p. 32 and illustrations.
148. V. Voina, '... i tvortsy vernutsia v otechestvo', *Nedelia*, 1987, 31, pp. 20–21.
149. On the Bacon exhibition, see Charles Darwin, 'Surreal encounter', *Guardian*, 26 September 1988; and Giles Auty, 'Formal fallacy', *Spectator*, 1 October 1988. On modern Western art see E. Kliavin'sh, [Klaviņš] 'Poslednie desiatiletiia zapadnogo iskusstva. Kakimi oni byli?', *Rodnik*, 1988, 5, pp. 33–38.
150. See Aleksandr Glezer, 'Tridstat' let bor'by i pobed', *Strelets*, 1988, 1, pp. 44–47. The paintings of Oskar Rabin were not allowed to be shown. On a 1988 Moscow exhibition of Soviet *avant-garde* painters, see Iurii Nechiporenko, 'Nad chem smeetsia avangard?', *Sobesednik*, 1988, 41, p. 16.
151. On Sidur, see Iu. Levitanskii, 'Pamiatnik pogibshim ot liubvi', *Iunost'*, 1988, 11, pp. 87–89. On the Sotheby's sale, see E. Bespalova, 'Auktsion Sotbiz: London-Moskva', *Ogonek*, 1988, 26, p. 8, infix, pp. 1–4, p. 25; and Aleksandr Glezer, 'God pereloma', *Russkaia mysl'*, 3735, 1988, p. 11, which also details other recent developments.
152. Il'ia Kabakov, 'Tsypliata belye, tsypliata chernye. Sub"ektivnye zametki', *Literaturnaia gazeta*, 1987, 34, p. 8.
153. On Kandaurov see Jeff Gleisner, 'Pictures at an exhibition', *Detente*, 9–10, 1987, pp. 40–41.
154. On Sysoev see 'Rasskazyvaet Viacheslav Sysoev', *Russkaia mysl'*, 3677, 1987, p. 7; I. Shelkovskii, 'Ekspozitsiia Viacheslava Sysoeva v Oslo', ibid., 3691, 1987, p. 11; A. Ginzburg, 'Kartinki s vystavki', ibid., 3714, 1988, p. 11. The cartoon is in *Moskovskie novosti*, 1988, 8, p. 11. There is another cartoon by Sysoev, ibid., 1988, 31, p. 8. It is in the unmistakable style of those for which Sysoev was arrested in the Brezhnev period. Almost exactly the same cartoon is in V. Sysoev, 'Khodite tikho, govorite tikho' (Paris–New York: 1983), p. 83.
155. On Khrushchev and Iankilevskii, see 'V iskusstve – stalinist', *Russkaia mysl'*, 3706, 1988, p. 39. On the *Ogonek* Bol'shoi ballet piece, see a report by Iurii Stepanov, reprinted from the unofficial journal *Referendum*, no. 6, in *Russkaia mysl'*, 3720, 1988, p. 12. For the study of Baryshnikov, see *Teatral'naia zhizn'*, 1988, pp. 20–3.
156. *Inostrannaia literatura*'s decline in circulation of 17 per cent to 400 000 is documented in *Moscow News* (see note 1.)

157. Franz Kafka, *Zamok*, translated by Rita Wright-Kovaleva, *Inostrannaia literatura*, 1988, nos 1–3; Franz Kafka, *Zamok*, translated by G. Notkin, *Neva*, 1988, nos. 1–4.
158. Aldous Huxley, *O divnyi novyi mir, Inostrannaia literatura*, 1988, 4, pp. 13–126. George Orwell, *Skotnyi dvor, Rodnik*, 1988, nos 3–6. Two chapters from Animal Farm appeared as 'Skotskii ugolok' in *Nedelia*, 1988, 37, pp. 22–23, Arthur Koestler, *Slepiashchaia t'ma, Neva*, 1988, nos 7–8. Some of Orwell's essays are to be published by Progress publishers; see V. Chalikova, 'Vstrecha s Oruellom', *Knizhnoe obozrenie*, 1988, 21, pp. 13–14. *1984* is also in *Kodry* (Kishinev) 1988, 9–1989, 1.
159. Sue Townsend, 'Tiazhkoe otrochestvo Adriana Moula', *Inostrannaia literarura*, 1988, 7; Umberto Eco, *Imia rozy*, ibid., 1988, nos 8–10.
160. This information from ibid., 1988, 6, pp. 254–55. Three chapters from *Ulysses* were published in *Literaturnaia ucheba*, 1988, 1, pp. 170–92.
161. Eliot's *Murder in the Cathedral* is in *V mire knig*, 1988, 4. Virginia Woolf's *To the Lighthouse* is in *Novyi mir*, 1988, nos 9–10. There are Lorca poems in *Don*. 1988, 7. Apollinaire's programme of surrealist theatre is in *Teatr*, 1988, 4. I. Diushen considers Artaud in *Sovremennaia dramaturgiia*. 1988, 4. There are Vian stories in *Rodnik*, 1988, 1; Borges's *Cabbalah* in *Daugava*, 1988, 7; and Cummings poems in *Rodnik*, 1988, 6. Ken Kesey's *One Flew Over the Cuckoo's Nest* is in *Novy mir*, 1987, nos 7–10; Updike's *Rabbit is Rich*, ibid., 1986, nos 9–12.
162. Raymond Chandler's *Farewell My Lovely* is in *Pod''em*, 1988, no. 8–1989,—no. 3. Dashiel Hammett's *The Maltese Falcon* in *Literaturnyi Kirgizstan*, 1987, 8–1988, 4; John Le Carré's *The Looking Glass War* has been announced by *Prostor*. Mario Puzo's *The Godfather* is in *Znamia*, 1987, nos. 10–12; his *The Sicilian* in *Zvezda*, 1988, nos. 4–7. Agatha Christie's *Sparkling Cyanide* is in *Volga*, 1988, nos. 5, 6, 8 and 9; her *Dead Man's Folly* in *Don*, 1988, nos. 7–9.
163. For information on translations of English writers see Lesley Chamberlain, 'Under Eastern Eyes', *The Times Literary Supplement*, 15–21 July 1988, pp. 780, 788.
164. I. S. Gol'denberg, 'Anatomiia knizhnogo defitsita', *Sotsiologicheskie issledovaniia*, 1987, 6, pp. 68–77.
165. Tat'iana Zhuchkova, 'Komu povem tsifir' svoiu?', *Knizhnoe obozrenie*, 1988, 23, p. 2. On the book deficit see also, for example, 'Kak reshaetsia problema knizhnogo defitsita?', *Argumenty i fakty*, 1988, 16, p. 2.
166. Lev Gudkov and Boris Dubin, 'Literaturnaia kul'tura: protsess i ratsion', *Druzhba narodov*, 1988, 2, pp. 168–88. It would be difficult to overestimate the value and timeliness of this analysis. In a second piece, 'Raznost' potentsialov', ibid., 10, pp. 204–17, Gudkov and Dubin consider reader responses to their article.
167. On the setting-up of *Zharki* see *Literaturnaia gazeta*, 1987, 24. On plans for *Vest'*, see *Glasnost'*, 1, June 1987, p. vi (in *Russkaia mysl'*, 3682, 1987). On difficulties, see *Glasnost'*, 12, November 1987, p. 40 (in *Russkaia mysl'*, 3726, 1988). According to Condee and Padunov (note 15), p. 8, the Council of Ministers refused, on 23 October 1987, to permit publishing cooperatives. Nevertheless, Viacheslav Trofimovich

Kabanov, in his introduction to the extract from Erofeev's *Moscow – Petushki* published in *Nedelia*, 1988, 36, p. 14, announces that the new publishing house of which he is editor-in-chief, *Knizhnaia palata*, does intend to publish 'soon' a *Vest'* collection, including *Moscow – Petushki*.

168. On Cherkinskii see G. Borisov, 'Avtorskoe izdanie; puti i puty', *Knizhnoe obozrenie*, 1988, 28, p. 2. For the proposal for authorial publication, see ibid., 1988, 16, p. 2. For resistance from publishing houses, see ibid., 1988, 33, p. 4.
169. See *The Times Literary Supplement*, 22–28 July 1988, p. 804.
170. On new publishing houses see *V mire knig*, 1988, 3, p. 74 (on the *Knizhnaia palata* house); and *Knizhnoe obozrenie*, 1988, 31, p. 2. On new attitudes at the *Khudozhestvennaia literatura* publishing house, see ibid., 1988, 8, p. 4.
171. On express publishing, see ibid., 1988, 5, pp. 1–2 and 23, p. 7. On readers' favourite books, see ibid., 1988, 13, p. 10; 18, pp. 8–9; 23, p. 5.
172. On pricing policy, see ibid., 1988, 14, pp. 2–3; 29, p. 2.
173. Ibid., 1988, 34, pp. 8–9.
174. *Sovetskaia kul'tura*, 9 July 1988.
175. See, for example, ' "Limit" na podpisku', *Ogonek*, 1988, 33, pp. 2–3; V. Lakshin, 'Ob iskusstvennom defitsite', *Moskovskie novosti*, 1988, 34, p. 3; A. Romanov, 'Pressa, kotoruiu my vybivaem', ibid., 1988, 35, pp. 4, 13.
176. See above, p. 125. I wish to thank Martin Dewhirst and David Saunders for drawing my attention to materials used in this survey. I am also particularly grateful to Mr Dewhirst for his exhaustive comments on a draft version of the article.

## POSTSCRIPT: SOME RECENT DEVELOPMENTS

The vociferous campaign against limits on print-runs and subscriptions for 1989 led to a compromise in which some papers and journals were allowed to raise their circulations, though not to the extent they would have wished. *Ogonek* was permitted to raise its 1989 circulation to 3 083 000 (almost all of it seemingly sold on subscription), *Novyi mir* to 1 556 000, *Druzhba narodov* to 1 095 000. Among newspapers, *Argumenty i fakty* reached 20 458 000, and *Literaturnaia gazeta* 6 277 000.[1]

It is not at all surprising that the journals should remain so popular, since they continue to provide a provocative and stimulating diet. There have been two more Nabokov novels, *Despair* in *Volga* (1989, 1–2) and *Pnin* in *Inostrannaia literatura* (1989, 2). Pil'niak's *Mahogany* is in *Druzhba narodov* (1989, 1) and Zabolotskii's prison letters in *Znamia* (1989, 1). Publication of Frederick Forsyth's thriller *The Day of the Jackal*, forcibly interrupted at the Alma Ata journal *Prostor* in February 1974, was restarted in December 1988, to the delight of readers, and completed by February 1989. There has been something of an Orwell boom. The long-awaited *Novyi mir* serialisation of *1984* ran from February to April 1989, but by then the Moldavian Russian language journal *Kodry* (Kishinev) had completed its own serialisation (1988, 9–1989, 1). *Animal Farm*, previously published in *Rodnik* (Riga; see note 158), was started by *Literaturnyi Kirgizstan* (Frunze) 1989, 1. There were two Orwell stories in *Znamia* (1989, 1), and a number of book publications are also announced. *Rodnik* caused a sensation by publishing in its October 1988 issue, as an illustration to Leonid Dobychin's story 'The Town of N', a cartoon of Lenin trapped in a mousetrap. The local Riga press rebuked *Rodnik*, and warned its editors to be always aware of their responsibilities on a journal intended for young people. *Rodnik* continues to show enterprise, however, including in its March 1989 issue an interview with the film director Aleksandr Sokurov taken from the unofficial Moscow cinema journal *Sine-fantom*. The serialisation of the New Testament by *V mire knig*, on the other hand, has been at least temporarily suspended. Despite indications in both the November and December issues (which included the Gospel according to Saint Matthew) that the publication would continue, neither the January nor the February issue did in fact do so.

Readers used to finding equally absorbing matter in the historico-political sections of the journals have not been disappointed either. Among articles of particular importance are Nikolai Shmelev's 'Either force or the rouble' in *Znamia* (1989, 1), S. Andreev's 'The structure of power and the tasks of society' in *Neva* (1989, 1) and Igor' Kliamkin's 'Why is it difficult to speak the truth? (Selected passages from the history of a certain illness)' in *Novyi mir* (1989, 2). Roi Medvedev has, no doubt to his own wry pleasure, become the journals' favourite historian: his 'On Stalin and Stalinism' is in *Znamia* (1989, 1–4), 'The Difficult Spring of 1918' in *Volga* (1989, 1–2), chapters from 'They Surrounded Stalin' (*All Stalin's Men*) in *Iunost'* (1989, 3), with the Khrushchev study to come in *Druzhba narodov*. In Robert Conquest's *The Great Terror* the literary bureaucrat N. V. Lesiuchevskii was described as 'generally supposed in the Soviet Union' to have denounced the writers Benedikt Livshits, Boris Kornilov, Elena Tager and Nikolai Zabolotskii.[2] A recent issue of the newspaper *Literaturnaia Rossiia* (1989, 10) under the banner headline *Denunciation* prints Lesiuchevskii's false and poisonous reports on Kornilov and Zabolotskii.

The most noticeable development in early 1989, however, was a spectacular increase in the number of publications of the work of living, third-wave émigrés. In December 1988 *Novyi mir* published three poems by Iuz Aleshkovskii, including the notorious 'Comrade Stalin, You're a Great Scholar', and *Iunost'* began serialisation of Voinovich's *The Life and Adventures of Private Ivan Chonkin* (1988, 12–1989, 2). After the death of Iulii Daniel', on 30 December 1988, Andrei Siniavskii and his wife, Mariia Rozanova, arrived in the USSR on a visit and were interviewed by both *Moscow News* ('Emigration is a horrible but instructive experience', 1989, 2) and *Knizhnoe obozrenie* (' "There they consider us Reds" ', 1989, 2). Also in January, *Druzhba narodov* published Voinovich's story 'By means of mutual correspondence', turned down by *Novyi mir* in 1987. February saw the appearance of Vladimov's *Faithful Ruslan* (*Znamia*, 1989, 2), and of Siniavskii's article 'The myths of Mikhail Zoshchenko' (*Voprosy literatury*, 1989, 2). (A stream of interesting publications in this journal over recent months makes the strictures expressed against it in the body of my article anachronistic). The Brodskii affair is examined at length by Ia. Gordon in *Neva* (1989, 2), and by N. Iakimchuk in *Iunost'* (1989, 2). At the same time *Inostrannaia literatura* began a series of interviews with émigré writers. Siniavskii, Vladimov, Voinovich, Korzhavin and Zinov'ev were interviewed in the February issue, to be followed in March by Aksenov, Etkind, Kopelev, Orlova, the returnee Odoevtseva, Sokolov, Dovlatov and Tsvetkov. March also saw Sokolov's *A School for Fools* in *Oktiabr'*, Korzhavin poems in *Novyi mir* and Voinovich's play *The Tribunal* in *Teatr*. Most remarkably, up to the time of writing, the ever-resourceful *Rodnik* published in *its* March issue a speech made by Aleksandr Solzhenitsyn in Zurich on 31 May 1974, three months after his expulsion from the USSR, on receiving a prize from Italian journalists. This is another small gain for those campaigning to see Solzhenitsyn's writings republished in the USSR.

The sudden influx of many alternative voices from Russian emigration into the Soviet press marks a further stage in the pluralising of officially tolerable opinion that the multiplicity of published readings of the Soviet past had already contributed to. Indeed, the pluralising of opinion can sometimes find startlingly complex expression. Soon after the émigré Andrei Siniavskii's interviews appeared in the official Soviet press, attacks on him in the unofficial Soviet press over an interview he had given to the French press were reprinted in a French émigré newspaper.[3] Clearly the strict barriers between Soviet and émigré voices, between official and unofficial voices, are under siege. The *Almanakh* group of poets, heard in London in March 1989 (themselves a microcosm of the new polyphony through their very different concerns and voices) have been published in the émigré press, in the unofficial Soviet press, and are beginning to appear in the official Soviet press.[4] But their 'Poets' Evening' at the Pushkin Theatre in Moscow is sponsored by the 'Creative Workshops' of the new Union of Theatre Workers, and their *Almanakh* is to be published by a new theatrical publishing house.

Monophony, a term used for decades to describe the voice of official Soviet culture, is at the time of writing no longer applicable. An ever greater, ever more 'normal' polyphony can now be detected. Readers both within the Soviet Union and abroad owe a debt of gratitude to Soviet writers, critics and editorial boards for seizing the opportunities that *glasnost'* has offered them.

### Notes to the Postscript

1. Figures taken from *Trud*, 25 December 1988, p. 4. See also *Sotsiologicheskie issledovaniia*, 1988, 6, pp. 60–63, for detailed analysis of rises in 1988 circulations and useful charts.
2. R. Conquest, *The Great Terror*, Penguin, Harmondsworth, 1971, p. 447.
3. Open letters to Siniavskii from Sergei Grigoriants (chief editor of *Glasnost'*), Aleksandr Podrabinek (chief editor of *Ekspress-khronika*) and Valerii Senderov, published in *Russkaia mysl'*, 3760, 27 January 1989, p. 13. Their main objection was to Siniavskii's description of Mr Gorbachev as 'the Soviet Union's Number One Dissident'. For further evidence of vitality of the Soviet independent press, see the detailed stenogramme of the first meeting of editors of independent journals reprinted in *Grani*, 148, 1988, pp. 276–309.
4. See especially 'Al'manakh', *Teatral'naia zhizn'*, 1988, 18, pp. 30–32.

# Index of Names

Abdrashitov, V.   45, 63, 64, 68
Abuladze, T.   46, 77, 128
Adamovich, A.   23, 64
Adylov, A.   17, 23
Adzhubei, A.   129, 150
Adzhubei, N.   149
Afanas'ev, Iu.   15, 121, 141, 145, 149
Aganbegian, A.   28, 40
Aigi, G.   116
Aitmatov, Ch.   113, 139, 141
Aizenberg, A.   18, 25
Akhmatova, A.   109, 110, 112, 124, 130
Aksenov, A.   6, 8, 24
Aksenov, V.   117, 118, 119, 121, 144, 146, 156
Albéra, F.   71, 73
Aldanov, M.   112
Aleksandrov, G.   74
Alekseev, M.   110, 121, 125, 126, 143
Aleshkovskii, Iu.   24, 156
Alimpiev, I.   71
*Alisa* (rock group)   106
Allen, W.   122
*Almanakh* (group of poets)   157
Alov, A.   65
Ambartsumov, E.   129, 149
Amiel, V.   70, 71
Amlinskii, V.   150
Anan'ev, A.   108, 136, 149
Andreev, G.   145
Andreev, S.   155
Andreeva, N.   4, 9, 30, 31, 37, 129
Andropov, Iu.   33
Antonov, S.   109, 113
Apollinaire, G.   133, 153
*Aquarium* (rock group)   101, 102
Arabov, Iu.   65
Arakelian, Iu.   35
Arbatov, G.   37
Arkhipova, I.   91

Aronov, G.   50
Arro, V.   116, 142
Artaud, A.   133, 153
Asanova, D.   56, 71
Askokova, L.   7, 23, 24
Askol'dov, A.   53, 54, 71
Astaf'ev, V.   108, 113, 149
Atlantov, V.   98
*Autograph* (rock group)   102
Auty, G.   152
Averbakh, I.   56, 71
Averchenko, A.   112
Averintsev, S.   148
Azarov, Iu.   151
Azhaev, V.   113

Babel', I.   112, 146
Bach, J. S.   96
Bacon, F.   131, 152
Baklanov, G.   107, 121, 136, 143
Balaian, R.   77
Baliazin, V.   149
Barber, J.   140
Barnet, B.   74
Barshchevskii, D.   14
Barthes, R.   122
Baruzdin, S.   108
Baryshnikov, M.   132, 152
Baturin, Iu.   42
Bazunov, O.   116
Beckett, S.   122
Bek, A.   107, 113, 114, 121, 140
Bek, T.   121
Belaia, G.   121, 145, 149
Beliaev, I.   14
Belinkov, A.   109, 119
Belov, V.   4, 111, 113
Belyi, A.   112
Berberova, N.   136
Berdiaev, N.   130, 150
Berggol'ts, O.   114
Bergman, I.   133
Beriia, L.   66, 129

Berman, B. 69
Bernshtein, A. 151
Bespalova, E. 152
Bibik, V. 96
Bitov, A. 107, 115
Blanchot, M. 122
Bocharov, A. 119, 122, 144, 145, 146
Bodrov, S. 65, 66
Bogatyreva, E. 91
Bogomolov, Iu. 77
Bokshitskaia, E. 151
Bondarchuk, S. 45, 46, 47, 52, 65, 75
Bondarev, Iu. 4
Borges, J.-L. 122, 133, 153
Borisov, G. 154
Borodin, L. 115
Borodin Quartet 98, 105
Bovin, A. 37
Bragg, B. 102
Brauns, M. 101
Bresson, R. 57
Brezhnev, L. I. 13, 15, 16, 19, 23, 26, 28, 33, 34, 45, 47, 60, 65, 79, 80, 109, 123, 125, 135, 152
Brodskii, I. 107, 118, 119, 121, 124, 137, 143, 144, 147, 156
Brokaw, T. 41
Bukharin, N. 14, 18, 28, 123, 130, 146, 150
Bukovskii, V. 117
Bulgakov, M. 23, 65, 79, 85, 107, 108, 109, 110, 112, 126, 139, 148
Bunin, I. 143
Buñuel, L. 68
Burlatskii, F. 28, 31, 37, 40, 41, 136
Burtin, Iu. 124, 125, 126, 129, 135, 140, 147, 148, 149
Bychkov, S. 152
Bykov, R. 48, 51, 54, 65, 70
Bykov, V. 60

Catherine the Great 136
Chagal, M. 54, 131, 151, 152
Chaianov, A. 112, 149
Chaliapin, F. 56, 71, 130, 151
Chalikova, V. 147, 153

Chamberlain, L. 153
Chandler, R. 133, 153
Chaplin, C. 54
Chekhov, A. 66, 85
Cherkinskii, Iu. 134, 154
Chernenko, K. 28
Chernyi, S. 112
Chernykh, V. 65
Chiaureli, M. 75
Christie, A. 133, 153
Christie, I. 4, 69, 72
Chudakova, M. 110, 112, 126, 148
Chukhontsev, O. 107
Chukhrai, G. 75
Chukovskaia, E. 145
Chukovskaia, L. 108, 114, 115, 121, 130, 141, 150
Chukovskii, K. 112
Chulaki, M. 116, 142
Chuprinin, S. 141, 142, 144, 146
Ciment, M. 72
Clark, K. 139
Condee, N. 138, 139, 143, 153
Connolly, R. 133
Conquest, R. 155, 157
*Copernicus* (rock group) 101
*Cruise* (rock group) 99, 102
cummings, e. e. 133, 153
Cushing, G. 5

Dali, S. 131
Dalrymple, S. 142
Daneliia, G. 46, 65
Daney, S. 72
Daniel', Iu. 115, 124, 141, 147, 156
Danilov, V. 128, 129, 149
Darwin, C. 152
Dashkevich, V. 94
Davies, R. W. 148
Davis, B. 50
Decaux, E. 70, 72
Dejevsky, M. 3
Dement'ev, A. 109
Dement'eva, I. 147
Demichev, P. 88
Demin, V. 77
Denisov, E. 94
Derobert, E. 70, 71
Dewhirst, M. 137, 154

# Index of Names

*Dialogue* (rock group) 102
Dimmock, M. 9
Dingley, J. 4
Diushen, I. 153
Dmitriev, V. 77
Dmitrii, Father 17
Dobrotvorskii, S. 151
Dobuzhinskii, M. 131
Dobychin, L. 155
Dodin, L. 84
Dolinina, N. 148
Dolmatovskaia, G. 69
Dombrovskii, Iu. 114
Donne, J. 144
Dorizo, N. 148
Dostoevskii, F. M. 79, 150
Dovlatov, S. 156
Dovzhenko, A. 54, 60, 74
Doyle, T. 20, 25
Drevin, A. 131
Dubin, B. 126, 134, 148, 153
Dudintsev, V. 108, 113, 122, 124, 141
Dunlop, J. 139, 151
Duras, M. 122
Durrell, G. 20
Dykhovichnyi, I. 66
Dzhordzhadze, N. 64
Dzhugashvili, Ia. 127, 148

Eco, U. 153
Efremov, O. 81, 83
Efros, A. 79
Einstein, A. 14
Eisenstein, S. 44, 54, 57, 73, 74, 75, 123, 130
Ekster, A. 131
Elagin, Iu. 146
Eliot, T. S. 133, 153
El'tsin, B. 37, 39, 40, 41
Epshtein, M. 116, 142
Erdman, N. 109, 112
Eresko, B. 100
Ermash, F. 47, 59, 62
Ermler, F. 75
Erofeev, Venedikt 116, 154
Erofeev, Viktor 143
Esenin, S. 150
Etkind, E. 119, 121, 149, 156

Evtushenko, E. 121, 123
Ezhov, N. 129

Fadeev, A. 124
Fedorenko, N. 133
Fedorov, S. 65
Fedosov, V. 52
Fedotov, A. 91
Feuchtwanger, L. 149
Filonov, P. 131, 151, 152
Florenskii, Father P. 130, 150
Fonvizin, D. 125
Forsyth, F. 155
Fowles, J. 133
Frank, H. 66
Frank, S. 151
Frayn, M. 84
Freidenberg, O. 108
Freidin, Iu. 72

Gabai 48, 72
Gakkel, S. 101
Galich, A. 13, 48, 106, 119, 144
Galin, A. 84, 117, 143
Gerasimov, G. 108
Gerasimov, S. 47
German, A. 50, 51, 52, 53, 60, 64, 70, 72, 73, 76, 77, 122, 130, 151
German, Iu. 50
Gershtein, E. 109
Gessen, E. 138, 145
Gillespie, D. 140
Ginzburg, A. 152
Ginzburg, E. 129, 150
Gippius, Z. 112
Glebova, E. 152
Gleisner, J. 152
Glenny, M. 3
Glezer, A. 152
Gluck, C. W. 96
Gnedin, E. 150
Gogol', N. V. 139, 141
Gol'denberg, I. 133, 153
Golovkov, A. 145
Goncharov, A. 18
Goncharova, N. 131
Gorbachev, M. S. 3, 5, 6, 8, 16, 22, 26, 27, 28, 29, 30, 31, 32, 33, 34, 37, 39, 40, 41, 42, 43, 44, 46, 66,

Gorbachev—*contd*
   78, 80, 86, 95, 117, 120, 148, 157
Gorbacheva, R.   36
Gorbanevskaia, N.   142
Gordon, Ia.   156
Gorelov, P.   117
Gor'kii, M.   68, 112
Goscillo, H.   141
Gracheva, A.   151
Gradskii, A.   20, 25, 101
Graffy, J.   3, 69, 70, 71, 146
Granin, D.   113, 124, 141, 147
Grebenshchikov, B.   102
Greene, G.   133
Grenkov, V.   92
Grigoriants, S.   38, 39, 157
Grishin, V.   33
Grodberg, G.   91
Grossman, V.   34, 54, 108, 113, 135, 145
Gubaidulina, S.   94, 105
Gubenko, N.   147
Gubin, D.   123
Gudkov, L.   126, 134, 148, 153
Gukovskii, G.   148
Gumilev, N.   58, 112, 121
Günther, H.   5
Gurchenko, L.   52

Haley, G.   8, 25
Hammett, D.   133, 153
Hesse, H.   122
Hitler, A.   14, 144
Hosking, G.   5, 140
Huxley, A.   133, 153

Iagoda, G.   129
Iakimchuk, N.   156
Iakovlev, A.   88
Iakovlev, E.   30, 40, 65, 108
Iakovlev, Ia.   128
Iampol'skii, M.   58, 71, 77
Iankilevskii, V.   132, 152
Iansons, M.   98, 105
Iensen, T.   151
Il'ina, N.   126, 138, 147
Ioseliani, O.   46, 60, 76

Iskander, F.   114, 121, 122, 134, 140, 145
Iskenderov, A.   128
Iurasov, D.   146, 147
Iur'enen, S.   139
Iutkevich, S.   47, 148
Ivanov, A.   23, 25, 111, 125, 139, 147
Ivanov, G. (Deputy Minister of Culture)   92
Ivanov, G. (émigré poet)   112
Ivanov, O.   91
Ivanov, Viacheslav   112
Ivanov, Viktor   111
Ivanov, Vsevolod   112
Ivanova, N.   140, 141, 143
Ivanova, V.   77
Ivnev, R.   150

John, E.   101
Joravsky, D.   140

Kabakov, I.   132, 152
Kabanov, V.   154
Kafka, F.   110, 133, 153
Kaganovich, L.   128
Kagarlitskii, B.   42, 146
Kaidanovskii, A.   67
Kalatozov, M.   58, 74, 75
Kaledin, S.   116, 142
Kamenev, L.   128
Kaminskii, G.   128
Kamshalov, A.   62
Kandaurov, O.   132, 152
Kandinskii, V.   131
Kapitsa, P.   14
Karaganov, A.   45
Karamzin, N.   110, 127, 148
Kariakin, Iu.   114, 124, 125, 126, 129, 141, 147, 150
Karpov, V.   92, 120, 121
Kasack, W.   145
Kasparov, G.   24
Kaverin, V.   147
Kesey, K.   153
Khachaturian, A.   92
Khanin, G.   128, 149
Kharitonov, E.   115
Kharms, D.   112

Kheifits, I.  64
Khlebnikov, V.  58, 112
Khodasevich, V.  112, 117, 145
Kholopov, G.  110, 111, 138
Khrennikov, T.  88, 92, 93, 106
Khrushchev, N. S.  3, 13, 28, 46, 59, 60, 61, 69, 79, 129, 132, 135, 136, 150, 152, 155
Khutsiev, M.  46, 61, 72, 75, 76
Kichin, V.  69, 70, 77
Kiiaschchenko, N.  91
Kiisk, K.  59, 60
Kinchev, K.  106
Kirov, S.  53
Kitson, C.  70, 73
Klavinš, E.  see under Kliavin'sh, E.
Kliamkin, I.  128, 149, 155
Kliavin'sh, E.  152
Klimov, E.  45, 46, 50, 54, 55, 60, 63, 64, 66, 68, 69, 70, 72, 77, 92
Klimov, V.  91
Kliuchevskii, V.  148
Kliuev, N.  112, 114
Koestler, A.  133, 153
Kolobov, A.  98
Kolosov, S.  65
Kol'tsov, M.  40, 146
Konchalovskii, A.  44, 46, 59, 61, 72, 76
Konchalovskii, M.  91
Kondrat'ev, V.  143
Kononykhin, S.  24
Kopelev, L.  136, 156
Korchnoi, V.  48
Kornilov, B.  155, 156
Kornilov, V.  115, 141
Korolev, S.  13
Korotich, V.  30, 41, 107
Korotkova, G.  92, 97
Korzhavin, N.  119, 144, 156
Kosygin, A.  79
Kovalenko, A.  16
Kozintsev, G.  57, 71, 74
Koz'min, M.  108
Kravchenko, L.  20, 21, 24, 25
Krivulin, V.  116, 142
Kublanovskii, Iu.  119, 136
Kuchment, M.  140
Kukushkin (Academician)  15

Kuleshov, L.  130
Kulidzhanov, L.  44, 45, 46, 69
Küng, H.  122
Kuniaev, S.  147
Kuraev, M.  116
Kushner, A.  118, 147
Kuzmin, M.  112
Kuz'minov, G.  148
Kuznetsov, E.  117
Kuznetsov, G.  9
Kuznetsova, N.  145

Lacan, J.  122
Laird, S.  142, 143
Lakshin, V.  107, 126, 143, 147, 148, 154
Larina, A.  150
Larionov, M.  131, 152
Latsis, O.  149
Latynina, A.  142, 148, 150
Laurent, N.  69
Le Carré, J.  133, 153
Leibovskii, V.  20, 24, 25
Lem, S.  122
Lenin, V. I.  1, 14, 18, 86, 87, 128, 130, 138, 143, 155
Lennon, J.  133
Leskov, N.  67
Lesnevskii, S.  142, 148
Lesiuchevskii, N.  155, 156
Levitanskii, Iu.  152
Leyda, J.  72
Liashenko, B.  24, 25
Liasko, K.  148
Ligachev, E.  30, 31, 40
Likhachev, D.  148
Limonov, E.  119
Lipkin, S.  108, 115, 141
Lipkov, A.  70, 151
Lisichkin, G.  136
Lisnianskaia, I.  115, 141
Liubimov, Iu.  3, 48, 79, 80, 117, 124, 147
Livshits, B.  155
Lobanov, M.  147
Lobanov-Rostovskii, Nikita  131, 152
Lobanov-Rostovskii, Nina  131, 152

Loginov, V.   18, 25
Lopushanskii, K.   66, 67
Lorca, F. Garcia   133, 153
Lotman, M.   144, 147
Lubarskii, C.   145
Lunacharskii, A.   56, 71

McLaughlin, S.   50
Machavariani, A.   94
Mahler, G.   96
Makanin, V.   107, 116, 142
Maksimov, Iu.   148
Maksimov, V.   117, 145
Malenkov, G.   124
Malevich, K.   131, 151, 152
Malikov, E.   24, 25
Malmstad, J.   146
Mamin, Iu.   67, 68
Mandel'shtam, N.   129, 150
Mandel'shtam, O.   62, 72, 109, 112, 121, 135, 145
Mao Tse Dun   144
Mark, Father   12
Martynenko, O.   140
Marx, K.   136
Maugham, S.   50
Medvedev, R.   13, 135, 136, 140, 155
Medvedev, V.   137
Medvedkin, A.   67, 74
Meierkhol'd, V.   78, 123, 146, 147
Mel'nikova, O.   7, 25
Men'shov, V.   65
Merezhkovskii, D.   112
Meshcherskaia, E.   150
Miagkov, B.   72
Mickiewicz, E.   8, 25
Mikael'ian, S.   65
Mikhalkov, N.   45, 58, 76, 77
Mikhalkov, S.   134
Mikhalkov-Konchalovskii, A.   see under Konchalovskii, A.
Mikhalkovich, V.   77
Miliband, R.   141, 148
Mindadze, A.   68
Mishima, Y.   133
Molchanov, V.   24
Molière, J.-B. P.   85
Molotov, V.   36, 128

Mozhaev, B.   109, 113, 124, 128, 140
Muratov, A.   49
Muratov, S.   70, 73
Muratova, K.   49, 50, 63, 68, 70, 71, 76
Murav'eva, I.   142

Nabokov, V.   108, 109, 110, 112, 133, 135, 139, 145
Naumov, V.   65
Nazarov, M.   139
Nechiporenko, Iu.   152
Neizvestnyi, E.   117
Nekrasov, V.   117, 119, 144
Nemirovich-Danchenko, V.   83
Nightingale, A.   106
Nikich, O.   19, 25
Nikishin, A.   151
Nikolaev, G.   111
Nikolai, Metropolitan   14
Nikol'skii, B.   108
Nikulin, Iu.   52
Norr, H.   23, 25
Norstein, Iu.   77
Notkin, G.   153
Nove, A.   146
Novikov, A.   151
Nuikin, A.   128, 149

Obolduev, G.   112
Obraztsova, E.   98
Odoevtseva, I.   110, 138, 156
Ogorodnikov, V.   66, 106
Oistrakh, D.   98
Oistrakh, I.   91
Okeev, T.   59, 60
Okudzhava, B.   113, 114, 134, 140, 143
Oleinikov, N.   112
Olenin, B.   10, 25
Olesha, Iu.   60, 72, 109
Olkhovsky, A.   105
Orlov, Iu.   117
Orlova, R.   156
Orwell, G.   110, 122, 133, 153, 155
Osorgin, M.   112
Otsup, N.   112
Ovcharov, S.   67

## Index of Names

Padunov, V.  138, 139, 143, 153
Panfilov, G.  61, 68, 76, 143
Panov, A.  20, 25
Paradzhanov, S.  59, 64, 75
Parkhomenko, S.  150
Passek, J.-L.  72
Pasternak, B.  34, 108, 109, 112, 124, 143, 147
Pasternak, Z.  112
Pauls, R.  101, 106
Peckinpah, S.  66
Peleshian, A.  58, 71, 72, 76
Pethybridge, R.  5
Petrov, N.  91
Petrov, V.  75
Petrushevskaia, L.  117, 142
P'etsukh, V.  116
Pichul, V.  67
Pikaizen, V.  91
Pil'niak, B.  107, 112, 114, 154
Pinter, H.  85, 122
Pirandello, L.  84, 85
Pistunova, A.  151
Pittman, R.  139
Plakhov, A.  45, 47, 77
Platonov, A.  55, 60, 107, 108, 109, 112, 114
Pliushch, L.  117
Podnieks, J.  47, 66
Podrabinek, A.  38, 157
Poliakov, Iurii (historian)  28, 41, 141
Poliakov, Iurii (writer)  12, 116
Polikarpov, V.  149
Poloka, G.  65
Popov, E.  115, 119, 141, 142, 144, 146
Popov, G.  149
Popov, V.  149
Porter, R.  139
Pound, E.  122
Pozner, V.  10
Prigov, D.  116
Pristavkin, A.  113, 136
Prokofiev, S.  92
Proshkin, A.  66
Proskurin, P.  125, 126
Pudovkin, V.  73, 74
Pugacheva, A.  102

Pushkin, A. S.  80
Puzo, M.  111, 133, 153

Rabin, O.  152
Radishchev, A.  125
Rahr, A.  41
Rainer, Y.  50
Raizman, Iu.  45, 63, 64, 65, 75
Rapoport, Ia.  148
Rapoport, N.  149
Rashidov, Sh.  123
Raskol'nikov, F.  149, 150
Rasputin, V.  4, 60, 113
Rassadin, S.  119, 147
Razlogov, K.  77
Razumovskaia, L.  12
Reddaway, P.  40, 41
Reed, J.  127
Rein, E.  141
Rekhviashvili, A.  64
Remizov, A.  112
Remnick, D.  24
Revault d'Allones, F.  72
Riazanov, E.  19, 20, 24, 25, 65, 66, 76, 119, 144
Riazantseva, N.  70, 71
Rice, C.  3, 4
Richter, S.  98
Rilke, R. M.  108
Robbe-Grillet, A.  122
Robinson, D.  70
Rodchenko, A.  131, 152
Romanov, General  54
Romanov, A.  154
Romanov, P.  112
Romanovich, S.  152
Romm, M.  75, 129, 130, 132, 150, 151
Room, A.  72, 73
Roshchin, S.  9
Rostotskii, S.  46
Rozanov, V.  130, 150
Rozanova, M.  41, 156
Rozenbaum, A.  12
Rubanova, I.  77
Rubinchik, V.  64
Rudnitskii, K.  123, 146
Russell, K.  55

Rybakov, A. 108, 113, 114, 141, 145
Rybnikov, A. 103
Rykov, A. 130, 150

Sakharov, Aleksei 66
Sakharov, Andrei 14, 22, 34, 141
Sakhnin, A. 147
Salutskii, A. 147
Sartre, J.-P. 133
Saunders, D. 154
Schmidt-Häuer, C. 41
Schnabel, J. 131
Schultz, B. 122
Schwarz, B. 105
Segal, Iu. 45
Seliunin, V. 127, 128, 149
Semeniuk, V. 71
Semenova, N. 151
Senderov, V. 157
Serebriakova, G. 150
*Seven Simeons, The* (musical ensemble) 35, 36
Severianin, I. 112
Shakespeare, W. 84
Shakhnazarov, K. 65, 66
Shalamov, V. 109, 114, 123, 140, 146
Shanin, T. 149
Sharapov, Iu. 18, 25
Shatrov, M. 86, 107, 109, 113, 114, 122, 140, 141, 149
Shaw, G. B. 55
Shchedrin, R. 92, 93, 103
Shekhovtsev, I. 23
Shelkovskii, I. 152
Shengelaia, E. 45
Shepit'ko, L. 46, 60, 76, 77
Shershenevich, V. 112
Shestov, L. 151
Shevelev, G. 9, 10, 24
Shilova, I. 69
Shklovskii, V. 43, 69
Shmelev, G. 128, 149
Shmelev, N. 28, 40, 116, 127, 142, 149, 155
Shnitke, A. 54, 94, 105
Sholokhov, M. 143
Shostakovich, D. 92
Shpikovskii, N. 62
Shtein, A. 149
Shukshin, V. 46, 59, 64, 72, 76, 113
Shumiatskii, B. 43, 68
Shvarts, Elena 116
Shvarts, Evgenii 112
Shved, S. 130, 150
Sidorov, I. 50
Sidur, V. 132, 152
Simanovich, G. 19, 25
Simonov, K. 52, 129, 149
Simonov, V. 147
Siniavskii, A. 115, 119, 121, 124, 141, 145, 147, 156, 157
*Sipoli* (rock group) 101
Slavkin, V. 85, 117, 143
Slusser, R. 134
Slutskii, B. 114
Smekhov, V. 124, 147
Smelianskii, A. 84
Smiley, X. 41
Smirnov, A. 45, 54, 60, 61, 65, 71
Smith, G. 140
Sokolov, S. 119, 144, 156
Sokurov, A. 50, 53, 54, 55, 56, 57, 58, 63, 65, 66, 68, 71, 130, 151, 155
Solov'ev, Sergei (film director) 65, 66
Solov'ev, Sergei (historian) 148
Solov'ev, V. 151
Solov'eva, I. 77
Solzhenitsyn, A. 117, 119, 120, 121, 137, 138, 140, 141, 143, 144, 145, 156
Solzhenitsyna, N. 120, 145
Somov, K. 131
Stalin, I. V. 2, 13, 14, 15, 23, 27, 28, 31, 44, 45, 62, 68, 78, 79, 86, 87, 114, 121, 124, 125, 127, 128, 129, 130, 134, 135, 136, 140, 143, 146, 148, 149, 151, 155
Stanislavskii, K. 78, 83
Starostin, A. 92
Starr, S. 105, 106
Stavronskii, A. 91
Stepanov, Iu. 152
Stratanovskii, S. 116
Strauss, R. 96

# Index of Names

Stravinsky, I. 96
Strelianyi, A. 107, 116, 119, 120, 136, 142, 144
Strugatskii, A. N. and B. N. 109
Sturua, R. 86
Suetnov, A. 119, 144
Svechnikova, E. 99
Sverdlov, Ia. 87, 130
Sysoev, V. 132, 152

Tabakov, O. 85
Tager, E. 155
Talalai, M. 38
Talankin, I. 46
Tariverdiev, M. 95
Tarkovskii, Andrei 45, 46, 53, 54, 56, 57, 58, 61, 66, 67, 71, 75, 76, 77, 117
Tarkovskii, Arsenii 114
Taylor, R. 69, 73
Tedstrom, J. 149
Temirkanov, Iu. 98, 105
Tendriakov, V. 114, 140
Terekhov, G. 121, 145
Tikhonov (academician) 14
Tolkien, J. R. 122
Tolmachev, V. 17
Tolstaia, T. 116, 141, 143, 144
Tolz, V. 41, 42, 149
Tovstonogov, G. 79
Townsend, S. 153
Trauberg, L. 71, 74
Trifonov, Iu. 113, 124, 147
Troepol'skaia, N. 152
Troitskii, A. 101, 105, 106, 151
Trotskii, L. 86, 128, 129, 130, 151
Trubetskoi, S. 151
Trukhanovskii, V. 128
Tsamutali, A. 148
Tsiv'ian, Iu. 151
Tsoffka, V. 151
Tsvetaeva, M. 108, 112, 124
Tsvetkov, A. 119, 156
Tsvetov, V. 20, 24, 25
Tsvik, V. 24, 25
Tucker, R. 5
Tukhachevskii, M. 130
Tukhmanov, D. 101, 103
Turovskaia, M. 77

Tvardovskaia, M. 126
Tvardovskii, A. 3, 14, 107, 110, 113, 124, 125, 126, 140, 144, 147, 148
Tvardovskii, I. 14

*UB 40* (rock group) 102
Udal'tsova, N. 131
Ul'ianov, M. 61
Updike, J. 153
Urnov, D. 108
Usanov, S. 91
Ustinova, E. 99

Vail', B. 145
Vaksberg, A. 123, 146
Vasilenko, S. 49
Vasil'ev, A. 85
Vasil'ev 'Brothers' (G. N. and S. D.) 74
Vasnetsov, A. 151
Verdi, G. 20, 96
Verina, T. 72
Vertov, D. 58, 72, 74
Vian, B. 122, 133, 153
Vikulov, S. 111, 125
Villien, B. 70, 72
Vinogradov, I. 144
Vinokurova, I. 144
Vishnevskaia, G. 48, 99, 106
Vladimov, G. 48, 117, 136, 144, 156
Voina, V. 152
Voinovich, V. 117, 118, 119, 136, 139, 143, 156
Volchek, D. 122
Volchok, M. 99
Volkogonov, D. 136
Voloshin, M. 112
von Ribbentrop, J. 36
Voronitsyn, S. 41
Voskresenskii, L. 145
Vozdvizhenskii, V. 147
Voznesenskii, A. 103
Vvedenskii, A. 112
Vyshinskii, A. 14
Vysotskii, V. 24, 49, 109, 115, 123, 124, 146

Walker, M.  106
Welles, O.  53
Wenders, W.  57
Wheatcroft, S.  148
Williamson, A.  71
Wishnevsky, J.  24, 25, 138, 139, 140, 143, 145, 151
Wolf, W.  71
Woolf, V.  133, 153
Wright-Kovaleva, R.  153
Wyler, W.  50

Yasmann, V.  6, 25, 42
Young, D.  70

Zabolotskii, N.  112, 124, 147, 154, 155, 156

Zaitsev, B.  112
Zaitseva, I.  12
Zaks, B.  147
Zalygin, S.  107, 118, 119, 144, 149
Zamiatin, E.  107, 109, 112, 117, 133, 135, 145
Zasurskii, Ia.  20, 25
Zbarskii, B.  149
Zerchaninov, Iu.  148
Zhdan, V.  45
Zhdanov, A.  2, 124, 129
Zhigulin, A.  114, 121, 140, 145
Zhuchkova, T.  134, 153
Zinov'ev, A.  117, 123, 156
Zinov'ev, G.  128
Zinov'eva, O.  117
*Zodiac* (rock group)  101
Zoshchenko, M.  112, 124, 147, 156